Bite Your Tongue

by

Alex Shepard

Rockwaller Books

Acknowledgments

To my parents,
for teaching me the wonder and
power of the words we use.

Contents

A...1

B...16

C...56

D...81

E...102

F...107

G...120

H...146

I...161

J...171

K...179

L...185

M...197

N...202

O...211

P...219

Q...234

R...235

S...247

T...277

U...291

V...294

W...296

X...305

Y...306

Z...309

— A —

143: (Internet/text) I love you.

4mer: (Internet/text) Former.

A bad dose: (Irish) A bad or unfortunate case of something.

A bit of a bumble: (UK) A state of confusion.

A bit of crumpet: (UK) An attractive woman.

A bit of how's your father: (UK) To have a sexual experience.

A bugger's muddle: (UK) A mess; a disorderly situation.

A button short: (UK) To be intellectually lacking.

A carse: (UK/Dorset) A variant of "of course."

A cold day in hell: (UK) Something that will never happen.

A grape on the business: (Australian) A person whose presence ruins things for other people.

A la: (UK) Pretentious.

A piece of crumpet: (UK) A sexually desirable woman.

A piece of goods: (UK) A person, but especially refers to a woman.

A roll Jack Rice couldn't jump over: (Australian) A large sum of money.

A skull: (UK) Per person.

A soda: (Australian) Something that is accomplished easily; a pushover.

a$$: (Internet/text) Ass.

a&f: (Internet/text) Always and forever.

a/l: (Internet/text) Age and location.

a/m: (Internet/text) Away message.

a/s/l/p: (Internet/text) Age/sex/location/picture.

a/s/l/r: (Internet/text) Age, sex, location, race.

a/s/l: (Internet/text) Age, sex, location.

a'ight: (Internet/text) All right.

a1t: (Internet/text) Anyone there.

a2a: (Internet/text) Ask to answer.

a3: (Internet/text) Anyplace, anywhere, anytime.

a4u: (Internet/text) All for you.

a7x: (Internet/text) Avenged sevenfold.

aabf: (Internet/text) As a best friend.

aaf: (Internet/text) As a friend.

aak: (Internet/text) Alive and kicking.

aamof: (Internet/text) As a matter of fact.

Aardvark: (UK) Hard (and often unpleasant) work.

aatf: (Internet/text) Always and totally forever.

aatw: (Internet/text) All around the world.

Ab: (Fitness) Abdominal muscle.

Abbess: (UK) The mistress of a brothel.

abd: (Internet/text) Already been done.

abend: (Internet/text) Absent by enforced net deprivation.

Abfab: (UK/Australian) Absolutely fabulous; first-rate; very attractive.

abft: (Internet/text) About fucking time.

aboot: (Internet/text) About.

About done: (UK) Tipsy; slightly drunk.

About right: (UK) Tipsy; slightly drunk.

abreev: (Internet/text) Abbreviation.

Abroad: (UK) To be out conducting illegal activities.

Absent without leave: (UK) A person who has escaped from prison.

absnt: (Internet/text) Absent.

Absorb: (UK) To drink or eat.

Absotively: (UK) A combination of "absolutely" and "positively."

abt: (Internet/text) About.

abwt: (Internet/text) About.

AC/DC: (UK) Bisexual.

Acc: (Internet/text) Account.

Acca: (Australian) Academic.

Accident: (UK) An arrest.

acct: (Internet/text) Account.

Ace hurler: (US) The best pitcher in a baseball team.

Ace in the hole: (US) An advantage one keeps hidden until the end that will likely ensure success.

Ace of trumps: (UK) A top-class person.

Ace out: (US) To get the best results in a test or exam.

Ace: (UK) 1) Excellent. 2) (US) To get the best results in a test or exam. 3) Asexual.

Ace-deuce: (UK) 1) Three. 2) A best friend.

Acey-deucy: (UK) Of uncertain quality.

acgaf: (Internet/text) Absolutely couldn't give a fuck.

Acid drops: (UK) Sarcastic comments; put-downs.

Acid house: (UK) A segment of youth culture that involves enjoying house music in combination with hallucinogenic drugs.

Acid trip: (UK) The experience of being under the influence of LSD (acid).

Acid: (UK) The drug LSD (lysergic acid diethylamide).

ack: (Internet/text) Acknowledged.

Ackers: (UK/military) Coins, notes; money.

Acorns: (UK) Testicles.

Across the board: All-inclusive.

Across the river: (US/military) The government (especially the White House and Congress).

Act dumb: (UK) To feign ignorance.

Act the jinnit: (Irish) To act foolishly.

Act the linnet: (Irish) To flirt.

Act the maggot: (Irish) To play the fool.

Act the mohawk: (Irish) To misbehave.

Act: (Australian) 1) Pretending to be something you aren't. 2) To throw a tantrum.

Action man: (UK) An overly macho man.

Action: (UK) Recreational activities, especially illicit ones (such as gambling and drug use).

Actual: (UK) Cash.

Adam and Eve ball: (UK) An early dance party that ends at midnight.

Adam and Eve on a raft and wreck 'em: (US) Scrambled eggs on toast.

Adam and Eve on a raft: (UK) Two poached eggs on toast.

Adam and Eve: (US) Two poached or fried eggs.

Adam and Eve's togs: (UK) Naked.

Adam's ale: (UK) Water.

Add fuel to the fire: (UK) To make a bad situation worse.

Add insult to injury: (UK) 1) To aggravate a situation that is already difficult. 2) To further upset someone.

Addiction medicine: (US) Psychiatric treatment that is used to treat people who suffer from an addiction.

Addled: (UK) Muddled or confused, especially owing to being drunk or high.

addy: (Internet/text) Address.

ADHD: (Internet/text) Attention deficit hyperactivity disorder.

adl: (Internet/text) All day long.

admin: (Internet/text) Administrator.

adn: (Internet/text) Any day now.

Adonis: (UK) An attractive man.

aeap: (Internet/text) As early as possible.

Aerial ping-pong: (Australian) Australian rules football.

Aerial: (UK) Area, region, district.

Aeroplane blond: (UK) A woman who has dyed her hair blonde.

Aeroplane skirt: (UK) A skirt that has a long slit up the side.

afaiaa: (Internet/text) As far as I am aware.

afaic: (Internet/text) 1) As far as I'm concerned. 2) As far as I care.

afaicr: (Internet/text) As far as I can remember.

afaicr4: (Internet/text) As far as I can remember for.

afaics: (Internet/text) As far as I can see.

afaict: (Internet/text) As far as I can tell.

afaik: (Internet/text) As far as I know.

afair: (Internet/text) As far as I recall.

afaiu: (Internet/text) As far as I understand.

afc: (Internet/text) Away from computer.

Affair: (UK/political) A reception held in order to fundraise and/or honor somebody's achievements.

afg: (Gaming) Away from game.

afk: (Internet/text) Away from keyboard.

afkb: (Internet/text) Away from keyboard.

Afraid of one's shadow: (UK) To be easily frightened.

Africa speaks: (Australian/New Zealand) Strong alcohol imported from South Africa.

African lager: (UK) Guinness beer.

African time: (South African) An expectation for unpunctuality.

African woodbine: (UK) A cigarette that contains cannabis.

After davy: (UK) Affidavit.

After hair: (UK) To pursue a woman for sex.

After one's own heart: Someone who has similar interests or sensibilities to the speaker.

After: (Australian) Afternoon.

Afterbirth: 1) (UK) Rhubarb. 2) (US) Excessive paperwork.

Afterglow: (UK) The cool-down period after sex.

Afternoon delight: (UK) Sex in the afternoon.

Afters: (UK) An after-hours drinking session.

Ag: (UK) Aggravation.

Against the clock: (UK) To have little time; to be in a hurry.

Against the wind: (UK) A struggle or difficult task.

Agate: (UK) A marble.

Agates: (UK) Testicles.

Aggie eyes: (UK) A person who hasn't had enough sleep.

Aggie: (UK) A marble.

Aggro: (UK/Australian) 1) Aggressive. 2) Aggravated.

Aggy: (UK) Edgy, with pointed corners.

Aginner: (Irish) A dissenter or contrarian.

agn: (Internet/text) Again.

Ah-ahs: (UK) Defecation.

Ahead of the game: To be in an advantageous position.

A-head: (US) A regular user of amphetamines.

AI: (Internet/text) Artificial intelligence.

aiadw: (Internet/text) All in a day's work.

aiamu: (Internet/text) And I'm a monkey's uncle.

aicmfp: (Internet/text) And I claim my five pounds.

aight: (Internet/text) All right.

aightz: (Internet/text) All right.

aiic: (Internet/text) As if I care.

aiid: (Internet/text) And if I did.

aiight: (Internet/text) All right.

Aim Archie at the Armitage: (Australian) To urinate.
AIM: (Internet/text) AOL Instant Messenger.
Aimed: (US) To be identified, singled out, or victimized.
aimmc: (Internet/text) Am I making myself clear.
Air dirty laundry: (US) To let others know of one's private matters.
Air hose: (US) Shoes worn without socks.
Air off oneself: (Jamaican) To show off or display one's superior status, especially at another person's expense.
Air out one's mouth on: (Jamaican) To speak aggressively or abusively.
Airball: (US) A slow, strange, or unpleasant person.
Airbrained: (US) Silly or frivolous.
Aircraft carrier: (US/basketball) A player whose driving force can carry the team to victory.
Airhead: A foolish or simple-minded person.
Airsick pigeon: (UK) To be useless.
aitr: (Internet/text) Adult in the room.
aiui: (Internet/text) As I understand it.
aiws: (Internet/text) As I was saying.
ajax: (Internet/text) Asynchronous Javascript and XML.
Aladdin's cave: (UK) A stash of stolen goods.
alaylm: (Internet/text) As long as you love me.
alaytm: (Internet/text) As long as you tell me.
Albatross: (UK) 1) An encumbrance. 2) Something that causes anxiety.
Alco: (Australian) Alcoholic.
Alec: 1) (UK) A swindler's victim. 2) (Australian) A foolish person.
Aled: (UK) Drunk.
Alf: (Australian) An uncultivated Australian.
Alfalfa: (US) 1) Money. 2) Tobacco. 3) Marijuana.
Algernon: (UK) A young upper-class man.
Ali Baba: (UK) An alibi.
Alias man: (Jamaican) A cheat or hypocrite.
Alias: (Jamaican) Dangerous or violent.
Alice: (Australian) Alice Springs.
Alight: (UK) Very drunk.
Alive: (UK) To have money.

Alkie (also "alky"): (UK) An alcoholic.

All arms and legs: (UK) Weak beer.

All beer and skittles: (UK) An easy life.

All behind like the cow's tail: (Irish) To be late.

All bets are off: The situation is entirely different than it was before; the outcome is impossible to predict, often because of something unexpected happening.

All buck-up goes: (Jamaican) To abandon all ethical standards.

All come on top: (UK) A disaster; for everything to go wrong.

All day and night: (UK) A life prison sentence.

All-dayer: (UK) An all-day drinking session.

All ears: (UK) To be attentive or listening closely.

All fruits ripe: (Jamaican) Everything is okay.

All hands: (Nautical) A ship's full crew.

All mouth and no trousers: (UK) All talk and no action.

All of a doodah: (UK) To be in a state of excitement.

All of one's dogs aren't barking: (US) Not in one's right mind; to be scatterbrained.

All on top: (UK) To be superficial.

All over the ballpark: (US) Disorganized or chaotic.

All over the lot: (US) Disorganized or chaotic.

All over the shop: (UK) Disorganized or chaotic.

All over the show: Disorganized or chaotic.

All piss and wind: (UK) To be full of bluster but have no substance.

All-rounder: (UK) Bisexual.

All same: (Jamaican) Something that makes no difference; to be all alike.

All snot and tears: (UK) To be mournful or remorseful.

All stations: (Australian) An Alsatian dog.

All systems go: Everything is functional and ready.

All the rage: Something that is in vogue.

All the way: 1) (UK) To have sexual intercourse. 2) (US) A snack or meal supplied with all the available extras.

All tits and teeth: (UK/derogatory) A woman who uses her physical attributes rather than her brain.

All to cock (also "all a-cock"): (UK) Unsatisfactory or mixed up.

All wet: (UK) Mistaken.

Allegro: (UK) Lively.

Alley apple: (US) A lump of horse manure.

Alley cat: (UK) Someone who prowls the streets at night looking for sexual partners.

All-fired: (US) Excessive or extreme.

Alligator spread: (US/Wall Street) A deal where the commissions are equal to, or larger than, the profit.

Alligator: 1) (UK) Later. 2) An investment property that does not bring in enough income to cover expenses.

All-out: (US) To work very hard at something.

alol: (Internet/text) Actually laughing out loud.

Along for the ride: (UK) To be unofficially associated with something.

alot: (Internet/text) A lot.

alrt: (Internet/text) Alright.

alryt: (Internet/text) Alright.

Alt: (Australian) A follower of an alternative lifestyle.

Alternative dentation: (UK) Dentures or false teeth.

Alvin: (US) An unsophisticated person, especially one who lives in a rural area.

AMA: (Internet/text) Ask me anything.

Amateur night: (US) A display of ineptitude.

Ambassador of Morocco: (UK) A shoemaker.

Amber fluid: (Australian) Beer.

Amber nectar: (Australian) Beer.

Ambidextrous: (UK) Bisexual.

Ambo: (Australian) 1) An ambulance. 2) An ambulance driver.

Ambulance chaser: (US) A lawyer who seeks profits from the lawsuits of accident victims.

American lad: (Irish) Fatty bacon imported from America.

Amidships: (UK) The tummy area.

amiic: (Internet/text) Ask me if I care.

aml: (Internet/text) All my love.

Amp joint: (UK) A marijuana cigarette laced with some form of narcotic.

Amp off: (UNIX) To run in the background.

Amped up: To be very excited.

Ampster: (Australian) A showman or conman's accomplice who starts buying their tickets or goods in order to draw in other people.

ams: (Internet/text) Ask me something.

Amscray: (UK) Go away.

amsp: (Internet/text) Ask me something personal.

Amy: (UK) Amyl nitrate.

Amyl: (UK) Amyl nitrate.

Anabols: (UK) Anabolic steroids.

Ananab: (UK) A banana.

Anarchists: (Australian) Non-safety matches.

Anchor: 1) (UK) A juror who has been bribed to influence other jurors, typically to vote for an acquittal. 2) (US) The main part of a shopping mall or complex.

Anchors: (UK) Brakes.

Andramartins: (Irish) Foolish behavior.

Angel crystal: (UK) Phencyclidine.

Angel dust: (UK) Phencyclidine.

Angel hair: (UK) Phencyclidine.

Angel: (Theatre) A primary financial backer.

Angry fruit salad: (Computer) An unattractive design that uses too many colors.

anim8: (Internet/text) Animate.

Animal companion: (UK) A pet.

Animal house: (US) A dwelling, particularly a college fraternity house.

Animal night: (Australian) A planned outing of bad or excessive behavior.

Animal: (UK) A crude or brutish person.

Animalist: (UK) An animal rights supporter.

Ankle slapper: (Surfing) A small wave.

Ankle: (Theatre) To quit.

Ankle-biter: (Australian) A young child.

anl: (Internet/text) All night long.

Annie no-rattle: (Irish) A person who waits until the end of a conversation to share their point of view.

Annie: (UK) A lorry.

Annihilated: (UK) Very drunk.

anon: (Internet/text) Anonymous.

Anorak: (UK) A socially inept person with no fashion sense.

Ant's bollock on a beach: (UK) Something that is almost impossible to find.

Ant's pants: (Australian) The height of fashion.

Ante up: (US) To pay one's contribution.

Antenna shop: (UK) A shop that displays prototype products in order to gauge consumer responses.

Anti-freeze: (UK) A strong alcoholic drink.

Antsy: (US) To be nervous or agitated.

anuda: (Internet/text) Another.

anw: (Internet/text) Anyways.

anwwi: (Internet/text) Alright now where was I?

Any Tom, Dick, or Harry: (UK) Anybody at all.

any1: (Internet/text) Anyone.

anywaz: (Internet/text) Anyways.

Anywhen: (UK) At any time.

aob: (Internet/text) Any other business.

aoe: (Internet/text) Age of Empires.

AOHell: (Internet/text) Derisive term for America Online (AOL).

A-okay: (UK) Fine; perfect.

aon: (Internet/text) All or nothing.

aos: (Internet/text) Adult over shoulder.

aota: (Internet/text) All of the above.

aoto: (Internet/text) Amen on that one.

aoys: (Internet/text) Angel on your shoulder.

Ape shit: (UK) Out of control.

Ape-hangers: (UK) Extra-high bicycle or motorbike handlebars.

API: (Internet/text) Application program interface.

Apiece: (UK) For each.

apoc: (Internet/text) Apocalypse.

apod: (Internet/text) Another point of discussion.

app: (Internet/text) Application.

Apple of one's eye: (US) A person of whom one is very fond or proud.

Apple pie order: (US) Neat and tidy.

Apple polish: (US) Flattery.

Apple shiner: (UK) An obsequious person.

Apple: (UK) The head.

Apple-polisher: (US) A flatterer.

Apples and oranges: (US) Completely different things that can't be compared.

Apples: (Australian) Fine; perfect.

Appleton talking: (Jamaican) A drunk person who is talking nonsense or aggressively.

Apply lawyer foot: (Jamaican) To run away.

Applying a band-aid: (US) An inadequate (often temporary) solution that won't solve the situation.

appt: (Internet/text) Appointment.

aprece8: (Internet/text) Appreciate.

apreci8: (Internet/text) Appreciate.

Apron: (US) A bartender.

apu: (Internet/text) As per usual.

aqap: (Internet/text) As quick as possible.

Arbuckle: (UK) An overweight person.

Archie: (UK) British Great War term for anti-aircraft fire.

Are your boots laced?: (US) An inquiry as to whether somebody understands the matter in question.

Argument ender: (UK) A fist.

Argy-bargy: (UK) 1) An argument or confrontation. 2) Pushing and shoving.

Arm: (UK) Power or influence.

Armchair quarterback: (US) A sports fan who thinks they could have made better decisions or plays than the players.

Armpit: (UK) An unpleasant place.

arnd: (Internet/text) Around.

Arnies: (UK) Anabolic steroids.

Arnold: (Jamaican) Pork.

Arnolds: (UK) Anabolic steroids.

Around the way: (Jamaican) The neighborhood.

Arse about face: (UK) Back to front; to be disorganized.

Arse about: (UK) 1) To fool around; to act irresponsibly. 2) To waste time.

Arse over tit (also "head over heels"): (UK) To fall over or go tumbling.

Arse up: (UK) To make a mess of something.

Arse wipe: (UK) An obnoxious or contemptible person.

Arse wiper: (UK) An obsequious person.

Arse: (UK) 1. The buttocks. 2. An unpleasant person.

Arsed: (Internet/text) Bothered (usually used negatively).

Arse-end: (UK) The back or bottom of something.

Arsy-versy: (UK) Backwards or upside down.

Arthur: (UK) A half pint.

Artical: (Jamaican) 1) Genuine; sincere. 2) Respected.

Artsy (also "artsy fartsy"): (US) Someone or something that has pretentious artistic qualities.

Arvo: (Australian) Afternoon.

As the crow flies: (US) In a straight line between two points.

asaik: (Internet/text) As soon as I know.

ASAP: (Internet/text) As soon as possible.

ase: (Internet/text) Age, sex, ethnicity.

asf: (Internet/text) And so forth.

Ash tray on a motorbike: (UK) Something that is useless.

ASIC: (Internet/text) Application specific integrated circuit.

asl: (Internet/text) Age, sex, location.

asln: (Internet/text) Age, sex, location, name.

aslo: (Internet/text) Age, sex, location, orientation.

asr: (Internet/text) Age, sex, race.

Ass over tincups: (US) Head over heels.

Astroturf: (UK) A police informer.

At it: (UK) To be committing a crime or engaged in a confidence trick.

At the post: (UK) Ready and waiting.

At the wash: (UK) Stealing from jackets in public washrooms or changing rooms.

atb: (Internet/text) All the best.

Ate-the-bolts: (Irish) A glutton for work.

atl: (Internet/text) Atlanta.

atm: (Internet/text) At the moment

ato: (Internet/text) Against the odds.

Atomic: (Unix) A set of operations that execute all at once and can't be interrupted.

ATOP: (Internet/text) At time of posting.

atp: (Internet/text) Answer the phone.

atq: (Internet/text) Answer the question.

atst: (Internet/text) At the same time.

Attaboy: An expression of approval or congratulations for a younger male.

attacc: (Internet/text) Attack.

Attic: (UK) The human head.

ATTN: (Internet/text) Attention.

atw: (Internet/text) All the way.

aty: (Internet/text) According to you.

audy: (Internet/text) Are you done yet?

Aunt Emma: (UK) Morphine.

Aunt Fanny: (UK) An expression of disbelief.

Aunt Hazel: (UK) Heroin.

Aunt Mary: (UK) Cannabis.

Aunt: (UK) The lavatory.

Auntie: 1) (UK) The British Broadcasting Corporation. 2) (Australian) The Australian Broadcasting Corporation.

Auntie's ruin: (UK) Gin.

AUP: (Internet/text) Acceptable Use Policy.

aupi: (Internet/text) And your point is.

Aussie salute: (Australian) Using one's hand to wave away flies.

Aussie: An Australian person.

Autograph: (UK) A signature.

av7x: (Internet/text) Avenged sevenfold.

avgn: (Internet/text) Angry video game nerd.

Avie (or "avvie"): (Internet/text) Avatar.

Avo: (Australian/South African) Avocado.

avsb: (Internet/text) A very special boy.

avtr: (Internet/text) Avatar.

avy: (Internet/text) Avatar.

Away and claw mould on yourself: (Irish) Go away.

Away for slates: (Irish) On the way to success.

Away on a hack: (Irish) To be lucky or successful.

Away the trip: (Scottish) To be pregnant.

Away to the hills: (Irish) To be crazy.

Away with the band: (Irish) To be drunk or intoxicated.

Away with the fairies: (Irish) To be crazy.

awb: (Internet/text) Acquaintance with benefits.

awes: (Internet/text) Awesome.

Awesome: Great, excellent.

awk: (Internet/text) Awkward.

awol: (Internet/text) Absent without leave.

awsic: (Internet/text) And why should I care.

awsm: (Internet/text) Awesome.

awty: (Internet/text) Are we there yet.

Axe: (US) A musical instrument, particularly a guitar.

Axeman: (US) Someone who plays a musical instrument, especially a guitar.

Axle grease: (UK) A bribe.

aybab2m: (Internet/text/gaming) All your base are belong to me.

aybab2u: (Internet/text/gaming) All your base are belong to us.

ayc: (Internet/text) Awaiting your comments.

ayd: (Internet/text) Are you done?

aydy: (Internet/text) Are you done yet?

ayec: (Internet/text) At your earliest convenience.

ayfr: (Internet/text) Are you for real?

aygs: (Internet/text) Are you going somewhere?

ayk: (Internet/text) Are you kidding?

aykm: (Internet/text) Are you kidding me?

ayl: (Internet/text) Are you listening?

ayok: (Internet/text) Are you okay?

AYOR: (Internet/text) At your own risk.

aypi: (Internet/text) And your point is?

ays: (Internet/text) Are you serious?

ayst: (Internet/text) Are you still there?

ayt: (Internet/text) Are you there?
ayte: (Internet/text) Alright.
ayw: (Internet/text) As you wish.
azn: (Internet/text) Asian.
Aztec two-step: (UK) Diarrhea, especially when suffered abroad.

B&: (Internet/text) Banned.

b/c: (Internet/text) Because.

b/cos: (Internet/text) Because.

b/g: (Internet/text) Background.

b/s/l: (Internet/text) Bisexual/straight/lesbian.

b/t: (Internet/text) Between.

b/w: (Internet/text) Between.

b@: (Internet/text) Banned.

b'day: (Internet/text) Birthday.

bOOn: (Internet/text) New person.

bOOt: (Internet/text) Boot (e.g., kicking people from game or chat servers).

BOrked; to bOrk: (Internet/text) Broken; to break.

B2B: (Internet/text) Business to business.

b2u: (Internet/text) Back to you.

b2w: (Internet/text) Back to work.

b3: (Internet/text) Be.

b4: (Internet/text) Before.

b4n: (Internet/text) Bye for now.

b4u: (Internet/text) Before you.

b4ug: (Internet/text) Before you go.

b4ul: (Internet/text) Before you leave.

b8: (Internet/text) Bait.

Baalebos: (Yiddish) A meddlesome person.

Bab: (UK) A kebab.

Babbler: (Australian) A cook or chef.

Babe lair: (US) A chic home that helps to impress women.

Babe magnet: (US) An item or person that attracts women.

Babe: (UK) A young woman, especially one who is attractive.

Baby Bells: (US) The regional telephone companies created by the break-up of American Telephone and Telegraph.

Baby blues: (UK) Eyes.

Baby boomer: A person born between 1946 and 1964.

Baby catcher: (US) An obstetrician.

Baby M laws: (US) Legislation regarding surrogate motherhood.

Baby pop: (US) A young man.

Baby: 1) A term of endearment. 2) A person who complains about petty matters.

Babycise class: (US) A parent-and-baby exercise class.

Baby-sitting: (UK) Looking after someone while they take illegal drugs.

Bacca box: (UK) The mouth.

Baccy: (UK) Tobacco.

Back blocks: (Australian) The outer suburbs.

Back door trots: (UK) Diarrhea.

Back door: (UK) The buttocks.

Back double: (UK) A back street.

Back end money: (US) A movie's final profits after all expenses have been paid.

Back end: (UK) The buttocks.

Back in the box: (US) Back in business after an arrest for drugs.

Back of bourke: (Australian) Anywhere far away.

Back off and let the breeze blow over me: (Jamaican) Leave me alone; go away.

Back street butcher: (UK) An abortionist, especially one operating illegally.

Back to square one: To start again; to return to the beginning of a process.

Backdoor man: (UK) An adulterer.

Backdoor: 1) To act covertly. 2) To act deceptively.

Backer: An investor.

Backhander: (UK) 1) A bribe. 2) A strike with the back of one's hand.

Backpedal: To reverse one's position, especially when the reactions to it are unfavorable.

Backseat driver: (US) A car passenger who offers the driver unwanted driving advice.

Bacon: Money.

Bad blood: (US) Relations that have soured or been severed between certain people.

Bad egg: (US) A troublemaker.

Bad news: Someone or something that is regarded as undesirable.

Baderbus: (UK) A wheelchair.

Badered: (UK) To be drunk or intoxicated.

Badge: (US) A police officer.

Badger crib: (UK) A cheap brothel where clients are often robbed.

Badger game: (UK) A con where a woman lures a man into a compromising position, at which point they are caught by her accomplice who pretends to be her husband. The couple then extort money from the victim.

Badger: (UK) A prostitute's accomplice who goes through her client's belongings while she keeps him occupied.

Badlands: (UK) A slum or dangerous urban area.

Bad-mouth: (UK) To speak ill about someone or something.

bae: (Internet/text) Before anyone else.

baf: (Internet/text) Bring a friend.

Bag and baggage: (US) Everything one owns.

Bag biter: (US) A troublemaker.

Bag job: (UK) A theft or burglary.

Bag man: (US) Someone who collects or distributes money for racketeers.

Bag of bones: (UK) A very thin person.

Bag of mystery: (UK) A sausage.

Bag of nails: (UK) To be in disarray.

Bag of shells: (Australian) A trifle; an unimportant object.

Bag of tripe: (UK) An unpleasant person.

Bag off: (UK) To pair off.

Bag on: (US) 1) To tease. 2) To chastise.

Bag one's face: (US) To hide one's face.

Bag some rays: (US) To sunbathe.

Bag up: (US) To divide marijuana into small amounts and packets.

Bag: (US) A package of a drug. 2) To conceal. 3) (Australian) To criticize.

Baggage: (UK) 1) A promiscuous woman. 2) A hanger-on.

Bagged: (UK) To be arrested.

Baggies: (UK) Swimming trunks, commonly worn by surfers.

Bagging: 1) (UK) A packed lunch. 2) (Australian) Criticism.

Baggy green: (Australian) A cricket player in the Australian national team.

Bagpipe: (UK) A boring or monotonous speaker.

Bags: 1) (Irish) To fail at or make a mess of something (e.g., "to make a bags of something"). 2) (UK) Loose-fitting trousers.

Bah: (Internet/text) I don't really care.

Bahookie: (Scottish) A person's backside.

bai: (Internet/text) Bye.

Baidie: (UK) Bad-tempered or aggressive.

Bail on someone: (UK) To suddenly cancel on agreed upon plans with someone.

Bail out: (UK) To help someone out of a difficult situation, particularly financially.

Bail up: (Australian) To rob or hold up; to delay.

Bail: (US/Australian) To leave or depart, especially abruptly.

Bait: (UK) An attractive potential sexual partner.

Bake it: (UK) To resist the urge to defecate.

Baking-spittle: (UK) The tongue.

Bakkie: (South African) A pick-up truck.

Baksheesh: (UK) A bribe, tip, or payment.

Balahu: (Jamaican) A noisy or boisterous person.

Bald tyre bandit: (UK) A traffic policeman.

Bald: (US) Terrible; awful.

Bale of straw: (US) A blonde woman.

Bales: (UK) Cannabis.

Bali belly: (Australian) Diarrhea.

Ball and chain: A spouse, especially a wife.

Ball tearer: (Australian) Something that is exceptional, for either its good or bad qualities.

Ball: (US) To behave in a lively and uninhibited way.

Ballast: (UK) Food, especially a heavy meal.

Ballbreaker: (US) An overpowering or threatening woman.

Ballistic: (UK) Furious; very angry.

Ball-less wonder: (UK) A timid or cowardly man.

Ballocks: (UK) 1) Testicles. 2) Nonsense.

Balloon juice: (US) Idle talk.

Balloon: 1) To try a new idea. 2) (Gambling) One hundred dollars.

Balloons: (UK) Large breasts.

Ballow: (US) To lay claim to something.

Balls up: (WWI) A botched or messed up situation.

Balls: 1) Testicles. 2) (UK) Nonsense. 3) Courage.

Balls-ache: (UK) Something or someone that is tedious or trying.

Balls-out: (US) All-out; full-scale.

Balls-up: (UK) A botched situation.

Ballsy: Courageous.

Bally: (UK) Very.

Baloney: (UK) Nonsense.

Bam: (UK) To cheat or wheedle.

Bama: (US) Abbreviation of Alabama. Also used to reference the South.

bamf: (Internet/text) Bad-ass motherfucker.

Banana truck: (US) A crazy person.

Banana: (UK) A foolish person.

Bananas: Crazy; to be out of one's mind.

Band rat: (UK) A groupie.

Band: (Australian) A prostitute.

Bandalu business: (Jamaican) A con or swindle.

Bandulu: (Jamaican) A con-artist or a trickster.

Bang on: 1) (Irish) Good; great. 2) (UK) To nag. 3) To speak incessantly.

Bang to rights: (UK) 1) Undeniable. 2) Caught in the act.

Banged out: (UK) Packed with people.

Banged up: (UK) Imprisoned.

Banger: (UK) 1) A sausage. 2) An old, worn-out vehicle.

Banjaxed: (Irish) 1) Defeated or overwhelmed. 2) To be drunk or intoxicated.

Banjo: 1) (UK) A guitar. 2) (Scottish) To hit someone with your full strength.

Banjo'd: (UK) Very drunk.

Banker: (UK/gambling) A certain or likely outcome.

Bankroll: To provide capital; to finance someone or something.

Banter play built on a coke frame: (US) An attractive young woman.

Bappo: (Australian) A Baptist.

Baps: (Irish) Female breasts.

Baptize: (UK) To water down spirits in a pub.

Bar bore: (UK) A regular pub customer who has their own seat (and often their own tankard too).

Bar stool preacher: (UK) A regular pub customer who thinks they know everything.

Barbie doll: A woman with dyed blonde and permed hair.

Barbie: (Australian) A barbecue.

Bareback: (US) Sexual intercourse without the use of a condom.

Barebum: (Australian) A short jacket, especially those worn by waiters.

Barf bag: (US) An airsickness bag.

Bar-fly: (US) A person who frequents cheap and seedy bars.

Bargain: (Australian) A phrase that conveys the speaker's approval.

Barges: (UK) Massive shoes.

Bark at ants: (US) To vomit.

Bark: 1) (UK) A miserable old man. 2) (Australian) To vomit.

Barker: (UK) A sausage.

Barker's egg: (Australian) Dog excrement.

Barking dogs: (UK) Aching or tired feet.

Barking irons: (US) A pair of pistols.

Barking: (UK) Crazy.

Barm pot: (UK) Crazy; foolish; eccentric.

Barmy army: (UK) A boisterous or enthusiastic group of people, especially fans of the English national cricket team.

Barmy: (UK) Crazy.

Barney: 1) (UK/Australian) An argument or fight. 2) (Irish) One's head or mind.

Baron: A prisoner who has power and influence over their fellow inmates.

Barra: (Australian) Barramundi fish.

Barrack: (Australian) To cheer loudly.

Barrel fever: (UK) A hangover.

Barrel: (US) To speed; to go very fast.

Barro: (Australian) Embarrassing.

Barry: (Scottish) Great.

Barse: (UK) The perineum.

Barsy: (UK) Crazy; a lunatic.

Bart: (Australian) A girl or young woman, especially an immoral one.

Barton: (UK) An enclosed yard for cows.

Base on: (US) To criticize.

Base: (US) 1) To disagree.

Bash up: (UK) To thrash or beat someone or something.

Basher: (UK) A thug or a bully.

Basic brown: (US/political) Someone with no real interest in or commitment to environmental issues.

Basin cut: (UK) A short-back-and-sides haircut made by placing a basin over the head and cutting around the rim.

Basin: (UK) Something that doesn't need a container.

Basket case: A person who is crazy or delusional.

Bassing: (UK) Getting loud.

Baste: (US) To speak ill of someone behind their back.

Baster: (US/Australian) A house thief.

Bat along: (US/Canadian) To discuss something informally.

Bat an eye: To show feeling; to respond.

Bat and bowl: (UK) To be bisexual.

Bat for the other side: (UK) To be gay.

Bat: (US/Canadian) A drinking spree; to binge.

Batch: (UK) A small rising in the ground.

Bate: (UK) A bad temper.

Batey: (UK) Bad-tempered.

Bath-dodger: (UK) An unwashed person; someone who is habitually dirty.

Bathers: (Australian) A swimming costume.

Bathtub: (Skiing) The indentation left in the snow by someone falling on their rear.

Bats in the belfry: (UK) Crazy; delusional.

Batten down the hatches: (UK) To secure everything, especially for terrible weather or a bad situation.

Batting a thousand: (US) To succeed in an extraordinary way.

Battle axe: (UK) A feisty or aggressive woman.

Battle bowler: (UK) A soldier's helmet.

Battle the subs: (Australian) To sell goods door-to-door in the suburbs.

Battler: (Australian) A financially poor person.

Batts: (UK) Shoes.

Batty: Crazy; strange; eccentric.

bau: (Internet/text) Back at you.

Baubles: (UK) Testicles.

Bawbag: (Scottish) A man's scrotum.

bb: (Internet/text) Bye-bye.

bb4h: (Internet/text) Bros before hoes.

bb4n: (Internet/text) Bye-bye for now.

bbe: (Internet/text) Baby.

bbf: (Internet/text) Best boy friend.

bbfn: (Internet/text) Bye-bye for now.

bbfs: (Internet/text) Best boy friends.

bbfu: (Internet/text) Be back for you.

bbg: (Internet/text) Baby girl.

bbi: (Internet/text) Baby.

bbiab: (Internet/text) Be back in a bit.

bbiaf: (Internet/text) Be back in a few.

bbim: (Internet/text) Be back in a minute.

bbk: (Internet/text) Be back, okay?

bbl (also "bbl8r"): (Internet/text) Be back later.

BBM: (Internet/text) BlackBerry Messenger.

bbml: (Internet/text) Be back much later.

bbn: (Internet/text) Be back never.

bbol: (Internet/text) Be back online later.

B-boy: A male fan of rap music.

bbp: (Internet/text) Banned by parents.

bbq: (Internet/text) Be back quick.

bbrs: (Internet/text) Be back really soon.

BBS: (Internet/text) 1) Be back soon. 2) Bulletin board system/service.

bbt: (Internet/text) Be back tomorrow.

bbtn: (Internet/text) Be back tonight.

bbw also ("bbwe"): (Internet/text) Be back whenever.

bbwl: (Internet/text) Be back way later.

bby: (Internet/text) Baby.

bbz: (Internet/text) Babes.

bc: (Internet/text) Because.

bck: (Internet/text) Back.

bcnu: (Internet/text) Be seeing you.

bcoz: (Internet/text) Because.

bcurl8: (Internet/text) Because you're late.

bcuz: (Internet/text) Because.

bd: (Internet/text) Birthday.

bday: (Internet/text) Birthday.

b-day: (Internet/text) Birthday.

Be a skinner: (New Zealand) 1) To be out of money. 2) To be used up.

Be all domino: (UK) The end; finished.

Be all over: To be enthusiastic or earnest.

Be dirty on: (Australian) To be offended by or hostile towards someone or something.

Be good: (US) A farewell expression.

Be hot for: To be attracted to someone.

Be lucky: (UK) Goodbye; farewell.

Be missing: (US) Go away.

Be my Georgie Best: (UK) An expression of encouragement.

Be my guest: An expression of encouragement.

be4: (Internet/text) Before.

Beacon: (UK) A red nose.

Beadle: (UK) A dock police officer.

Beagle: (UK) A heavy smoker.

Beak off: (Irish) To play truant.

Beak: (UK) 1) A magistrate or judge. 2) A person's nose, especially one that has a long, hooked shape.

Beaker: (UK) A fowl or chicken.

Beaker-hauler: (UK) A poultry thief.

Beam: (US) To look.

Beamer: (US) A BMW car.

Bean counter: An accountant.

Bean: (UK) 1) The head. 2) A coin.

Bean-bag: (UK) An unpleasant person.

Beanie: (UK/Australian) A wool hat.

Beano: (UK) A celebration or party.

Beanpole: (UK) A tall, thin person.

Beans: (US) Money.

Bear trap: (US) A difficult situation.

Bear: (US) A large, often hairy, male homosexual.

Beard: A male escort who poses as a romantic partner, often to help conceal a lesbian's sexual orientation.

Beardie: (UK) A bearded beatnik.

Bear-leader: (UK) An expert who teaches by example.

Bear-tracker: (UK) A detective.

Beast: (UK) 1) A sex criminal. 2) An unattractive woman. 3) (South African) Someone who is very strong or good at what they do.

Beastie: (UK) Disgusting or coarse. 2) (US) Impressive or powerful.

Beastmaster: (UK) An unattractive woman's husband.

Beat for the yolk: (US) To be short of cash.

Beat one's chops: (US) To talk.

Beat one's meat: (UK) To masturbate.

Beat one's skin: (US) To clap.

Beat the rap: (US) To escape punishment, especially in terms of the law.

Beat the rocks: (US) To walk the sidewalk.

Beat to the socks: (US) Weariness.

Beat: 1) (UK) To puzzle or baffle. 2) (US/Canadian) To cheat or defraud.

Beats me: (US) I don't know.

Beaut: (Australian/New Zealand) Excellent; distinctive.

Beauty: (Australian/New Zealand) An expression of agreement or approval.

Beaver: (UK) A long or luxuriant beard.

bebe: (Internet/text) Baby.

Bebop glasses: (US) Fashionable sunglasses.

Bebop: A style of jazz that features nonsense lyrics.

Becker: (UK) A quick act of sexual intercourse.

becuz: (Internet/text) Because.

Bedfordshire: (UK) 1) Bed. 2) Bedtime.

Bedworthy: (UK) A sexually attractive woman.

Bee stings: (UK) Small female breasts.

Bee: (US) An idea.

Bee's bollocks: (UK) Something that is excellent; the best.

Bee's knees: (UK) Something that is excellent; the best.

Beechams: (UK) Testicles.

Beef brain: (UK) A dim-witted person.

Beef head: (UK) A dim-witted person.

Beef up: To intensify.

Beef: A complaint or argument.

Beefcake: A man with a large, muscular body.

Beefy: Muscular.

Beemal: (UK) Lamb.

Beemob: (UK) A bomb.

Been round the block: (UK) Experienced.

Beer barrel: (UK) The stomach.

Beer belly: (US) A large stomach caused from drinking too much beer.

Beer eater: (UK) A person who loves beer.

Beer gut: (UK) A large stomach caused from drinking beer.

Beer me up, Scotty: (UK) A request for a beer.

Beer scooter: (UK) To get home after a night out drinking and not remember how one got made the trip.

Beer shop: (UK) A pub.

Beer trap: (UK) The mouth.

Beered up: (UK) To be drunk or intoxicated.

Beersucker: (UK) 1) The mouth. 2) A heavy drinker.

Beer-tokens: (UK) One-pound coins; money.

Beer-up: (Australian) A bout of drinking.

Beer-vouchers: (UK) One-pound coins; money.

Beery nose: (UK) A drunk.

Beery: (UK) Tipsy.

Beetle brain: (UK) A dim-witted person.

Beetle off: (UK) To depart, often quickly.

Beetle: (UK) To hurry.

Beetle's blood: (UK) Stout beer.

Beetle-crushers: (UK) Heavy work boots.

Beetle-sticker: (UK) An entomologist.

Beetroot mug: (UK) A red face.

Beevo: (US) Beer.

Beeza: A BSA motorcycle.

Beezer: (UK) 1) A person or chap. 2) The nose. 3) Excellent or attractive. 4) (Scottish) An extreme example of its kind.

Beezonker: (UK) The nose.

Before day creep: (US) A stealthy late-night or early-morning visit to one's lover.

Before one can say Jack Robinson: (UK) Very quickly; instantly.

Beggar maker: (UK) A publican or bookmaker.

Beggar's lagging: (UK) Three weeks in prison.

Belch water: (US) Soda water.

Belcher: (UK) 1) A spotted handkerchief. 2) A dedicated beer drinker.

Belfry: (UK) The head.

Bell the cat: (UK) To do something dangerous.

Bell: (UK) A telephone call.

Belled up: (UK) To be protected by a burglar alarm.

Bellman: (UK) A burglar who is good at disarming alarms.

Bellows to mend: (UK) To be out of breath.

Bellows: (UK) The lungs.

Bellowsed: (UK) To be transported as a convict.

Bell-ringer: (US) A great success.

Bells and whistles: 1) Embellishments or gimmicks. 2) For all features to be included.

Bells: (UK) Annabel's nightclub.

Bellswagger: (UK) A loud braggart or a bully.

Belly fiddler: (US) Guitar.

Bellyache: (UK) To complain frequently.

Bellyflop: 1) To land stomach-first on a surface of water. 2) To result in total failure.

Bellyful: (UK) More than one can tolerate.

Below the belt: Underhanded or vindictive.

Belsen victim: (UK) A very thin person.

Belt and braces man: (UK) An overly cautious person.

Belt loosener: (UK) A very large meal.

Belt strainer: (UK) A very large meal.

Belt up: (UK) To stop talking.

Belt: (UK) 1) To give a sharp blow or punch. 2) To hurry.

Belter: (UK) A popular song that is sung enthusiastically. 2) (South African) An attractive young woman. 3) (Scottish) Something great. 4) Something painful.

Belyando spew: (Australian) Sickness, which results in vomiting after one eats.

Bemused: (UK) To be drunk or intoxicated.

Bench points: (UK) Physical advantages.

Bencher: (US) An idle or incompetent person.

Bench-legged: (US) Bowlegged.

Bench-man: (US) A judge.

Bench-warmer: (US) 1) An idle or incompetent person. 2) A substitute in a sports team.

Bend down: To allow something to happen.

Bend one's ear: (UK) To nag or speak incessantly.

Bend over backwards: To go out of one's way to accommodate someone or something.

Bend the elbow: (UK) To drink alcohol.

Bender: (UK) A drinking binge.

Benny: (UK) A simpleton.

Bent as a nine-bob note: (UK) Dishonest or corrupt.

Bent: (UK) 1. Dishonest or corrupt. 2) Gay (derogatory).

Benty: (UK) Twenty.

Beresk: (UK) Berserk; out of control.

Berk (also "burk"): (UK) A fool; an idiot.

Berko: (Australian) To go berserk.

Berley: (Australian) Nonsense; rubbish.

Bernie: (UK) One million pounds sterling (short for Bernie Ecclestone).

Berries: (UK) Testicles.

Berry: 1) (UK) An easy victim for a con-artist. 2) (US) An easy opponent.

Bertie Smalls: (UK) An informer.

Berzonkers: (UK) An intense rage.

besos: (Internet/text) Kisses.

Best bib and tucker: (UK) One's finest clothes.

Bestie (US): Best friend.

Bet your bollocks: (UK) A certainty.

Bet your boots: (UK) A certainty.

Betcha: (Internet/text) Bet you.

Better half: One's husband, wife, or romantic partner.

Better to be blown up than shown up: (UK) Better to be brave and fail than to be cowardly.

bettr: (Internet/text) Better.

Betty: (UK) A girl, especially one who doesn't play a sport.

Between the horns: (US) In the center of the forehead.

Between the jigs and the reels: (Irish) Between one thing and another.

Between the sheets: In bed.

Between the two Ws: (UK) To be infected with a venereal disease.

Bev: (UK) An alcoholic beverage.

Bevvied: (UK) To be drunk or intoxicated.

Bevvy shop: (UK) A pub.

Bevvy: (UK) An alcoholic drink.

Bevvypint: (UK) A pint of beer.

Bevvy-up: (UK) A bout of heavy drinking.

bewbs (also "bewbz"): (Internet/text) Boobs.

Beyond the beyonds: (Irish) Excessive or unreasonable.

Beyond the rabbit-proof fence: (Australian) The wild countryside.

bezzie: (Internet/text) Best friend.

bf: (Internet/text) 1) Boyfriend. 2) Best friend.

bf4e: (Internet/text) Best friends forever.

bf4eva: (Internet/text) Best friends forever.

bf4l: (Internet/text) Best friends for life.

bfam: (Internet/text) Brother from another mother.

bfd: (Internet/text) Big fucking deal.

bff: (Internet/text) Best friend forever.

bffa: (Internet/text) Best friends for always.

bffl: (Internet/text) Best friends for life.

bfn: (Internet/text) Bye for now.

bg: (Internet/text) Background.

B-girl: (US) Female fan of rap music.
bh: (Internet/text) Bloody hell.
bhwu: (Internet/text) Back home with you.
bi: (Internet/text) Bye.
Bi: Bisexual.
biab: (Internet/text) Back in a bit.
biaf: (Internet/text) Back in a few.
bibi: (Internet/text) Bye-bye.
Bibleback: (UK) A pious person who frowns on ordinary people.
Bible-basher: (UK) An overly enthusiastic or aggressive advocate of the Bible.
Bible-pounder: (UK) An overly enthusiastic or aggressive advocate of the Bible.
Bible-puncher: (UK) An overly enthusiastic or aggressive advocate of the Bible.
Bible-thumper: (UK) An overly enthusiastic or aggressive advocate of the Bible.
bicbw: (Internet/text) But I could be wrong.
Biccy: (UK) A biscuit.
Bice of tenners: (UK) Twenty pounds sterling.
Bice: (UK) A two-year prison sentence.
Bicycle: (UK) A promiscuous woman.
Bide quiet: (UK) To be still and listen.
Biff: 1) (UK) To strike with the hand. 2) (Irish) A punishment involving a strike to the palm of the hand with a strap or cane.
Biffo: (Australian) A fight.
Biftad: (US) A male student of a preparatory school.
Big A: AIDS.
Big alley: (US) A main street.
Big B: (US) Baltimore, Maryland.
Big bickies: (Australian) A large sum of money.
Big blink: (UK) Death.
Big blue: (US) IBM (International Business Machines).
Big Brother: The government.
Big bucks: A large amount of money.

Big cheese: An important person.

Big deal: (US) 1) A serious issue. 2) Something that is worthy of attention.

Big enchilada: (US) An important (or self-important) person.

Big eye: (UK) A stare.

Big figure: (UK) A large, muscular person.

Big gates: (UK) Prison; jail.

Big girl's blouse: (UK) A weak or ineffectual man.

Big Green: (US) Dartmouth College, USA.

Big guy: (US) An affectionate term of address, typically for large male friends.

Big house: (UK) Prison; jail.

Big I am: (UK) A self-important or self-centered person.

Big job: (UK) A murder or a contract killing.

Big jobs: (UK) Excrement.

Big jump: (US) Death.

Big money: (US) A very large amount of money.

Big mover: (Australian) A successful person, particularly in regard to a man being successful with women.

Big noise: (UK) An important person.

Big one: (UK) One hundred pounds sterling.

Big potato: (UK) An important person.

Big red switch: (UK) The power switch.

Big red: (US) Cornell University, USA.

Big sleep: Death.

Big smoke: (Australian) The city.

Big time: (UK) Very.

Big wheel: (UK) An important person.

Big wig: An important person.

bigd: (Internet/text) Big deal.

Bigger state than China: (UK) A state of total chaos or confusion.

Bigger state than Texas: (UK) A state of total chaos or confusion.

Bighead: (UK) An egoist or self-centered person.

Bigitty: (UK) Arrogant or conceited.

Bigmouth: An indiscreet or boastful person.

Bignote: (Australian) An arrogant person.

Big-note: (Australian) To boast or praise.

Big-noter: (Australian) A boastful person.

bii: (Internet/text) Bye.

Bike: 1) (UK) A promiscuous woman. 2) (Boxing) A boxer going backwards around the ring.

Bikie: (Australian/New Zealand) A motorcycle rider or member of a motorcycle gang.

Bikkie: (Australian) A biscuit.

Bilge: (UK) Nonsense; rubbish.

Bilgewater: (UK) 1) A bad-tasting drink. 2) A flat beer.

Bilingual: (UK) A deceitful or boastful person.

Bilk: (UK) To cheat someone, particularly by withholding a payment.

Bill shop: (UK) A police station.

Bill: (UK) 1) The nose. 2) The police.

Billabong: (Australian) Waterhole.

Billet: (UK) To heckle or jeer.

Billies: (US) Money; dollar bills.

Bill-on-a-bike: (UK) A motorcycle police officer; a traffic cop.

Billy Button: (UK) A tailor.

Billy man: (UK) A police officer.

Billy Muggins: (UK) An idiot; a fool.

Billy no mates: (UK) A contemptible or friendless person.

Billy two sheds: (UK) A person who always has to be one better than everyone else.

Billy: 1) (UK) A police officer. 2) (Australian) A teapot.

Billy-O: (UK) Very; a great amount.

bilu: (Internet/text) Baby, I love you.

Bimbette: (UK) A silly, airheaded young girl.

Bimbo: (UK) An attractive but airheaded woman.

Bin: (UK) 1) To throw away or reject. 2) An asylum. 3) A jail cell.

Bind: (UK) 1) Something irritating. 2) To complain.

Bingle: (Australian) A car accident.

Bins: (UK) 1) Binoculars. 2) Spectacles. 3) Headphones or loud speakers.

Bint: (UK) Derogatory term for a girl or woman.

bio: (Internet/text) Biological break (e.g., bathroom break).

bion: (Internet/text) Believe it or not.

Birch broom in a fit: (UK) Wild and unruly hair.

Bird bandit: (UK) Someone who steals another person's woman.

Bird droppings: (UK) Something derisory or pitiful.

Bird: (UK) A woman.

Birdbath: (UK) A foolish person.

Bird-batten: (UK) To catch birds with nets.

Birdbrain: (UK) A foolish or airheaded person.

Birding: (UK) Chasing women.

Bird-kippy: (UK) To keep birds away from corn.

Birf: (UK) Birthday.

Birmingham screwdriver: (UK) A hammer.

Birthday suit: Naked.

Bis: (US) A handgun or pistol.

Biscuit: (UK) A young woman.

Bish: (UK) A mistake.

Bish-bash-bosh: (UK) To do something quickly or efficiently.

bisly: (Internet/text) But I still love you.

Bit of a brothel: (Australian) A mess.

Bit of crackling: (UK) An attractive woman.

Bit of fluff: (UK) A woman, especially a girlfriend.

Bit of rough: (UK) A male romantic partner whose toughness or lack of refinement makes them attractive.

Bit of skirt: (UK) A girl or woman.

Bit of slap and tickle: (UK) Sexual activities.

Bit of spare: (UK) A married person's additional lover.

Bit of stuff: (UK) 1) One's romantic partner. 2) A potential romantic partner.

Bit of the other: (UK) Sexual activity.

Bit on the side: (UK) An extramarital relationship.

Bit previous: (UK) Too early; premature.

Bit spit: (US) To vomit.

bitd: (Internet/text) Back in the day.

Bite the bullet: To do something (usually unpleasant) in order to get it over with.

Bite the dust: To die.

Bite: (UK) To be taken in by something.

Biter: (UK) An extortionist or scrounger.

Bities: (Australian) Biting insects.

Bits and bobs: (UK) Possessions; material objects.

Bitsa: (UK) A mongrel.

Bitser: (Australian) A mongrel.

Bitter oath: (UK) A definite oath.

Bitterzweet: (UK) Cider apple.

bitz: (Internet/text) Neighborhood.

Bivvy: (UK) A small tent or shelter.

biw: (Internet/text) Boss is watching.

biz: (Internet/text) Business.

bizi: (Internet/text) Busy.

Bizzie: (UK) Police officer.

Bizzies: (UK) The police.

Bizzo: (UK/Australian) 1) Business. 2) What needs to be done.

bk: (Internet/text) Back.

bka: (Internet/text) Better known as.

bl: (Internet/text) 1) Bad luck. 2) Boys love (yaoi).

Blab: To inform on someone; to reveal secrets.

Blabber: (Australian) A TV remote control.

Blabbermouth: A person who talks indiscreetly and shares private information.

Black bag job: (US) A break-in or covert operation performed by a government agency.

Black food: (UK) Guinness beer.

Black job: (UK) A funeral.

Black maria: (UK) A police car or prison van.

Black money box: (UK) A London taxi.

Black Peter: (Australian) A solitary confinement cell.

Black rat: (UK) 1) A London taxi. 2) A police officer in uniform.

Black Rock Day: (UK) An awful day when everything goes wrong.

Black stuff: (Irish) Guinness beer.

Black stump: (Australian) 1) A long way away. 2) The horizon.

Black velvet: (UK) A mixture of Guinness and champagne, or Guinness and cider.

Black widow: (UK) A woman who has had several husbands who passed away.

Black-bob: (UK) A cockroach.

Bladdered: (UK) To be very drunk or intoxicated.

Blade: (UK) A quick-witted person.

Blag: (UK) 1) A robbery. 2) To rob. 3) To bluff or mislead.

Blagger: (UK) A major thief.

Blah blah blah: 1) Describes someone talking verbosely. 2) Used in conversation to leave out details that the listener already knows.

Blah: (UK) Boring or meaningless details.

Blanch: (US) To vomit.

Blank: 1) (UK) To snub or refuse to speak to someone. 2) A rejection or defeat3) (US) Extremely low-grade.

Blanker: (UK) A spark; a cinder.

Blanket fever: (UK) A strong desire to stay in bed.

Blanket treatment: (UK) To be beaten up by prison officers.

Blanket: (UK) 1) A bed. 2) A thick skin on the top of custard.

Blast from the past: (UK) Refers to something nostalgic.

Blast: (UK) 1) A party or celebration. 2) A good time.

Blasted: (UK) 1) To be very drunk or intoxicated. 2) Heavily criticized.

Blatherskite: (UK) 1) A boastful person. 2) A disreputable person.

Blazes: (UK) Hell.

Bleat: (UK) 1) To complain. 2) To inform on others, especially to the police.

Bleeder: (UK) A contemptible person.

Bleeding: (UK) Very.

bleme: (Internet/text) Blog meme.

Blert: (UK) A contemptible or unpleasant person.

Blether: (Scottish) To speak for a long time.

bleve: (Internet/text) Believe.

blg: (Internet/text) Blog.

blh: (Internet/text) Bored like hell.

Blighted: (UK) To be drunk or intoxicated.

Blighty: (UK) Britain.

Blimey: (UK) An expression to express shock or surprise.

Blimp out: (US) To overeat.

Blimp: (UK) 1) A pompous, old-fashioned person. 2) An overweight person.

Blind: 1) (UK) A cover-up; something designed to conceal the truth. 2) (Gambling) To gamble without looking at one's cards. 3) To be very drunk or intoxicated.

Blinder: (UK) Something impressive or exciting.

Blindo: (UK) To be drunk or intoxicated.

Bling: (US) Jewelry or expensive (typically flashy) decorative items.

Blink: (UK) An alcoholic drink.

Blinker: (UK) A punch in the eye.

Blinkers: (UK) The eyes.

Blissed-out: (UK) Ecstatic; elated.

Blister: 1) (UK) A painful punishment. 2) An unpleasant person. 3) (New Zealand) A rebuke. 4) (UK/Australian/New Zealand) A court summons.

Blitz out: (UK) To escape from confinement.

Blitz: (UK) To break into a building for a robbery.

Blitzed: (UK) To be very drunk or intoxicated.

Blivet: (Computer) A problem or important piece of hardware that can't be fixed.

blnt: (Internet/text) Better luck next time.

Bloat: (UK) A worthless or immoral person.

Bloater: (UK) 1) An overweight person. 2) Something large and swollen.

Blob wagon: (UK) Ambulance.

Blob: (UK) 1) A corpse. 2) An ulcer. 3) A score of naught in cricket.

Block in: (UK) To have sex with someone.

Block it: (UK) To take illicit drugs.

Block: (UK) 1) The head. 2) The section of a prison that houses the punishment cells.

Blocked: (UK) To be drunk or intoxicated.

Blockhead: (UK) A foolish person.

Blog: (Internet/text) Web log.

Blogger: (Internet/text) Web logger.

Bloke: (UK) 1) A man. 2) Boyfriend.

Bloke-bird: (UK) A masculine woman.

Blokess: (UK) A woman who acts in a masculine way.

Blokey: (Australian) Male-orientated.

Blokish: (UK) Boisterous ("masculine") female behavior.

Blood alley: (US) An area where a four-lane highway narrows to two lanes.

Blood box: (US) An ambulance.

Blood bucket: (UK) A notoriously unruly bar.

Blood medicine: (US) Alcohol.

Blood or beer: (UK) A street challenge.

Blood wagon: (UK) An ambulance.

Bloodhound: (UK) A police officer.

Bloodhouse: (Australian) A public house with an unsavory reputation.

Blood-red fancy: (UK) A bright-red handkerchief.

Blood-worm: (UK) Black pudding.

Bloody flag is out: (UK) To be drunk or intoxicated.

Bloody Monday: (UK) The last day of a school term.

Bloody: (UK) Very.

Bloomer: (UK) A mistake.

Blooming: (UK) Very.

Blooper: (US) A mistake.

Blootered: (Scottish) To be drunk or intoxicated.

Blooth: (UK) Blossom.

Blops: (Gaming) Back Ops.

Blotto: (UK) To be drunk or intoxicated.

Blow a fuse: To lose one's temper.

Blow a gasket: To lose one's temper.

Blow a gut: (UK) To explode with laughter.

Blow away: (US) 1) To kill by shooting. 2) To defeat one's opponent overwhelmingly. 3) To make a big impression.

Blow beets: (US) To vomit.

Blow bile: (US) To vomit.

Blow breakfast: (US) To vomit.

Blow bubbles: (UK) To inform on others.

Blow chow: (US) To vomit.

Blow chowder: (US) To vomit.

Blow chunks: (US) To vomit.

Blow fire: (US) To do something well.

Blow it in: (UK) 1) To halt or abandon a project. 2) To take a break.

Blow one's cork: (UK) To lose one's temper.

Blow one's mind: Something that is surprising or very impressive.

Blow one's radiator cap: (UK) To lose one's temper.

Blow one's top: To lose one's temper.

Blow out: (UK) 1) Cancel; fail. 2) To reject someone.

Blow the gaff: (UK) To disclose a secret.

Blow: (Australian/New Zealand) To boast or brag.

Blower: (UK) 1) A braggart or loudmouth. 2) A telephone.

Blowhard: (UK) A braggart or loudmouth.

Blowhole: 1) (UK) The mouth. 2) (Australian) A talkative person.

Blowies: (Australian) Blowflies.

Blown away: 1) Killed. 2) Surprised or amazed.

Blown out: (UK) 1) Rejected. 2) Tired or exhausted. 3) (US) Ruined; failed.

Blow-out: (UK) An occasion to overindulge.

Blowser: (UK) An untidy woman.

Blub: (UK) To cry.

Blubber head: (UK) An idiot.

Blubber: 1) Fat. 2) An overweight person.

Bludge: (Australian) 1) To not do anything. 2) To beg.

Bludger: (Australian) A scrounger.

Blue Broadway: (US) Heaven.

Blue film to a man with no arms: (UK) Something that is useless.

Blue funk: 1) A state of fear. 2) A lack of courage.

Blue pipe: (UK) A vein.

Blue plum: (UK) A bullet.

Blue ribboner: (UK) A teetotaler.

Blue room: (UK) A punishment cell.

Blue ruin: (UK) Cheap gin.

Blue slop: (UK) A thin overall jacket.

Blue: (UK) 1) Police officer. 2) A Tory. 3) (Australian) A fight or argument.

Bluebottle: (UK) A police officer.

Bluenose: (US) 1) A puritanical or prudish person. 2) A sycophant. 3) Someone with a self-inflated opinion of themselves.

Blues and twos: (UK) An emergency vehicle's flashing lights and siren.

Blues: (UK) Depression; feeling sad.

Bluey: 1) (UK) A five pound note. 2) (Australian) A redheaded man.

bm&y: (Internet/text) Between you and me.

bm: (Internet/text) Bite me.

bm4l: (Internet/text) Best mates for life.

bma: (Internet/text) Best mates always.

bmay: (Internet/text) Between me and you.

bmf: (Internet/text) Be my friend.

bmfe: (Internet/text) Best mates forever.

bmfl: (Internet/text) Best mates for life.

bml: (Internet/text) Bless my life.

bn: (Internet/text) Been.

bng: (Internet/text) Being.

bnib: (Internet/text) Brand new in box.

bnol: (Internet/text) Be nice or leave.

bnr: (Internet/text) Banner.

bo (also "B.O."): (Internet/text) Body odor.

Boak: (Scottish) To vomit.

Boards: (UK) Playing cards.

Boat person: (UK) An illegal immigrant.

Boat: (UK) Big shoes or boots.

Bob: (UK) A shilling.

Bob's your uncle: (UK) Expresses that a situation can be handled with ease.

Bobbing and weaving: (UK) Getting by; getting along.

Bobbins: (UK) Nonsense; rubbish; useless.

Bobby: (UK) 1) A police officer. 2) Twenty pounds sterling.

Bobbydazzler: (UK) Something or someone impressive.

bobw: (Internet/text) Best of both worlds.

Bock: (UK) A jinx.

Bod: (UK) 1) An irritating person. 2) Body.

Bodes dodgy: (UK) Bad omens.

Bodge: (UK) 1) To make a mess of something. 2) To do a slapdash job.

Bodge-up: (UK) 1) A mess or disaster. 2) A slapdash repair.

Bodgie: (Australian) A male member of a youth cult.

Bodgy: (UK) 1) Inferior. 2) Malfunctioning.

Bodyshop: (UK) An employment agency.

Boff: (UK) To hit or punch. 2) (US) A loud laugh.

Boffo: (UK) Very good or successful.

Boffola: (US) A funny joke.

boffum: (Internet/text) Both of them.

Bog blocker: (UK) Something that makes you feel sick.

Bog eyed: (UK) Eyes that are puffy, especially from a lack of sleep.

Bog off: (UK) Go away!

Bog up: (UK) To make a mess of things.

Bog: (UK) 1) A lavatory. 2) A mess or disaster.

Bogan: (Australian) A foolish and ineffectual person.

Bogart: (UK) To monopolize a cigarette.

Bog-brush: (UK) A person with spiky hair.

Bogey team: (UK) A sports team that usually manages to win despite not being the best.

Bogey: 1) Snot. 2) (UK) A jinx. 3) A police officer or detective. 4) (US) An enemy aircraft.

Bogger: (UK) A peeping Tom; a voyeur.

Boggin: (Scottish) Something that is foul-smelling.

bogo: (Internet/text) Buy one, get one.

bogof: (Internet/text) Buy one, get one free.

Bogon: (US/computer) Someone who is considered fake and says untrue things.

Bogosity: (US/computer) The extent to which something is considered untrue.

Bog-roll: (UK) 1) Toilet paper. 2) Paperwork.

Bogsatt: (Internet/text) A group of guys sitting around a table.

Bog-standard: (UK) Normal; unremarkable.

Bogue: (US) 1) A period of withdrawal. 2) A cigarette.

Bogulate: (US) Surfing without skill.

Bogus beef: (US) A baseless complaint.

Bogus: (US) Fake.
Boho: (UK) A scruffy, careless person.
boi: (Internet/text) Boy.
Boiler room: (US) A room in which salespeople sell overpriced or misleading services or products over the telephone.
Boiler: (UK) A woman.
Boilermaker: 1) (UK) A beer that consists half of draught mild and half of bottled brown ale. 2) (US) A whisky followed by a beer chaser.
Boilerplate: (US) Standard; plain; ordinary.
Boink: (US) To have sex with someone.
Boko: (UK) The nose.
bol: (Internet/text) Barking out loud.
Bold: (UK) Flamboyant; audacious; fashionable.
Bolic: (UK) Anabolic steroids.
Boll weevils: (US) Conservative Southern democrats.
Bollitics: (UK) Political correctness that is overextended into absurdity.
Bollixed: (UK) Messed up.
Bollo: (UK) Bollocks.
Bollock brain: (UK) An idiot.
Bollock buster: (UK) A heavy weight to carry.
Bollock: (UK) 1) A dance. 2) To chastise someone harshly.
Bollockache: (UK) An unpleasant situation.
Bollock-head: (UK) A shaved head.
Bollocking: (UK) A harsh rebuke or dressing down.
Bollock-naked: (UK) Totally nude.
Bollocks in brackets: (UK) A bow-legged man.
Bollocks: (UK) Nonsense.
Bollocksed: (UK) Broken; messed up.
Bollocks-up: (UK) A mistake.
Bollocky: (Australian) Totally nude.
Bolo: (US/police) To be on the lookout for something or someone.
Bolt: To leave in a hurry; to run away.
Bolted-up: (UK) Falsely accused of a crime.
Bomb thrower: (UK) Someone unwilling to compromise on an issue or discuss it in good faith.

Bomb: (UK) 1) A large amount of money. 2) A major storm at sea. 3) To make a splash when jumping into water. 4) (Australian/New Zealand) An old or worn-out vehicle. 5) (US) To cover a wall with graffiti. 6) To fail badly. 7) The best.

Bombadier: (UK) A potato.

Bomber: A graffiti artist.

Bombhead: (UK) A person with a large head.

Bona: (UK) Excellent; great.

Bonce ponce: (UK) A parasite that lives in the hair.

Bonce: (UK) 1) The head. 2) A large playing marble.

Bone box: 1) (UK) A coffin. 2) (US) A hearse. 3) An ambulance.

Bone factory: (UK) A hospital.

Bone orchard: (US) A cemetery.

Bone shaker: (UK) A bumpy form of transport.

Bone: 1) (UK) To steal or to take possession of something. 2) (US) To victimize someone. 3) To have sexual intercourse.

Bone-ache: (UK) Aches and pains.

Bonehead: (UK) A dim-witted or stubborn person.

Boner: (UK) A blunder or mistake.

Bones: (UK) 1) Dice. 2) A ship's surgeon.

Boneshaker: (UK) An unsteady vehicle.

Boneyard: (UK) A cemetery.

Bonk: To have sex.

Bonkers: (UK) Crazy; delusional.

Bonnie: (Scottish) Beautiful.

Bonus: (UK) A bribe.

Bonzer: (Australian/New Zealand) Excellent.

Boob tube: 1) (UK) A close-fitting strapless top for women. 2) (Australian) A strapless, shapeless brassiere made of stretchy fabric. 3) (US/Canadian) A television receiver.

Boob: (UK) 1) A female breast. 2) A mistake. 3) An idiot.

Boo-boo: (UK) A mistake.

Boobs: Female breasts.

Booby: (UK) An idiot or foolish person.

Boofhead: (Australian) 1) An idiot. 2) A person or animal with a big head.

Booger: Snot.

Boogie box: (UK) A cassette player or stereo.

Boogie: To dance to pop music.

Book: (US) 1) To place a reservation. 2) To leave in a hurry; to run away.

Boolie: (UK) An enema.

Boom: (US) 1) A car music system. 2) A party.

Boomer: 1) (US) Someone born during a baby boom. 2) (Australian) A large male kangaroo.

boomm: (Internet/text) Bored out of my mind.

Boondocks: (US) A rural, often isolated, community.

Boost: (US) To steal.

Booster: (US) A shoplifter.

Boot trees: (UK) The feet.

Boot: (US) A navy or marine recruit, typically one who is still in training.

Booted: (US) Expelled or fired.

Bootface: (UK) A miserable face.

Bootie: (UK) A Royal Marine.

Bootlicker: An obsequious person.

Bootnose: (UK) A person with a broken or misshapen nose.

Boots: (UK) Tires.

Boot-snitch: (US) Information.

Booty: (US) The buttocks.

Bootylicious: (US) Sexually attractive.

Booze: An alcoholic drink.

Boozed: To be drunk or intoxicated.

Boozer: (UK) 1) A pub or bar. 2) A heavy drinker.

Booze-up: (UK) An occasion to drink heavily.

Bop: 1) A dance. 2) To hit or punch.

Borak: (Australian/New Zealand) Nonsense; rubbish.

bord: (Internet/text) Bored.

Bored out of one's skull: (UK) Incredibly bored.

Born again virgin: A person who hasn't had sex in a long time.

Boron: (UK) An ignorant bore who acts like a know-it-all.

bos: (Internet/text) Boss over shoulder.

Boss: Excellent; great.

Boss-eyed: (UK) Awry; muddled.

Bot: (Australian) To irritate. 2) (UK) The bottom.

Bother: (UK) Trouble; aggression.

Botheration: (UK) A small annoyance.

Botherments: (UK) Problems or minor annoyances.

botoh: (Internet/text) But on the other hand.

Bottle blonde: (UK) A person with dyed blonde hair.

Bottle of milk: (UK) A very pale white person.

Bottle opener: (UK) A laxative.

Bottle out: (UK) To lose one's nerve.

Bottle up and go: (US) To leave.

Bottle: (UK) 1) Courage; nerve. 2) Money that is collected by street performers.

Bottled promise: (UK) A promise given while drinking alcohol and which is unlikely to be kept when sober.

Bottled: (UK) To be drunk or intoxicated.

Bottom of a birdcage: (UK) Very dry.

Bottom: A submissive sexual partner.

Boulder bonce: (UK) A bald person.

Bounce: (UK) 1) To trick someone into believing or doing something. 2) Swagger or cockiness. 3) For a check to be refused by the bank. 4) To leave; to head out.

Bounced: (UK) To be expelled or fired.

Bounce-up: (UK) A fight or brawl.

Bounder: (UK) A contemptible person.

Bounding: (UK) To act impudently.

Bout: (Internet/text) About.

Bovered: (Internet/text) Bothered.

Bovver boots: (UK) Heavy boots, often with a steel toecap.

Bovver boy: (UK) A young male who seeks out trouble.

Bovver: (UK) Unruliness, particularly resulting from teenage youths.

Bovver-boy: (UK) A youth who likes causing trouble.

Bow down before the porcelain god: (US) To vomit.

Bow locks: (UK) Nonsense; rubbish.

Bowl a wide: (UK) To make a mistake.

Bowl: (UK) Walk; gait.

Bowser: (UK) An unattractive woman.

Bowt: (Internet/text) About.

Bow-wow: (UK) 1) An unattractive woman. 2) A dog.

Box of birds: (UK) A state of joy; happiness.

Box the fox: (Irish) To rob an orchard.

Box: (Australian) Female genitals.

boxor: (Internet/text) Box.

Boy racer: (UK) A young male who drives dangerously fast.

Boy scout with agorophobia: (UK) Describes something useless.

Boysie: (UK) 1) A term of address for a man. 2) A kiss on the cheek.

Boystown: (UK) The male homosexual scene.

Bozo: (US) A fool; a chump.

br: (Internet/text) Bathroom.

Brace of horned corns: (US) Aching feet.

Brace: (US) Accost.

Bracelets: (UK) Handcuffs.

Brackers: (UK) To be without money.

Bracket: (UK) The nose and mouth.

Bradbury: (UK) A one-pound note.

Brads: (UK) Money.

Brady: (US) A white middle-class person from the suburbs.

Brah: (Internet/text) Brother.

Brahma: (UK) 1) An attractive girl or girlfriend. 2) Money or wealth. 3) Good.

Brain failure: (UK) An instance of forgetfulness.

Brain(s): 1) Intelligence. 2) A clever person.

Brain: To hit someone hard on the head.

Brainbox: (UK) 1) The skull. 2) An intelligent person.

Brains: (UK) 1) The Criminal Investigation Department. 2) An idiot.

Brainstem: (US) An eccentric person.

Brainwave: (UK) A sudden idea that is great.

Brass hat: (UK) A senior officer in the armed forces or police.

Brass monkeys: (UK) Very cold weather.

Brass neck: (UK) Impertinent; very cheeky.

Brassed off: (UK) Fed up; disgruntled.
Brassick: (UK) Penniless.
Brasswork: (UK) A promiscuous woman.
Brassy: (UK) A flashy, loud woman.
Brat: A badly behaved child.
Brattery: (UK) A nursery; a creche.
Braveheart: (UK) A Scotsman.
Braw: (Scottish) Attractive; good-looking.
Brawl: (US/Canadian) An uproarious party.
brb: (Internet/text) Be right back.
brbl: (Internet/text) Be right back later.
brbs: (Internet/text) Be right back soon.
brd: (Internet/text) Bored.
Bread and scrape: (UK) A slice of bread with a thin spread of butter.
Bread hooks: (UK) The hands or fingers.
Bread: Money.
Breadbasket: (UK) The stomach.
Breadhead: (UK) Someone motivated by money.
Breadspread: (UK) A fat that can be spread on bread.
Break one's duck: (UK) For a man to lose his virginity.
Break shins: (UK) To borrow money.
Break up: (UK) To cause or be overcome with laughter.
Breakneck speed: Very fast.
Breeze: Very easy.
Brekkers: (UK) Breakfast.
Brekkie: (Australian) Breakfast.
Brekky: (UK) Breakfast.
Brew: 1) (UK) Tea. 2) (US) Beer.
Brewer's droop: (UK) Temporary impotence owing to excessive alcohol consumption.
Brewski: (US) Beer.
brgds: (Internet/text) Best regards.
brh: (Internet/text) Be right here.
Brian: (UK) A boring, inane person.
Brick in one's hat: (UK) To be drunk.

Brick it: (UK) 1) A smash-and-grab robbery. 2) To be scared.

Brick: (UK) 1) A good fellow. 2) To castrate.

Bricked: (UK) To be castrated.

Bricking it: (UK) To be scared.

Bridge: (US) A quantity of four.

Bridger: (UK) Constipation.

Bridget Joneses: (UK) Large women's knickers.

Bridgets: (UK) Large women's knickers.

Brief: (UK) 1) A lawyer (especially a barrister). 2) A passport. 3) A pawnbroker's ticket. 4) A driving license. 5) A membership card.

Brig: (UK) A prison.

Brill: (UK) Brilliant; awesome.

Bring down: (UK) To cause someone's mood to lower.

Bringdown: (UK) A disappointment.

Brinny: (Australian) A stone, especially on that is thrown.

Briny: (UK) The sea.

Bristles: (UK) A moustache.

Brit: A British person.

Brixton briefcase: (UK) A portable radio or cassette player.

brk: (Internet/text) Break.

Bro: Brother.

Broads: (UK) 1) Playing cards. 2) Credit cards.

Broke: (UK) To not have any money.

Bromide: (UK) Someone who is conventional in their thoughts and speech.

Bromidiom: (UK) A conventional comment or saying.

Bronze: (UK) Non-silver coins.

Broom off: (UK) To get rid of something.

Broomhead: (UK) An idiot.

Bros: Brothers.

Broseph: (Internet/text) Brother.

Brothel creepers: (US) Shoes with thick crepe soles.

Brothel stompers: (US) Shoes with thick crepe soles.

Brother of the badge: (UK) A London taxi driver.

Brover: (Internet/text) Brother.

Brown bottle: (UK) Beer.

Brown food: (UK) Beer; ale.
Brown tongue: (UK) To be obsequious.
Brown trousers: (UK) Very frightening.
Browned off: (UK) 1) Bored. 2) Angry. 3) Disgusted.
Brownie points: (UK) Credit for doing something good.
Brownie: (UK) A whisky.
Brown-nose: (UK) To be subservient to someone; to be a sycophant.
brt: (Internet/text) Be right there.
Bruh: (Internet/text) Brother.
Brum: (UK) Birmingham.
Brummagem screwdriver: (UK) A hammer.
Brummagem: (UK) 1) Birmingham. 2) Counterfeit. 3) Flashy but cheap.
Brummie: (UK) 1) Someone from Birmingham. 2) The dialect spoken in Birmingham.
Bruno: (US) Brown University.
Brush off: To dismiss or ignore someone.
Brush: 1) (Australian) A woman. 2) (UK) Sexual activity.
Brutal: (Irish) 1) Terrible; awful. 2) Difficult.
Bruv: (Internet/text) Brother.
Bruva: (Internet/text) Brother.
Bruz: (Internet/text) Brothers.
Bryant and May: (UK) Light ale.
BSOD: (Computer) Blue screen of death.
bsx: (Internet/text) Bisexual.
bt: (Internet/text) Bit torrent.
btb: (Internet/text) By the by.
btcn: (Internet/text) Better than Chuck Norris.
btd: (Internet/text) Bored to death.
btdt: (Internet/text) Been there, done that.
btdtgtts: (Internet/text) Been there, done that, got the T-shirt.
btfl: (Internet/text) Beautiful.
bth: (Internet/text) Be totally honest.
btias: (Internet/text) Be there in a second.
btm: (Internet/text) Bottom.
btr: (Internet/text) Better.

bts: (Internet/text) Be there soon.

bttt: (Internet/text) Been there, tried that.

btw: (Internet/text) By the way.

btwn: (Internet/text) Between.

bty: (Internet/text) Back to you.

Bub: (Australian/New Zealand) A baby.

bubar: (Internet/text) Beyond all recognition.

Bubbies: (UK) Breasts.

Bubble up: (UK) To inform on others.

Bubble: (UK) 1) A sham company. 2) To swindle. 3) A simpleton. 4) To inform on others.

Bubblebrain: (UK) A simpleton.

Bubbled up: (UK) Informed upon.

Bubbled: (UK) Informed upon.

Bubblegum: (UK) Overly commercial pop music that targets a very young audience.

Bubbly: Champagne.

bubi: (Internet/text) Bye-bye.

Buck house: (UK) Buckingham Palace.

Buck: 1) (US/Canadian/Australian) A dollar. 2) A young male member of a street gang.

Bucket of cold mud: (US) Chocolate ice cream.

Bucket of hail: (US) A glass of ice.

Bucket shop: (US) A place where facilities are given for betting small sums of money. 2) A place that sells cheap airline seats.

Bucket: (UK) A ship or boat. 2) An old car. 3) To rain heavily.

Bucketing down: (Irish) To be raining hard.

Bucketing: (Australian) To criticize someone or something harshly.

Buckley's chance: (Australian/New Zealand) Something that has no chance at all.

Buckshee: (UK) Without charge; free.

Budgie: (UK) A talkative person.

Buff: (UK) 1) Naked. 2) A muscular figure. 3) An enthusiast or aficionado of something. 4) (Irish) A self-important person.

Buffaloed: (US) Bullied; overwhelmed.

Buffoon: A foolish person.

Bug house: (US) A mental hospital.

Bug out: To leave in a hurry; to run away.

Bug path: (UK) A hair parting.

Bug rake: (UK) A comb.

Bug run: (UK) A hair parting.

Bug walk: (UK) A hair parting.

Bug: 1) An insect. 2) A covert listening device. 3) A virus or infection. 4) To annoy someone.

Bug-a-lug: (UK) 1) A scarecrow. 2) A scruffy-looking person.

Bugged: Irritated or angry.

Bugger about (or around): (UK) 1) To act frivolously. 2) To waste time.

Bugger all: (UK) Nothing.

Bugger off: (UK) Go away!

Buggeration: (UK) Ruin; disorder.

Buggered: (UK) Exhausted; ruined; broken.

Buggery grips: (UK) Sideburns.

Buggy: (US) Crazy; insane.

Bughouse: 1) (UK) A decrepit building. 2) (US) A mental hospital or asylum.

Bugle: (UK) The nose.

Bugle-duster: (UK) A handkerchief.

Bug-smasher: (US) A light aircraft.

Bugsy: (UK) A crazy person.

buhbi: (Internet/text) Bye-bye.

Build a sconce: (UK) To run up a score.

Built for comfort: (UK) An overweight person.

Built: A muscular physique.

Bull artist: (UK) A person who spouts nonsense while trying to impress or hoodwink others.

Bull dust: (Australian) Nonsense.

Bull fiddle: (UK) A double bass.

Bull merchant: (UK) A person who spouts nonsense while trying to impress or hoodwink others.

Bull session: (UK) An earnest but shallow conversation.

Bull: 1) (US/Australian) A police officer in uniform. 2) Nonsense; something that is untrue.

Bull's eye: (UK) Fifty pounds sterling.

Bulldoze: To force things to go your preferred way.

Bullet: (UK) 1) A playing card with one pip. 2) A dismissal, often without notice.

Bullets: (UK) Hard peas.

Bullock's blood: (UK) A cocktail of beer and rum.

Bullshine: (UK/military) An unnecessary regimental routine.

Bullywayo: (UK) A bully.

Bum (one) Out: To sadden someone.

Bum bag: (UK) A bag or pouch that is worn around the waist.

Bum fodder: (UK) 1) Toilet paper. 2) Newspaper.

Bum freezer: (UK) An Eton jacket (or one of similar style), typically worn by men.

Bum rap: A false charge or unjust punishment.

Bum up: (UK) To praise; to speak highly of someone or something.

Bum's rush: (UK) 1) A quick dismissal. 2) A forceful ejection.

Bumbershoot: (UK) An umbrella.

Bumf: (UK) 1) Toilet paper. 2) Information on paper.

Bumfluff: (UK) Light facial hair, especially on a young teenager.

Bumfreezer: (UK) A short jacket, especially an Eton Jacket.

Bummed out: (US) Disappointed; dejected.

Bummer: (US) 1) An idle or worthless person. 2) Something that is disappointing or sad.

Bump off: (UK) To murder or kill.

Bump start: (UK) A sudden rousing to action.

Bump tummies: (UK) To have sex.

Bump: 1) (Internet/text) To comment in a thread in order to bring it to the top of the page. 2) To remove someone from a waiting list.

Bumpers: (UK) Tennis shoes.

Bumph: (UK) 1) Toilet paper. 2) Information on paper.

Bumsucker: (UK) Someone who acts in an obsequious manner.

Bumsucking: (UK) Obsequious behavior.

Bumswizzled: (UK) To be drunk or intoxicated.

Bumwad: (UK) Toilet paper.

Bun fight: (UK) 1) A tea party. 2) An official function.

Bun in the oven: Pregnant.

Bunce: (UK) Money or profit; perks; bonuses.

Bunch of fives: (UK) A fist.

Bunco: (US) A scam or fraud.

Bundle: 1) (US) A large amount of money or something desirable. 2) (UK) A fight.

Bung in the bottle: (UK) Constipation.

Bung: (UK) 1) A bribe or gratuity, especially given to the police. 2) To throw or hand something over. 3) (Australian/New Zealand) Dead; ruined; useless.

Bungalow Bill: (UK) An idiotic man.

Bungalow: (UK) A well-endowered but foolish man.

Bunger: (Australian) A firework.

Bungie: (UK) A rubber eraser.

Bungy: (UK) A rubber eraser.

Bunk in: (UK) To enter somewhere illicitly.

Bunk off: (UK) To play truant.

Bunk: 1) (UK) To abscond. 2) Nonsense; rubbish. 3) (US) Unfashionable. 4) To cheat.

Bunkies: (UK) Sexual intercourse.

Bunk-up: (UK) To have sexual intercourse.

Bunny boiler: (UK) An overly possessive woman.

Bunny: 1) (UK) Incessant chatter. 2) (Australian) A mug; a dupe.

Buns: 1) (UK) Food. 2) (US) The buttocks. 3) (Australian) Sanitary products.

Bup: (UK) 1) A slice of bread and butter. 2) Money.

Burg: (US) A town or place.

Buried: (UK) Imprisoned.

Burk: (UK) An idiot; a jerk.

Burl: (Australian) An attempt.

Burleycue: (US) Burlesque theatre.

Burly: 1) (US) Something difficult. 2) (UK) A large, muscular physique.

Burn off: (UK) To overtake and humiliate another driver.

Burn oil: (UK) To drive an old car.

Burn rubber: To drive very fast.

Burn smoke: (US) To drive very fast.

Burn someone's goat: (US) To annoy or anger someone.

Burn the British: (US) A toasted muffin.

Burn: 1) (UK/prison) Tobacco; a cigarette. 2) To kill by shooting.

Burned: To be cheated; for your expectations to have been far greater than the result.

Burner: (UK) A venereal disease.

Burnout: Mental or physical exhaustion, especially from overwork or stress.

Burnt offering: (UK) Overcooked food.

Burn-toast: (UK) A useless cook.

Burn-up: (UK) Fast driving.

Bury the hatchet: To let bygones be bygones.

Bury: To win by a wide margin.

Bush lawyer: (Australian) A person who tries to enforce rules without having the authority to do so.

Bush parole: (US/prison) An escape.

Bush: (UK) Provincial or rural.

Bush-bashing: (Australian/New Zealand) Forging a path through the bush.

Bushed: (UK) Exhausted.

Busher: (US) 1) An amateur. 2) An uncultured person.

Bushie: (Australian) A rural or unsophisticated person; a yokel.

Bushwhacker: (Australian) An unsophisticated person; a yokel.

Busk it: (UK) To improvise.

Bust one's buns: (US) To exhaust oneself working.

Bust one's conk: (US) To work hard.

Bust: 1) An arrest. 2) An escape from prison. 3) To burgle. 4) (US/army) A demotion. 5) (Australian) A burglary or break-in.

Buster: 1) (UK) A man or boy. 2) A bet of four or more accumulators. 3) (US/Canadian) Someone who breaks horses.

Busting: (UK/Midlands) Good; excellent.

buszay: (Internet/text) Busy.

Butch up: (UK) To become more assertive or masculine.

Butch: 1) Distinctly masculine. 2) A masculine lesbian.

Butt out: (US) Stop interfering!

Butt: 1) The buttocks. 2) A jerk.

Butterball: (US) An overweight person.

Butterboy: (UK) A novice.

Butterface: (Internet/text) Everything is hot but her face.

Butthead: (UK) A jerk or stupid person.

Buttie: (UK) A sandwich.

Buttinski (also "buttinsky"): A person who frequently interrupts others.

Button it: (UK) To shut up; to keep quiet.

Button one's lip: (UK) To shut up; to keep quiet.

Buttoned up: To be taciturn.

Butty: 1) (UK) A sandwich. 2) (Welsh) A close friend.

buwu: (Internet/text) Breaking up with you.

Buy a pup: (UK) To be swindled.

Buy it: To die; to be killed.

Buy the farm: (US) To die; to be killed.

Buy the rabbit: (UK) To fare badly.

Buy: (UK) To accept something as true.

Buyer: (UK) A receiver of stolen goods.

Buzz off: (UK) Go away!

Buzz: 1) A rumor. 2) A pleasant sensation, especially from caffeine or intoxication. 3) A sense of excitement or adrenaline.

Buzzard: (UK) A cantankerous old person.

Buzzcocks: (UK) Bollocks.

Buzz-crusher: (UK) A killjoy; a person who ruins the mood.

Buzzer: (UK) A pickpocket.

Buzzing: (UK) To be intoxicated.

bw3: (Internet/text) Buffalo Wild Wings.

bwim: (Internet/text) By which I mean.

bwt: (Internet/text) But when though?

By a jugful: (US) By a long way; by a good deal.

By a long chalk: (UK) By a long way; by a good deal.

By a long shot: By a long way; by a good deal.

By a long sight: (US) By a long way; by a good deal.

By a street: (UK) By a long way.

By chalks: (Australian) By a long way.

By the neck: (Scottish/Irish) A beer served in the bottle.

By'n-by: (UK) Later on.

byak: (Internet/text) Blowing you a kiss.

byeas: (Internet/text) Goodbye.

Bye-byes: (UK) 1) Sleep. 2) Unconsciousness.

byes: (Internet/text) Bye-bye.

bykt: (Internet/text) But you knew that.

byob: (Internet/text) Bring your own beer/booze.

byoc: (Internet/text) Bring your own computer.

byself: (Internet/text) By myself.

bz: (Internet/text) Busy.

bzns: (Internet/text) Business.

bzy: (Internet/text) Busy.

bzzy: (Internet/text) Busy.

C&C: (Gaming) Command & Conquer.
C&V: (Internet/text) Chapter & verse.
c/b: (Internet/text) Comment back.
c/t: (Internet/text) Can't talk.
c: (Internet/text) See.
c@: (Internet/text) Cat.
c|n>k: (Internet/text) Coffee through nose into keyboard.
c'mon: (Internet/text) Come on.
c14n: (Internet/text) Canonicalization.
c2: (Internet/text) Come to.
c2c: (Internet/text) Cam to cam.
c2c: (Internet/text) Care to chat?
c2tc: (Internet/text) Cut to the chase.
c4y: (Internet/text) Cool for you.
Cab yab: (UK) Money; bank notes.
Cabbage head: (UK) A fool; a dim-witted person.
Cabbage: (UK) 1) A dim-witted person. 2) To pilfer or steal.
Cabbaged: (UK) To be drunk or intoxicated.
Caboose: (UK) A prison; a jail.
Ca-ca (also "caca"): (UK) Excrement.
Cacatorium: (UK) A lavatory.
Cack-catchers: (Australian) Trousers.
Cack-handed: (UK) Clumsy; unskilled.
Cad: (UK)A contemptible person.
Caddle: (UK) Confusion; a muddle.
Caddy: Cadillac.
Cady: (UK) A hat.
Cafeteria: (UK/cricket) An easy-to-hit ball.
Caff: (UK) Cafe.
Cag mag: (UK) An annoying person.

Cage: (UK) A prison cell.

Cake hole: (Australian) A person's mouth.

Cakery: (UK) A bakery.

Calaboose: (UK) A prison; a jail.

Calendar: (UK) A year in prison.

California special: (US) An artificially enhanced coin.

Call a copper!: (UK) A cry of alarm.

Call it quits: 1) To stop working; to take a break. 2) To give up.

Call the shots: To be in a leadership position; to make the decisions.

cam: (Internet/text) 1) Webcam. 2) Camera.

Camister: (UK) A priest; a vicar.

Camp: (UK) 1) To carry oneself in an effeminate or theatrical way. 2) Homosexual.

Can do: (US) Totally possible.

Can it: (UK) Be quiet!

Can of worms: A very complicated situation.

Can: (UK) 1) A lavatory. 2) A prison or police cell. 3) (US) To dismiss from employment. 4) To suppress or conceal something. 5) To imprison.

Can't take a trick: (Australian) To be consistently unsuccessful.

Cancer stick: (UK) A cigarette.

Candle basher: (UK) A spinster.

Candles: (UK) Discharge from the nose running toward the mouth.

Candyass: (US) A weak or effete person.

Cane: (UK) 1) Assault; beat. 2) To criticize harshly.

Caned: (UK) To be drunk or intoxicated.

Caner: (UK) A school teacher.

Canister: (UK) The head.

Canned: (UK) 1) To be drunk or intoxicated. 2) Arrested; caught.

Canny: (UK) 1) Quick-witted. 2) Attractive.

Canoodle: (UK) To kiss and cuddle.

Cans: (UK) Headphones.

Canteen medal: (UK) A food stain on one's clothes.

Canvas: (UK) The skin.

Capeesh: (UK) Understand?

Caper: (UK) An activity. 2) (US/Canadian) An organized crime.

Capon: A red herring; a false trail.
Capper: (US) A by-bidder; a decoy for gamblers.
Captain sensible: (UK) A responsible, level-headed man.
Capture: (UK) To seduce someone.
Car surfing: (US) Riding on the roof of a moving car.
Carbolic naked: (UK) Naked; nude.
Carcass trade: (UK) Repurposing old furniture to pass them off as antiques.
Cardie: (UK) A cardigan.
Cark: (Australian) 1) To break down. 2) To die.
Cark it: (New Zealand) To die.
Carn: (UK) Money; cash.
Carny (also "carney" or "carnie"): 1) (UK) Hypocritical. 2) (US/Canadian) A carnival; a person who works in a carnival.
Caroon: (UK) Twenty-five pence.
Carrot cruncher: (UK) Someone who lives in the countryside.
Carrot-top: A redhead.
Carry: 1) (US) To be in possession of illicit drugs. 2) (UK) To have plenty of money on oneself.
Carry-out: (UK) An alcoholic drink bought as a pub or bar is closing to be consumed off the premises.
Carve up: (UK) 1) To deliberately ruin a person's chances at something. 2) To cut in front of another driver.
Carve: (UK) To attack with a knife.
Carver: (UK) A knife used as a weapon.
Carve-up: (UK) 1) The distribution of something. 2) A scam that ruins one's chances at something.
Cas: (US) Relaxed; nonchalant.
Case: 1) A crazy person. 2) To inspect a place, especially as the target for a crime.
Cased up: (UK) To be dressed.
Caser: (UK) Twenty-five pence.
Cash in: (UK) To die.
Caso: (UK) Crazy; unpredictable.
Cassava: (US) A woman, especially one who is available.
Cat lick: (UK) Catholic.

Cat: (UK) 1) Bad; terrible. 2) A vindictive woman.

Cat's breakfast: (UK) A mess; something done very poorly.

Cat's lick: (UK) A quick wash.

Cat's pyjamas: (UK) Someone or something that is excellent.

Cat's whiskers: (UK) Someone or something that is excellent.

Catch a cold: (UK) To make a loss; lose one's investment.

Catch a few Zs: (US) To get some sleep.

Catch on: To understand something.

Catch some rays: To sunbathe.

Catch some Zs: (US) To get some sleep.

Catch-22: (US) An impossible situation with no simple solution.

Cathouse: (UK) A brothel.

Cats and dogs: (UK) Heavy rain.

Catting: (UK) To search for a sexual partner.

Cattle market: (UK) A place where women gather.

Cattle train: (US) A Cadillac.

Catty: 1) (UK) A catapult. 2) Spiteful.

catwot: (Internet/text) Complete and total waste of time.

Caught short: (UK) A sudden need to go to the toilet.

Cavalier: (UK) An uncircumcised male.

Cave in: To submit or yield, especially to pressure.

Cavy: (UK) Beware.

cayc: (Internet/text) Call at your convenience.

cb: (Internet/text) Come back.

cba: (Internet/text) Can't be arsed.

cbb: (Internet/text) Can't be bothered.

cbi: (Internet/text) Can't believe it.

cc: (Social media) Carbon copy.

ccl: (Internet/text) Couldn't care less.

ccna: (Internet/text) Cisco certified network associate.

cd9: (Internet/text) Code 9 (a warning that other people are nearby).

Cec: (Internet/text) Sex.

Cecil: (UK) Pounds sterling.

Celestial discharge: (UK/nursing) Death.

Celestial transfer: (UK/nursing) Death.

celly: (Internet/text) Cell phone.
Cementhead: (US) An idiot; a dim-witted person.
Centre forward: (UK) A nine playing card.
Cereb: (US) A person who studies hard.
Cess: (Irish) Luck.
Cessy: (UK) Foul; objectionable.
cex: (Internet/text) Sex.
cexy: (Internet/text) Sexy.
cfas: (Internet/text) Care for a secret?
cfid: (Internet/text) Check for identification.
cg: (Internet/text) Congratulations.
cgad: (Internet/text) Couldn't give a damn.
cgf: (Internet/text) Cute guy friend.
ch@: (Internet/text) Chat.
Chain gang: (UK) Married men.
Champers: (UK) Champagne.
Champion: (UK) Brilliant.
Champs: (Internet/text) Champions.
Chancer: 1) (Irish) Someone who takes risks. 2) (UK) An unscrupulous opportunist.
Chandu: (US) To vomit.
char: 1) (Internet/text) Character. 2) (UK) A cup of tea.
Chara: (UK) A motor coach.
Charge: (UK) A thrill.
Charles Atlas: (UK) A small man.
Charlie's dead: (UK) For someone's underwear or petticoat to be showing.
Charra: (UK) A coach.
Charver (also "charva"): (UK) 1) Sexual intercourse 2) An easy lay. 3) To mess up or spoil something.
Charvered: (UK) Exhausted.
Chase one's tail: (UK) To be very busy.
Chase the dog end: (UK) To urinate.
Chase: (UK) To carry on gambling after a losing streak.
Chassis: (UK) A person's body, especially in reference to a woman.
Chateau'd: (UK) To be drunk or intoxicated.

Chattermag: (UK) 1) A magpie. 2) A talkative woman.

Chaunter: (UK) Someone who sells newspapers on the street.

Chav: (UK) 1) A person who is (or feigns to be) of low social standing and dresses accordingly, often in sports clothing. 2) Council-housed and violent.

Chavvy lavvy: (UK) A child's potty.

Chavvy: (UK) A child.

Chaw: (UK) To steal.

Chawry goods: (UK) Stolen goods.

Cheapo: (UK) Cheap; simple.

Cheat the worms: (UK) To recover from a bad accident or illness.

Check it out: (US) Pay attention.

Check out: To die.

Check the war: (US) An order to stop arguing.

Check your nerves: (US) An order to keep cool.

Cheek: Impudent; impertinent; sassy.

Cheerful earful: (UK) Bad news.

Cheers: 1) (UK) An expression of appreciation or acknowledgement. 2) A toast before drinking.

Cheese effect: (UK) A false smile.

Cheese it: (US) 1) Run away. 2) Exploit a situation.

Cheese: 1) (UK) Detest. 2) (Australian) A wife.

Cheeseball: (US) A corny or silly person.

Cheesebox: (US) A run-down vehicle.

Cheesecake: (US) Pin-up pictures.

Cheesecaker: (US) A photographer who specializes in producing pin-ups.

Cheese-cutter: (UK) 1) A curved, aquiline nose. 2) A large square peak on a cap.

Cheesecutter: (UK) A flat cap.

Cheese-cutters: (UK) Bandy legs.

Cheesed off: Irritated; angry.

Cheesy: Hackneyed or trite.

Chelsea smile: (UK) A scar running from the mouth to the ear.

Chernobyl packet: (Computer) A network packet that causes a network meltdown.

Cherries: (US) A police car's flashing lights.

Cherry: A virgin; virginity. 2) Brand new.

Chestnut: (UK) An old joke or story.

Chesty: (UK) To be heavy-chested.

Chevy: (UK) A Chevrolet car.

Chew someone out: (US) To chastise someone.

Chew up: (UK) To make someone nervous or anxious.

Chewers: (US) Teeth.

Chi-ack: (UK) Tease; taunt.

Chic: Good form; stylish.

Chi-chi: 1) Posh; pretentious. 2) Overly cute.

Chick: A girl or young woman, especially an attractive one.

Chicken feed: A small amount of money.

Chicken ranch: (US) A rural brothel.

Chicken soup: (UK) Acceptable; fine.

Chicken: 1) A coward. 2) A young, inexperienced person.

Chickie: (UK) A young girl.

chik: (Internet/text) Chick.

Children: (UK) A housebreaker's tools.

Chill out: Relax; be calm.

Chill: 1) Relax. 2) To kill.

Chillax: (Internet/text) Chill and relax.

Chillin (also "chillin'"): (Internet/text) Relaxing.

Chimney: (UK) A heavy smoker.

Chin: (UK) To hit someone hard.

China pot: (UK) Great riches.

Ching: (UK) A five-pound note.

Chinker: (UK) Five.

Chinkers: (UK) Coins.

Chinless wonder: (UK) A gormless person.

Chinny: (UK/boxing) 1) An opponent who is knocked down easily. 2) (US) Talkative.

Chin-prop: (UK) A brooch.

Chin-splitter: (US) A goatee beard that is narrow.

Chinstrap: 1) (UK) The buttocks. 2) (Irish) A tide mark around the neck.

Chintz: (UK) A bedbug.

Chintzy: (US) Mean; miserly. 2) Second-rate.

Chinwag: (UK) To chat.

Chip in: To contribute, especially financially.

Chip together: (US) To contribute or cooperate.

Chip: (UK) A child.

Chiphead: (UK) A technical person.

Chippens: (Irish) Money.

Chipper: Lively; cheerful.

Chipping: (Australian) Cheeky; impertinent.

Chippy: 1) A fish and chip shop. 2) (UK/New Zealand) A carpenter.

Chips: (UK) A carpenter. 2) Money.

Chipsy: (US) Arrogant; superficial.

Chirky: (US) Cheerful.

Chirpy: Cheerful; in an upbeat mood.

Chisel: (UK) To cut something close, as in a bargain or to swindle someone.

Chiseller: 1) (UK) A swindler. 2) (Irish) A child.

Chiv: (UK) A knife.

Chivey: (UK) 1) To tease. 2) Noisy. 3) To chase about.

Chiv-man: (UK) Someone skilled at handling a knife.

Chivver: (UK) Someone skilled at handling a knife.

chk: (Internet/text) Check.

Chocaholic: Somebody who loves to eat chocolate.

Chocka: (New Zealand) To be very full.

Chocker: (UK) Irritated; fed up.

Choco: (Australian) A member of the citizen army during WWII; a conscript.

Chocolate fireguard: (UK) Useless.

Chocolate teapot: (UK) Useless.

chohw: (Internet/text) Come hell or high water.

Choice: (New Zealand) 1) Thanks. 2) Great; awesome.

Choirboy: (US) An innocent, naive young man. 2) Someone pretending to be innocent.

Choke: 1) To die. 2) To make a mistake under pressure, often at a critical moment, such as on the verge of victory.

Choked: (UK) To be upset or disappointed.

Choker: (US) A neck tie.

Chokey: (UK) Prison; jail.

Chomp: To eat or take a bite of something.

Chompers: (UK) Teeth.

Chomping gear: (UK) Teeth.

Choo-choo: A train, especially a steam train.

Choof off: (Australian) To leave; to go away.

Chook: (Australian) A chicken.

Choom: (Australian) An Englishman.

Choose off: (US) To challenge someone to a fight.

Chooser: (UK) A plagiarist.

Chop shop: (US) A workshop that customizes cars.

Chop: (UK) 1) A customized motorbike. 2) To give up doing something. 3) (Australian/New Zealand) Share. 4) (South African) An idiot.

Chopped hog: (UK) A customized motorbike.

Chopper: A helicopter. 2) A customized motorbike. 3) (US) A submachine gun.

Choppers: (UK) Teeth; dentures.

Chops: 1) The jaws, lips, and mouth. 2) The skill to do something.

Chopsy: (UK) Argumentative.

Chow down: (US) To start to eat.

Chozzer: (UK) A police officer.

chr: (Internet/text) Character.

Chrissie: (Australian/UK) Christmas.

Christen: To use something for the first time.

Chrome-dome: A bald person.

Chronic (US): Cannabis.

chu: (Internet/text) You.

Chubb: (UK/prison) To lock.

Chubbette: (UK) A stocky young woman.

Chubby chops: (UK) An overweight person.

Chubby-chaser: Someone who is attracted to overweight people.

Chuck a cheesy: (Australian) To grin.

Chuck up: (UK) 1) To vomit. 2) To have bad body odor.

Chuck you, Farley: (US) An exclamation of contempt or cheek.

Chuck: (UK) 1) Chicken. 2) A term of endearment. 3) To vomit.

Chuckaway Charlie: (UK) A person who is careful with their money.

Chucking-out time: (UK) The closing time of a pub or bar.

Chucklehead: (US) A foolish or silly person.

Chuddy: (Australian/New Zealand) Chewing gum.

Chuff: (UK) 1) To pleasure or delight. 2) The backside.

Chuffed: (UK) Proud; pleased.

Chuffer: (UK) A train.

Chuffing: (UK) Very.

Chug: To take large gulps of a drink, especially beer.

Chum: (UK) A friend; a buddy.

Chummy: (UK) Being on friendly terms with someone.

Chump: (UK) 1) The head. 2) An idiot.

Chunder circuit: (Australian) A pub crawl.

Chunder: (US/Australian) To vomit.

Chunderous: (Australian) Nauseating.

Chunderspew: (US) To vomit.

Chunnel: (UK) The Channel Tunnel.

Chunter: (UK) To nag or complain.

Chur: (New Zealand) 1) Thank you. 2) Great; no problem.

Church Key: (UK) A bottle opener.

Churchwarden: (UK) A clay tobacco pipe.

Churchyard cough: (UK) A bad cough.

Chute: (UK) The rectum.

Chutzpah: (UK) Bold effrontery; spunky; spirited cheek.

cid: (Internet/text) Consider it done.

Cig: (UK) Cigarette.

Ciggie: (UK) Cigarette.

Cigs: (UK) Cigarettes.

cihyn: (Internet/text) Can I have your number?

Cinch: Something that is easy to accomplish.

Cincies: (US) Cincinnati commemorative half dollars.

cing: (Internet/text) Seeing.

Circling the drain: To be close to passing away.

cis: (Internet/text) 1) Chuckling in silence. 2) Computer information science. 3) Someone who identifies with the gender they were assigned at birth.

Civilian: (UK/criminal) A person who is neither a criminal nor a police officer.

Civvies: (UK) Civilian clothes.

Civvy street: (UK) Civilian life.

Civvy: (UK) Civilian.

ciwwaf: (Internet/text) Cute is what we aim for.

Clack: (UK) To chatter endlessly.

Clack-box: (UK) The mouth.

Clackers: (UK) False teeth; dentures.

Clag: (UK) Bad weather.

Claim: (UK) 1) To grab someone. 2) To arrest someone.

Claimo: (UK) An accident without injury and the insurance claim is paid.

Clam up: 1) To refuse to talk. 2) To stop talking.

Clam: 1) (UK) The mouth. 2) (US) A dollar.

Clambrain: (US) A dim-witted person.

Clams: (US) The hands.

Clamshell: (US) A one-dollar bill. 2) The mouth.

Clamshells: (US) The lips.

Clang: (UK) To make a mistake.

Clanger: (UK) A big mistake.

Clap eyes on: (UK) To observe; to watch or see.

Clap: Gonorrhea; a venereal disease.

Clapped out: (UK) Exhausted; worn out.

Clapped up: (UK) Infected with a venereal disease.

Clapper: (UK) The tongue.

Clappers: (UK) The testicles.

Clapster: (UK) A promiscuous man.

Class act: (US) 1) An impressive performance, service, or person. 2) Someone who conducts themselves professionally.

Classy chassis: (US) An attractive woman's body.

Classy: Stylish; elegant.

Clat-tale: (UK) A tell-tale.

Claw hammer coat: (UK) A dress coat with a swallowtail pattern.

Clay pigeon: (US) Someone in a defenseless or vulnerable position.

Clean: 1) Innocent. 2) Not carrying anything illicit, such as illegal weapons or drugs.

Cleaned out: To be left penniless.

Cleanskin: (Australian) Someone without a criminal record.

Clear as mud: (UK) Something that is incomprehensible.

Clear out: 1) To leave someone with no money. 2) To use all of a resource.

Cleety: (Irish) Awkward.

Clemmed: (UK) Very hungry.

cless: (Gaming) Clanless.

Clever-clogs: (UK) A know-it-all.

Click: 1) (UK) A big success. 2) A relationship that runs smoothly; for people to be very compatible. 3) (UK) A robbery. 4) (US/military) A kilometer.

Cliffdweller: (US) A person who lives in a high-rise block of apartments.

Cliffhanger: (UK) A story with an unresolved ending.

Climb the rigging: (UK) To lose one's temper.

Climb the wall: To be too anxious or agitated to keep still.

Clinch: (UK) A lover's embrace.

Clink: Prison; jail.

Clinker: (US/Canadian) A mistake, especially when playing music.

Clip artist: (US) A fraudster or confidence trickster.

Clip joint: A business that overcharges or cheats its customers.

Clip one's wings: To restrict someone's behavior.

Clip: (UK) To swindle, especially by overcharging. 2) To hit someone with a glancing blow. 3) (US) To move at a high speed. 4) Each.

Clippie: (UK) A bus conductor.

clm: (Internet/text) Cool like me.

Cloak and dagger: 1) Espionage activities. 2) A matter that involves intrigue and secrecy.

Cloakroom: (US) An anteroom to the side of each main chamber in Congress where informal meetings can be held by legislators.

Clobber: To beat or hit someone. 2) (UK) Personal belongings, such as clothing.

Clobbered up: (UK) 1) Dressed up. 2) Burdened.

Clock: (UK) 1) The face. 2) To hit someone, especially in the head.

Clodhopper: (UK) A clumsy or uncouth person.

Clog: (UK/soccer) To foul an opponent. 2) To kick. 3) Virility.

Clogger: (UK) 1) Someone who kicks others. 2) A soccer player who frequently commits fouls.

Clone: 1) A fashion or trend follower. 2) An imitator.

Close doors: (US) To go out of business.

Close ranks: To set aside differences in order to accomplish or defend a common interest.

Close the book: To end something; to lay a matter to rest.

Closeted: 1) A matter that is kept secret. 2) To not publicly reveal oneself as gay.

Clot: (UK) A fool; an idiot.

Clothesline: (UK/US/sports) Hitting an opponent's neck with an outstretched arm.

Clothesliner: (UK) A petty thief.

Cloud: (US/real estate) Preventing a sale or transfer of deeds from taking place until an unpaid debt has been settled on the property.

Clown: A foolish person; a jokester.

Cloy: (UK) A pickpocket.

clt: (Internet/text) Cool like that.

Club fed: (US) Prison; jail.

Clucky: (Australian) Pregnant.

Cludgie: (Scottish) A toilet.

cluebie: (Internet/text) A clueless newbie.

Clueless: (US) To have no understanding of something.

Clum: (UK) An awkward person.

Clump: (UK) To hit someone.

Clunk: (US) 1) A dim-witted person. 2) A worn-out vehicle.

Clutchfist: (UK) A miser.

Clutey: (Irish) Awkward; clumsy.

Clydesdale: (US) An attractive man.

cm: (Internet/text) Call me.

cma: (Internet/text) Cover my ass.

cmao: (Internet/text) Crying my ass off.

cmar: (Internet/text) Cry me a river.

cmb: (Internet/text) Comment me back.

cmbo: (Internet/text) Combo.

cmeo: (Internet/text) Crying my eyes out.

cmh: (Internet/text) Call my house.

cmiiw: (Internet/text) Correct me if I'm wrong.

cml: (Internet/text) Call me later.

cml8r: (Internet/text) Call me later.

cmn: (Internet/text) Call me now.

cmon (also "c'mon"): (Internet/text) Come on.

cms: (Internet/text) Content management system.

cmt: (Internet/text) Comment.

cn: (Internet/text) Can.

CnC: (Gaming) Command & Conquer.

C-note: One hundred pounds; one hundred dollars.

cnt: (Internet/text) Can't.

Coal sack: (UK) A cul-de-sac.

Coalboxed: (UK) Ruined; wrecked.

Coasting: Getting by with the least amount of effort.

Coat: (UK) To rebuke; to scold.

cob: (Internet/text) Close of business.

Cob: (UK) A bad mood.

Cobbler: (Australian/New Zealand) A sheep that puts up a struggle during shearing.

Cobblers: (UK) Nonsense; rubbish.

Cock a deaf one: (UK) To pretend not to hear something or someone.

Cockeye bob: (Australian) A storm or cyclone that emerges very quickly.

Cocktail: (UK) A coward; someone who is half-hearted.

Cock-up: (UK) To botch something; to make a mess of things.

Cocky: 1) Arrogant; overly confident. 2) (Australian) A cockatoo. 3) A small farmer.

Cocky's joy: (Australian) Golden syrup.

Cocooning: (US) Staying at home rather than going out to socialize.

COD: (Gaming) Call of Duty.

Cod: (UK/Irish) To tease; to make fun of someone or something. 2) Fake; a sham.

codbo: (Gaming) Call of Duty: Black Ops.

Code brown: (Nursing) When a patient defecates in bed.

Code yellow: (Nursing) When a patient's catheter breaks or leaks.

Codswallop: (UK) Nonsense; rubbish.

cof: (Internet/text) Crying on the floor.

Coffin dodger: (UK) An old person.

Coffin nail: (UK) A cigarette.

Cog: (UK) 1) To cheat, especially in a game of dice. 2) A gear.

Coit: (Australian) The buttocks.

coiwta: (Internet/text) Come on, I won't tell anyone.

Cojones: 1) Courage. 2) The testicles.

Cokies: (UK) Old-fashioned baggy trousers.

col: (Internet/text) Crying out loud.

Cold enough to freeze the balls off a brass monkey: Very cold weather.

Cold fish: (UK) Someone who is unemotional or uncaring.

Cold turkey: To cure an addiction or break a habit by stopping it completely.

Cold: 1) Untraceable. 2) Unemotional.

Coldie: (Australian) A cold can or bottle of beer.

Collar: (UK) 1) Hard work. 2) Arrest. 3) The head on a pint of beer.

Collared: (UK) Arrested.

Collect: (UK) To receive money or some form of payment.

Collins street farmer: (Australian) A businessperson who invests in farms or land.

Collywobbles: (UK) An upset stomach; nervousness or anxiety.

Colonic: (UK) A mix of Coca-Cola and tonic.

Coloring the patio: (US) To vomit.

Combo: Combination.

Come a cropper: (UK) To have an accident; to meet with misfortune.

Come a gutser: (Australian/New Zealand) 1) To fall down heavily. 2) To fail because of a mistake or misfortune.

Come a stumer: (Australian) To crash financially.

Come at: (Australian) To agree to do something. 2) To presume or impose something. 3) To tolerate something.

Come hard: (UK) To behave aggressively.

Come it hard: (UK) To behave aggressively.

Come it: (UK) 1) To pretend. 2) To exaggerate.

Come off: (US) To appear as being a certain way; to give an impression.

Come on: To flirt; to show romantic interest.

Come one's guts: (UK) To confess.

Come out: To reveal oneself as part of the LGBTQ+ community.

Come the acid: (UK) 1) For something to be unpleasant or offensive. 2) To speak in a scathing way.

Come the raw prawn: (Australian) To try to take advantage of someone; to deceive someone.

Comeback: (UK) A repercussion.

Comedown: A state of depression or low spirits after being in an elevated mood.

Come-on: (UK) A flirtatious comment.

Commo: (UK/Australian) Communist.

Comp.: Complimentary; free.

Compo: (Australian) Unemployment compensation.

Compy: (Internet/text) Computer.

Con: 1) A convict. 2) To deceive or swindle someone.

Concertinas: (UK) Trousers that are too long.

Conch: (US) A hard-working student.

Con-charge: (UK) Congestion charge.

Condo: (US) Condominium.

Conehead: (US) Someone who is strange and/or foolish.

Coner: (UK) A pickpocket who operates by dropping an ice-cream at the mark's feet to serve as a distraction.

Congrats: (Internet/text) Congratulations.

Conk out: (UK) 1) A mechanical breakdown. 2) To fall unconscious. 3) To fall asleep.

Conk: (UK/Australian) To hit someone on the head. 2) (UK/New Zealand) The nose.

Conker: (UK) A nut from a horse chestnut tree.

Conniption: (US/Canadian) To be very angry; to be in a fit of rage.

Conshie: (UK) A conscientious objector.

Constipated: (UK) To be blocked, especially in reference to a road.

Contrib: (Internet/text) Contribution.

Convo: (Internet/text/Australian) Conversation.

Coo: (Internet/text) Cool.

Cood: (Internet/text) Could.

Cooey: (UK) A pigeon.

Cook: To happen.

Cooked: (UK) To be drunk or intoxicated.

Cooking: 1) (UK) Beer. 2) (US) For something to be going well.

Cool it: A warning for the listener to calm down.

Cool off: Calm down.

Cool: (US) Calm; fine. 2) Interesting; good; popular.

Cooler: Prison.

Coombe: (UK) A small valley.

Coot: (UK) An old foolish person.

Cootie (also "cooty"): 1) (US/Australian) Body louse. 2) (US) An imaginary germ (usually used in its plural form).

Cop a broom: (US) To leave in a hurry.

Cop a drill: (US) To leave by foot.

Cop a flower pot: (UK) To be reprimanded harshly.

Cop a plea: (US) To plead guilty to a lesser offence than the one you are being charged with.

Cop a squat: (US) To sit down.

Cop off: (UK) To find a sexual partner.

Cop out: To fail to uphold one's commitment or responsibility.

Cop shop: A police station.

Cop some Zs: (US) To sleep.

Cop the brewery: (UK) To get drunk or intoxicated.

Cop the currant: (UK) 1) To surpass. 2) To be highly unlikely.

Cop: A police officer.

Copacetic: (US/Canadian) Excellent; highly satisfactory.

Copper: (UK) A police officer.

Copper-nob: (UK) A person with red hair.

Coppers: (Australian) Police officers.

Copshop: (UK) A police station.

Copyvio: (Internet/text) Copyright violation.

Core: (Computer) Main storage or RAM.

Corgis: (UK) A couple of awful people.

Cork it: (UK) Keep quiet.

Cork up: (UK) Shut up; keep quiet.

Corked: (UK) 1) To be drunk or intoxicated. 2) Constipated.

Corker: (UK) Someone or something that is remarkable.

Corking: (UK) Excellent.

Corkscrew: 1) (UK) A laxative. 2) (Boxing) A punch that ends by twisting one's fist.

Corn juice: (US) Whisky.

Corn squeezings: (US) Illegally distilled whisky.

Corn up: (US) To get drunk or intoxicated.

Corned beef city: (UK) A large council housing estate.

Corned beef legs: (UK) Legs that are red and blotchy.

Corner-boy: (UK) An idle youngster.

Cornflake: (US) Someone who is strange or foolish.

Cornhusker: (US) A farmer.

Cornish duck: (UK) A pilchard.

Cornish pasties: (UK) A style of men's shoe that has a molded sole and which is considered unfashionable.

Cornpone: (US) A rustic person, particularly one who lives in the South.

Cornpopper: (US) 1) A large truck. 2) A cheap and noisy car.

Cornstalk: (Australian) 1) A native Australian. 2) A man who is tall and thin.

Corny: (UK) Something that is trite or overly sentimental.

Corporal: (UK) Two pounds sterling.

Corpse-reviver: (US) A stimulant alcoholic drink taken as a hangover remedy.

Cos: (Internet/text) Because.

Cosh boy: (UK) A young male thug.

Cosmic: (UK) Awesome; out-of-this-world.

Cossie: (Australian/South African) A swimsuit.

Costard: (UK) The head.

cotf: (Internet/text) Crying on the floor.

Cottage: (UK) A public lavatory.

Cotton on: To reach an understanding of something.

Cottontail: (US) An attractive woman.

Couch case: (UK) An eccentric or crazy person.

Couch potato: Someone who is lazy and does little but sit in front of their TV.

Couch slouch: (UK) A lazy person who watches a lot of TV.

Cough up: (US) To give something over, especially with reluctance.

Cough: (UK) To confess; to give up information.

Coulda: Could have.

Couldn't give a candy: (UK) To not care.

Counterjumper: (UK) A salesperson in a shop.

Country pancake: (UK) A cowpat.

Coupon: (Scottish) The face.

Cousins: (UK) Americans.

Cove: (UK) 1) A man or boy. 2) Old-fashioned.

Cover with the moon: (US) To sleep in the open.

Cow cocky: (Australian) A small-scale cattle farmer.

Cow college: (US) A college that is in a remote area.

Cow juice: (UK) Milk.

Cow pie: (UK) A cowpat.

Cow: 1) An unpleasant lady. 2) (Australian) A hard task. 3) (Australian/New Zealand) Something that is objectionable.

Cowboy choker: (Internet/text) Cigarette.

Cowboy job: (UK) Workmanship that is poorly done.

Cowboy outfit: (UK) A company that provides poor workmanship or operates with dubious legality.

Cowboy: 1) (US) A reckless person. 2) (UK) A bad workman.

Cow-horns: (UK) Handlebars on a bicycle or motorbike that are high and curved.

Cowing: (UK) Laughing.

Coyote: (US) A person who preys on illegal immigrants crossing the USA–Mexico border; typically an unscrupulous border agent.

Coz: (Internet/text) Because.

Cozzer: (UK) A police officer.

Cozzie: (Australian/South African) A swimsuit.

c-p: (Internet/text) Sleepy.

cptn: (Internet/text) Captain.

CPU: (Computer) Central processing unit.

cpy: (Internet/text) Copy.

cr: (Internet/text) Can't remember.

cr8: (Internet/text) Crate.

Crab: (UK) 1) An unpleasant person. 2) Somebody who regularly borrows money.

Crabs: Pubic lice.

Crack a crib: (US) To commit burglary.

Crack it: To solve a difficult problem.

Crack on: 1) (Irish) Carry on; persist at something. 2) (UK) To talk ceaselessly or boastfully.

Crack up: To be overcome with laughter.

Crack wise: To make a witty or cheeky comment.

Crack: 1) A joke or jeer. 2) A person who excels at something.

Crackajack: (UK) Someone who is extremely good at something.

Cracker: (UK) A person or thing with remarkable qualities.

Crackers: (UK) Insane; crazy.

Cracking: (Irish/UK) Very good; great; excellent.

Crackle: (UK) Money.

Crackling: (UK) An attractive woman.

Crackpot: A person or idea that is crazy.

Cracksman: (UK) A burglar, especially one who breaks into safes.

Cradle snatcher: An older person who dates someone who is young.

Crakalakin: (Internet/text) Happening.

Cranberry eye: (US) A bloodshot eye.

Crank the chicken switch: (Military) To eject from an aircraft.

Crap out: (US) To fail at something; to withdraw. 2) To rest.

Crap: 1) Excrement. 2) To defecate. 3) Something that is rubbish.

Crapology: (UK) Talk that is utter nonsense.

Crappo: (UK) Something that is cheap or of poor quality.

Crappy: (UK) Something that is rubbish or of poor quality.

Crap-rack: (UK) A car park.

Crash cart: (Nursing) A wheeled unit with a defibrillator and supplies for emergency resuscitations.

Crash out: 1) (US) To sleep. 2) To spend the night away from home.

Crash pad (also "crashpad"): (US) A temporary place to sleep or live.

Crash: (Computer) A sudden error that results in a program or the whole system shutting down or restarting.

Crasher: (UK) Someone who is a bore.

Crash-hot: (Australian) Excellent.

Cratehead: (UK) An idiot or foolish person.

Crawler: (UK) A sycophant.

Cray-cray: (Internet/text) Crazy.

crazn: (Internet/text) Crazy Asian.

Crazy rim: (US) A stylish hat.

Crazy: Excellent.

cre8or: (Internet/text) Creator.

Cream: To thoroughly defeat an opponent.

Crease up: (UK) To be amused; to cause amusement.

Cred: Street credibility.

Creep: Someone who is obnoxious or socially unsettling.

Creeper: (UK) 1) A thief who robs hotels or brothels. 2) A shoe with a soft sole.

Creepers: (UK) Body lice.

Creeping Jesus: 1) An obsequious or sycophantic person. 2) A religious person who behaves hypocritically.

Creeps: A feeling of fear or unease.

Creepshow: Something that is unpleasant or grotesque.

Cremated: (UK) Ruined; defeated.

Crew: 1) (UK) A street gang. 2) (US) Members of a group.

Crib: (US) A house or apartment.

Crikey: (Australian) An exclamation of surprise.

Crim: (Australian/New Zealand) A criminal. 2) (UK) Christmas.

Crimbo: (UK) Christmas.

Cringe: (UK) Embarrassing.

Cringe-making: (UK) Embarrassing; nauseating.

Crinkle: (UK) Money, especially banknotes.

Crinkly: (UK) An old person.

Crippleware: (Computer) A program that is offered for free but is missing important features in order to coerce the customer into paying for a "pro" version.

Crispy: (US) To be suffering from a hangover.

crm: (Internet/text) Customer relationship management.

Croak: To die; to pass away.

Crock: (UK) Someone or something that is old or decrepit. 2) (US) Nonsense; worthless.

Crocked: 1) (UK) Injured. 2) (US/Canadian) Drunk.

Crocus: (UK) A bad doctor.

Cronk: (UK) An old, worn-out car.

Crook: (Australian/New Zealand) 1) Feeling ill. 2) Unpleasant. 3) Low quality.

Cropper: (UK) 1) A fall on one's head. 2) A sudden failure.

Crow: 1) (UK) A lookout. 2) (UK/Australian) An old or unattractive woman.

Crown: To hit someone over the head.

crp: (Internet/text) Crap.

Crucify: To thoroughly defeat or ridicule.

Crud: (UK) 1) A crusty, dirty substance. 2) Someone or something that is worthless or awful.

Cruddy: (UK) Worthless or unpleasant.

Crumb: 1) (UK) An awful person. 2) (US) To ruin or mess up something.

Crumble rumble: (UK) An altercation between old people.

Crumble: (UK) Old people.

Crumbly: (UK) An old person.

Crummy: (UK) 1) To be inferior or of little value. 2) To feel unwell or dispirited.

Crumpet man: (UK) A womanizer.

Crumpet: (UK) A woman.

Crunk: (Internet/text) Crazy and drunk.

Crush: 1) To harbor romantic feelings for someone without being in a relationship with them. 2) To be disappointed (typically used passively).

Crusher: (UK) A boring or dull person.

Crust: (UK) 1) Money; a wage. 2) Impertinence. 3) The head.

Crusty: (UK) A very dirty person.

Crut: (UK) Dirt.

Crutch: (Australian/New Zealand) To clip wool from a sheep's hindquarters.

Cry beef: (UK) To shout an alarm at the scene of a crime.

crzy: (Internet/text) Crazy.

CS: (Gaming) Counter-Strike.

csi: (Internet/text) Crime Scene Investigation (TV show).

csl: (Internet/text) Can't stop laughing.

css: (Internet/text) Cascading style sheets.

ct: (Internet/text) Can't talk.

ctc: (Internet/text) Call the cell.

CTD: (Computer) Crash to desktop.

ctf: (Internet/text) Capture the flag (a popular online mode in FPS video games).

ctm: (Internet/text) Chuckling to myself.

ctn: (Internet/text) Can't talk now.

ctncl: (Internet/text) Can't talk now, call later.

ctpc: (Internet/text) Can't talk, parent(s) coming.

ctpos: (Internet/text) Can't talk, parent over shoulder.

ctrl: (Computer) Control.

ctrn: (Internet/text) Can't talk right now.

cts: (Internet/text) Change the subject.

ctt: (Internet/text) Change the topic.

cu: (Internet/text) See you (e.g., goodbye).

cu2: (Internet/text) See you too.

cu2nit: (Internet/text) See you tonight.

Cube: Someone who conforms in all ways.

cubi: (Internet/text) Can you believe it.

Cuckoo: Crazy; insane.

Cuckoo's nest: A mental institution.

cud: (Internet/text) Could.

Cuff: To handcuff someone.

cuic: (Internet/text) See you in class.

Cujo: (US) Someone whose reckless behavior endangers other people.

cul: (Internet/text) See you later.

cul83r (also "cul8er"): (Internet/text) See you later.

cul8r (also "cul8tr"): (Internet/text) See you later.

culd: (Internet/text) Could.

Cully: (UK) Friend.

cuom: (Internet/text) See you on Monday.

Cupcake: (US) A cute young woman.

Cupid stunt: (UK) A foolish or contemptible person.

Cupid's itch: (US) A venereal disease.

cuple: (Internet/text) Couple.

Cuppa: (UK) A cup of something (usually tea).

curn: (Internet/text) Calling you right now.

Curtains: The end of something.

Cushdy: (UK) Wonderful; fine.

Cushti manti: (UK) Wonderful; excellent.

Cushti rye: (UK) Top man.

Cushti: (UK) Wonderful; excellent.

Cushy: 1) Easy; comfortable. 2) Lucrative.

Cut a chuckle: (UK) To laugh.

Cut a melon: (US/Canadian) To declare a very high dividend to shareholders.

Cut a rug: To dance.

Cut it out: (US) To stop something immediately.

Cut it: To succeed at something.

Cut lunch: (Australian) Sandwiches.

Cut of one's jib: (UK) A person's personality or character.

Cut some slack: To give someone a chance; to be lenient or understanding in terms of one's expectations for someone.

Cut stick: (UK) To make off stealthily or hurriedly.

Cut the cheese: (US) To fart.

Cut the mustard: (US) To meet expectations.

Cut yourself a big slice of cake: (UK) To boast; to flatter oneself.

Cut: To dilute something. 2) A music track. 3) (UK) To be drunk or intoxicated.

cut3: (Internet/text) Cute.

Cutaways: Blue jeans made shorter by cutting off the legs.

Cut-downs: (UK) Trousers made shorter by cutting off the legs.

Cutesy: (UK) Exaggeratedly cute.

Cutie: (UK) An attractive person, especially a girl or woman.

Cut-offs: (UK) Blue jeans made shorter by cutting off the legs.

Cutout: (Australian) The end of shearing an animal.

Cut-purse: (UK) A pickpocket who would cut a purse free from a person's bag or belt.

Cutter: (UK) A knife or blade.

cuwul: (Internet/text) Catch up with you later.

cuz: (Internet/text) Because.

cw2cu: (Internet/text) Can't wait to see you.

cwd: (Internet/text) Comment when done.

cwot: (Internet/text) Complete waste of time.

cwyl: (Internet/text) Chat with you later.

cy2: (Internet/text) See you too.

cya: (Internet/text) See you (e.g., goodbye).

cyal ("cyal8r"): (Internet/text) See you later.

cyas: (Internet/text) See you soon.

cyb: (Internet/text) Cyber.

cyberbug: (Internet/text) A person who spends too much time online.

cybl: (Internet/text) Call you back later.

cybr: (Internet/text) Cyber.

cyla: (Internet/text) See you later, alligator.

cyl: (Internet/text) See you later.

cyl8 (also "cyl8er"): (Internet/text) See you later.

cym: (Internet/text) Check your mail.

cyt: (Internet/text) See you tomorrow.

cyu: (Internet/text) See you (e.g., goodbye).

— D —

D and D: (UK) Drunk and disorderly.

D&C: (Internet/text) Divide and conquer.

D&D: (Internet/text) Dungeons & Dragons (role-playing game).

D.K.: (US) 1) To snub someone. 2) To feign ignorance.

D.M.'s: (UK) Doctor Marten's shoes.

D.O.A.: 1) Dead on arrival. 2) To be unconscious or inert.

D.O.M.: (UK) Dirty old man; a lecherous person.

d/c: (Internet/text) Disconnected.

d/l: (Internet/text) Download.

d/m: (Internet/text) Doesn't matter.

d/w: (Internet/text) Don't worry.

d00d: (Internet/text) Dude.

D2: (Gaming) Diablo 2.

d2m: (Internet/text) Dead to me.

d2t: (Internet/text) Drink to that.

d8: (Internet/text) Date.

da: (Internet/text) The.

Dab on: (UK) To apply at the unemployment benefit office.

Dab: (UK) 1) Fingerprint. 2) Bad.

Dabs: (UK) Fingerprints.

Dad's Army: (UK) The Home Guard during World War II.

Daddio: A man.

Daddler: (UK) A small coin.

dadt: (Internet/text) Don't ask, don't tell.

Daffodil: (UK) Someone who is naive and innocent.

Daffy: (UK) 1) A large amount of money. 2) Eccentric, crazy.

Daft: (UK) Foolish; idiotic.

Dafty: (Scottish) An idiot; a fool.

Dag: (Australian) 1) Dried sheep dung. 2) A foolish or horrible person. 3) (New Zealand) A quirky or eccentric person.

Daggy: (Australian) Foolish or unpleasant.

dah: (Internet/text) Dumb as hell.

daii: (Internet/text) Day.

Dainties: (US/Australian) Women's underwear.

Daisy beaters: (UK) The feet.

Daisy cutter: (Cricket) A ball that is bowled to stay close to the ground.

Daisy dormer: (UK) A bed warmer.

Daisy: (UK) An excellent person or thing.

Daks: (Australian/New Zealand) Trousers.

Damage: Expense; cost.

damhik: (Internet/text) Don't ask me how I know.

damhikt: (Internet/text) Don't ask me how I know this.

Damn all: (UK) Nothing at all.

Damp: (UK) 1) To be ineffectual or weak. 2) A drink.

Damper: (US) A savings bank.

Dance: (UK) 1) A flight of stairs. 2) To steal from a building's upper floors.

Dancer cases: (UK) Footwear.

Dang: (US) An expression of frustration or astonishment.

Dangler: 1) (UK) A trailer attached to another vehicle. 2) (US) A trapeze artist.

Dapper Dan: (UK) A man who is well dressed.

Daps: (UK) Tennis shoes.

Darbies: (UK) 1) Handcuffs. 2) Hands. 3) Fingerprints.

Darkers: (UK) Sunglasses.

Darkmans: (UK) Night-time.

Darks: (UK) Night.

Dash: (UK) Money, especially a bribe or tip.

dass: (Internet/text) Dumb ass.

dat: (Internet/text) That.

Date roll: (Australian) A toilet roll.

dats: (Internet/text) That's.

Davy Jones' locker: (Nautical) The bottom of the sea, especially as a grave.

dawg: (Internet/text) Friend.

Day-glo: (UK) Gaudy; garish.

Daylighting: To work a second job during the day.

dayum: (Internet/text) Damn.

Dazzler: (UK) The sun.

db: (Internet/text) Database.

db4l: (Internet/text) Drinking buddy for life.

dbh: (Internet/text) Don't be hating.

dbm: (Internet/text) Don't bother me.

DBZ: (Internet/text) Dragon Ball Z (an anime).

dc: (Internet/text) Don't care.

DC'd (also "D/C"): (Internet/text) Disconnected.

dcw: (Internet/text) Doing class work.

dd: (Internet/text) Don't die.

ddg: (Internet/text) Drop-dead gorgeous.

ddl: (Internet/text) Direct download.

ddt: (Internet/text) Don't do that.

De facto: (Australian) A live-in lover.

Dead and alive: (UK) A miserable person.

Dead bang: (US) To be caught red-handed.

Dead body: (UK) Someone who is boring and doesn't like to socialize.

Dead duck: (UK) Someone or something that is in big trouble, especially because of poor judgment or a mistake.

Dead from the neck up: (UK) To be stupid or foolish.

Dead meat: (UK) Someone who is inevitably doomed.

Dead presidents: (US) Paper money.

Dead to rights: (US) Caught in the act; guilty without doubt.

Dead weight: (UK) Someone who is unneeded or who doesn't contribute.

Dead-and-alive hole: (UK) A glum, depressing place.

Deadass: (UK) Someone who is very boring or lazy.

Deadbeat: Someone who avoids paying their debts. 2) An idle or worthless person.

Deadhead: (UK) A dull, lifeless person.

Deadleg: (UK) A lazy or disappointing person.

Deadly: (Irish) 1) Great. 2) Desirable.

Deal: To sell illegal drugs.

Dealer: Someone who sells illegal drugs.

Deaner: (UK) A five-penny piece.

Death seat: (US/Australian) The seat beside the driver of a vehicle.

Death warmed up: (UK) To feel very ill; to be very tired.

Deb: 1) (UK) A debutante. 2) (US) A female member of a gang.

Deb's delight: (UK) An eligible bachelor who is rather simple.

Decent: (Scottish) Good; pleasing.

Deck it: (UK) To accelerate quickly; to drive at top speed.

Deck: 1) To punch someone. 2) A skateboard. 3) A surfboard.

Decko: (UK) To have a look.

ded: (Internet/text) Dead.

Deedle: (UK) A foolish person.

Deelab: (UK) Bald.

Deelybopper: (UK) A pair of fake antennae worn on the head.

Deenah: (UK) Assistance; a helping hand.

Deep pockets: To have plenty of money or resources at one's disposal.

Deep six: (UK) A grave.

Deep-sea fisherman: (UK) A confidence trickster on an ocean liner.

Deep-six: 1) (UK) To bury someone. 2) (US) To dispose of or destroy something.

Deeracks: (UK) Playing cards.

Deeray: (UK) A yard; three feet.

Deerib: (UK) A woman.

Deerut: (UK) Excrement.

deets: (Internet/text) Details.

deez: (Internet/text) These.

def (also "defs"): (Internet/text) Definitely.

Def: (US) Excellent; very good.

Defo: (Australian) Definitely.

Defrosted: 1) (US) Agitated; heated. 2) (UK) Angry.

degmt: (Internet/text) Don't even give me that.

Dekko: (UK) A look; a glance.

Deli: A delicatessen.

Delo lib: (UK) The police.

Delo nam: (UK) A husband; an old man.

Delo nammow: (UK) Wife; an old woman.

Delo: (UK) Old.

Deloes: (UK) Old people.

Delog: (UK) Gold.

dem: (Internet/text) Them.

Dementoid: (UK) Crazy; insane.

Demo: Demonstration.

Demon: (Australian) A detective.

Denis: (UK) The police.

Dept: (Internet/text) Department.

Depth charge: (UK) A pint of beer with a small glass of spirits dropped inside and drunk in one go.

der: (Internet/text) There.

Deri (also "derry"): (UK) A derelict building, especially one used by vagrants.

dernoe: (Internet/text) I don't know.

Dero: (Australian) A vagrant or destitute person.

Derro: (UK) An unfortunate or unpleasant person.

Des res: (UK) A desirable residence.

Desdy: (UK) A constant moaner.

Destroyed: (UK) To be drunk or intoxicated.

detai: (Internet/text) Don't even think about it.

Detox: (UK) A course of withdrawal from something, especially a substance.

Deuce: Two dollars; two pounds.

Devil's buckie: (UK) A perverse or rebellious youth.

Devo: (Australian) Devastated.

dewd: (Internet/text) Dude.

Dewdrop: (UK) Fluid leaking from the nose.

Dewey: (UK) The number two.

dey: (Internet/text) They.

dftc: (Internet/text) Down for the count.

dfw: (Internet/text) Down for whatever.

dg: (Internet/text) Don't go.

dga: (Internet/text) Don't go anywhere.

dgac: (Internet/text) Don't give a crap.

dgara: (Internet/text) Don't give a rat's ass.

dgms: (Internet/text) Don't get me started.

dgt: (Internet/text) Don't go there.

dgu: (Internet/text) Don't give up.

DH: (Internet/text) Dear husband.

dhac: (Internet/text) Don't have a clue.

Dhobying: (UK) Washing clothes.

dhv: (Internet/text) Demonstration of higher value.

diaf: (Internet/text) Die in a fire.

diah: (Internet/text) Die in a hole.

Dial: (UK) The face.

Diamond: (UK) Superb; first-rate; awesome.

Diamond-cracking: (Australian) Breaking rocks as part of a prison sentence.

Dib: 1) (US) A contribution or amount of money. 2) (UK) A partly-smoked cigarette that is saved for later.

Dibble: (UK) A police officer.

Dibs (to have dibs on): (US) To claim ownership of something before someone else gets it.

dic: (Internet/text) Do I care?

Dicey: Risky.

Dick around: (UK) Mess around with something.

Dick up: (UK) To make a mess of something.

Dickey: (UK) A hat.

Dicky up: (UK) To get dressed up smartly or nicely.

Dicky: (UK) 1) Insecure; shaky; unreliable. 2) Unwell.

Dicky-bow: (UK) A bow tie.

Diddle: (UK) 1) To cheat; to swindle. 2) To molest.

Diddley diddley band: (UK) An Irish folk group.

Diddlo: (UK) Silly; crazy.

Diddly squat: Nothing at all.

Diddly-dum: (UK) Fine; perfect.

Diddy: (UK) 1) A fool. 2) Cute and appealing.

Diesel boots: (UK) Cheap footwear.

diez: (Internet/text) Dies.

diff: (Internet/text) Difference.

Dig out: (UK) To criticize; to abuse.

Dig: (US) To understand or enjoy something.

Digs: (UK) Temporary accommodation.

diku: (Internet/text) Do I know you?

diky: (Internet/text) Do I know you?

dil: (Internet/text) Daughter-in-law.

Dilbert: (UK) A foolish person.

Dill: (UK/Australian/New Zealand) An idiot; a fool.

dillic: (Internet/text) Do I look like I care?

Dilly: (US/Canadian) A remarkable person or thing.

Dim bulb: (US) A dim-witted person.

Dimbo: (UK) A foolish person.

Dime dropper: (US) An informer.

Dime someone: (US) To inform on someone.

Dimmo: (UK) A dim-witted person.

Dimp: (UK) A partially smoked cigarette that can be re-used.

Dimwit: A fool; an idiot.

din: (Internet/text) Didn't.

din't: (Internet/text) Didn't.

Din-dins: Dinner; a meal.

Ding dongs: (UK) Bell-bottomed trousers.

Dingaling: (UK) A crazy or eccentric person.

Dingbat: (US) A crazy or eccentric person.

Ding-dong: (US) A stupid or contemptible person.

Dingo: (Australian) A cheat; a coward.

Dingo's breakfast: (Australian) To urinate and look around.

Dink: (UK) 1) A foolish person. 2) A member of a wealthy couple who doesn't have any children. 3) To hit someone with a weapon. 4) (Australian/New Zealand) To carry a second person on a vehicle or animal, such as a bicycle or horse.

Dinkum: (Australian) Genuine; sincere; honest.

Dinky: (UK) 1) A car. 2) A member of a wealthy couple who doesn't have any children.

Dinky-di: 1) (Australian) The real thing. 2) (UK) Perfect; fine.

Dinnyhazer: (UK) A knockout punch.

Dip and drive: (UK) To drive.

Dip one's wick: (UK) To have sex.

Dip your bread in: (UK) To try; to make an attempt.

Dip: (UK) 1) A pickpocket. 2) An idiot.

Dipping: (UK) Picking pockets.

Dippy: (UK) Eccentric; crazy; strange.

Dipso: (UK) An alcoholic; a drunkard.

Dipstick: A fool; an idiot.

Dipsy: (US) 1) An alcoholic; a drunkard. 2) An idiot.

Dipsy-doo: (US) A fraud or deceit.

dirl: (Internet/text) Die in real life.

Dirt: Scandalous information.

Dirtbag: (US) A lowlife; a contemptible person.

Dirty money: (UK) Money gained through illegal means.

Dirty water: (UK) Brown ale.

Dirtybones: (UK) A very dirty person.

dis: (Internet/text) This.

Disgusto: (UK) A repellent person or thing.

Dish it out: (US) To give someone a hard time.

Dish the dirt: (US) To spread scandalous or malicious rumors or information.

Dish: 1) (UK) An attractive person. 2) To defeat or destroy. 3) (US) Gossip.

Dishy: Very attractive.

Dismal Desmond: (UK) A miserable person.

Disneyland: A state of delusion; to be disconnected from reality.

Diss: To disrespect.

dit: (Internet/text) Details in thread.

Ditch: To abandon or discard something.

Ditsy: Silly; airheaded; frivolous.

Ditz: (UK) A silly or airheaded person.

Div: (UK) 1) A foolish person. 2) To swindle.

Dive: A disreputable or seedy place.

Divebombing: (UK) Attacking something with spray-painted graffiti. 2) Retrieving cigarette ends from the street to re-use them.

Diver: (UK) A pickpocket.

Diving: (UK) Picking pockets.

Divot: (UK) A toupee.

Divulge dinner: (US) To vomit.

Divvy up: (UK) To divide something and share it out.

Divvy: (UK) 1) Strange. 2) Stupid; pathetic. 3) Deviant.

DIY: Do it yourself.

dju: (Internet/text) Did you?

dk: (Internet/text) Don't know.

dkdc: (Internet/text) Don't know, don't care.

dl (also "d/l"): (Internet/text) Download.

dlf: (Internet/text) Dropping like flies.

dlibu: (Internet/text) Don't let it bother you.

dln: (Internet/text) Don't look now.

dm: (Internet/text) Death match (video game mode).

DM: (Social media) Direct message.

dmaf: (Internet/text) Do me a favor.

dmi: (Internet/text) Don't mention it.

dmn: (Internet/text) Damn.

dmu: (Internet/text) Don't mess up.

dmwm: (Internet/text) Don't mess with me.

dnd: (Internet/text) Do not disturb.

DnD: (Internet/text) Dungeons & Dragons (role-playing game).

dndp: (Internet/text) Do not double post.

dnk: (Internet/text) Do not know.

dno: (Internet/text) Don't know.

dnrta: (Internet/text) Did not read the article.

dnt: (Internet/text) Don't.

dnw: (Internet/text) Do not want.

Do a Bertie: (UK) To inform on one's accomplices.

Do a bunk: (UK) To leave in a hurry; to skip out on school or work.

Do a job on someone: (UK) To deceive or devastate someone.

Do a melba: (Australian) To make repeated farewell appearances.

Do a number: (US) To manipulate or deceive.

Do a runner: (UK) 1) To run away. 2) To leave a restaurant after eating without paying for one's meal.

Do for: (UK) 1) To beat up someone. 2) To murder.

Do in: (UK) 1) To murder. 2) To exhaust.

Do it: To have sex.

Do one's crust: (UK) To lose one's temper.

Do one's head in: (UK) To annoy; to madden.

Do one's nut: (UK) To lose one's temper.

Do one's scone: (Australian/New Zealand) To lose one's temper.

Do over: (UK/Australian/New Zealand) To beat up someone.

Do some metalwork: (UK) To leave quickly.

Do someone dirt: (UK) To do something vicious or malicious.

Do the book and cover: (US) To be imprisoned for life.

Do the book: (US) To serve a life sentence.

Do the dance: (US) To be hanged.

Do the deed: (US) To have sex.

Do the do: (US) To have sex.

Do the downy: (UK) To lie in bed.

Do the full sesh: (US) To indulge in something completely.

Do the gentleman: (UK) To urinate.

Do the graceful: (UK) To charm; to fascinate.

Do the grand: (UK) To act ostentatiously.

Do the handsome: (UK) To behave in an honorable way.

Do the heavy: (UK) To show off; to act with swagger.

Do time: To serve a prison sentence.

Do up: (UK) To assault someone.

Do your block: (Australian/New Zealand) To lose one's temper.

Do your nut: (UK) To get angry.

DOA: (Internet/text) Dead on arrival.

Dob in: (Australian/New Zealand) 1) To inform on others, especially to the police. 2) To make a financial contribution towards a purpose.

Dob: (Australian) To inform on others, especially to the police.

dob: (Internet/text) Date of birth.

Dobber: (Australian) An informant or traitor.

Dock asthma: (UK) Feigned gasps of astonishment.

Docker: (UK) A partially smoked cigarette that is kept to be used later.

Doctor: To falsify documents or forms of media.

dod: (Internet/text) Day of defeat.

Do-dad: (UK) A phrase that refers to something one can't remember at the time.

Doddle: (UK) Something that is easy to accomplish.

Dodgements: (UK) Doubtful; suspect.

Dodgework: (UK) Someone who is lazy or idle.

Dodgy job: (UK) A criminal case that is hard to prove.

Dodgy: (UK) 1) Doubtful; suspect. 2) Illegal or illicit. 3) Risky.

Dodo: (UK) 1) A fool; an idiot. 2) A conservative or old-fashioned person.

Dog breath: Bad breath.

Dog burger: (UK) A cheap hamburger.

Dog collar: (UK) An oversized head on a pint of Guinness.

Dog it: (US) To perform badly at something.

Dog out: (US) To dress smartly.

Dog someone around: (US) 1) To pester someone. 2) To behave badly or unfaithfully.

Dog trick: (UK) An act of treachery.

Dog: 1) (UK) A sausage. 2) To follow. 3) (Australian) A police informer. 4) (US) To discard; to get rid of something.

Dog's bollocks: (UK) Excellent; awesome.

Dog's breakfast: (Australian/UK) A complete mess or muddle; a chaotic situation.

Dog's breath: (UK) An awful person.

Dog's dinner: (UK) 1) A showy display. 2) A mess; a muddle.

Dog-ass: (US) Inferior; low-quality; worthless.

doge: (Internet/text) Dog.

Dog-end: (UK) A cigarette butt.

dogg: (Internet/text) Friend.

Dogged-up: (UK) Smartly dressed.

Doggie-do: Dog excrement.

Doggy bag: A bag for taking home one's unfinished food from a restaurant.

Dogs: (UK) The feet.

Do-hickey: (US) A phrase that refers to an unspecified thing.

Doink: (UK) A foolish person.

Dole bludger: (Australian) Someone who claims unemployment benefits without trying to find work.

Doley: (Australian) Someone who claims unemployment benefits.

Doll up: To dress up smartly or stylishly.

Dollface: (US) An attractive young woman.

Dollop: (UK) Excrement.

Dolly bag: (UK) A hidden pocket that dockers use for smuggling.

Dolly bird: (UK) A pretty, stylish girl or woman, especially one who is thought to be unintelligent.

Dolly dimple: (UK) An overweight person.

Dolly shop: (UK) An unlicensed pawnbroker.

Dolly: (UK) A pretty, stylish girl or woman, especially one who is thought to be unintelligent.

Dome: The head.

Domkop: (South African) An idiot.

Don Juan: (UK) A womanizer.

don: (Internet/text) Denial of normal.

Don: (US) A high-ranking member of the Mafia.

Dona: (UK) A woman or girlfriend.

Donah: (UK) A girl.

doncha: (Internet/text) Don't you.

Done for: (UK) 1) To have no chance of success. 2) To be defeated, ruined, or doomed.

Done like a kipper: (UK) Deceived or framed.

Done up like a kipper: (UK) 1) Beaten up. 2) Deceived or framed. 3) Caught in the act by the police.

Donk: (Australian) 1) A car engine. 2) An idiot.

Donkey deep: (New Zealand) To be heavily involved in something.

Donkey: (UK) A slow or clumsy person.

Donkey's breakfast: (UK) A straw mattress.

Donkey's years: (Irish/UK) A very long time.

Donkey-lick: (Australian) To overwhelmingly defeat an opponent.

Donnybrook: (UK) A brawl; a fight.

Dontcha: (Internet/text) Don't you?

Dooby: (Australian) Shabby; unglamorous.

Dood: (Internet/text) Dude.

Doodad: (UK) Refers to an unspecified object.

Doodah: (UK) Refers to an unspecified object.

Doodle: (UK) Nonsense.

Doodly-squat: (UK) Nothing at all.

Doody: (US) Excrement.

Doodz: (Internet/text) Dudes.

Doofer: (UK) 1) Refers to an unspecified object. 2) A partly smoked cigarette.

Doog: (UK) Good.

Dook: (UK) A hand; a fist.

Doolally: (UK) Crazy; out of one's mind.

Doolan: (New Zealand) A Roman Catholic, usually an Irish one. 2) (Australian) A police officer.

Doombrain: (UK) A dim-witted person.

Doon: (UK) A novice or incompetent person.

Doorstep baby: (UK) An illegitimate or unwanted baby.

Doorstep: (UK) 1) A thick slice of bread. 2) To wait around a private house; to bother someone at home.

Dooze: (US) Something that is easy to accomplish. 2) To flatter; to swindle.

Doozer: (US) Someone or something that is impressive.

Doozy: (UK) Excellent; amazing.

Dope out: (US) To devise; to plan.

Dope sheet: (Horse racing) A publication that provides information on the horses running in races.

Dope: 1) A fool. 2) Awesome; cool.

Dope-book: (Horse racing) A chart that details race horses' past performances.

Dopester: (US/Canadian) Someone who makes predictions, especially in sport or politics.

Dopey: Dim-witted; foolish.

Dork: A fool; a geek.

Dorky: Geeky; gauche.

DoS: (Internet/text) Denial of service.

Dose: (UK) A venereal infection.

Dosed up: (UK) To be infected with a venereal disease.

Dosh: (UK/Australian) Money.

Doss around: (UK) To idle about; to do nothing in particular.

Doss down: (UK) To lie down to sleep.

Doss money: (UK) The money needed for a night's lodging.

Doss: (UK) 1) A place to sleep. 2) To sleep. 3) A contemptible person.

Dossbag: (UK) 1) A sleeping bag. 2) A lazy or unkempt person.

Dosser: 1) (Irish) Someone who idles or messes about. 2) (UK) A vagrant.

Dosshouse: (UK) A cheap lodging house frequented by vagrant.

Dossy: (UK) Foolish; simple.

Dot and carry one: (UK) To limp.

Dot on the card: (UK) A certainty; a sure thing.

Dot: (UK) To hit; to punch.

dotc: (Internet/text) Dancing on the ceiling.

Dots and carefuls: (UK) To be warned about something.

Dotty about: (UK) To be extremely fond of something.

Dotty: (UK) A bit crazy; not quite right in the head.

Double bubble: (UK) Twice the usual rate of pay.

Double Dutch: (UK) Unintelligible; incomprehensible.

Double event: (Scottish) To order a glass of whisky and a pint of beer.

Double fair: (UK) Very satisfactory.

Double handful: (UK) Ten pounds sterling.

Double take: To be surprised; to look at something twice out of astonishment.

Double top: (UK) Forty pounds sterling.

Double up: (US) To share something with another person, especially to split the costs.

Double whammy: Two blows delivered one after the other.

Double: (UK) Very; extremely.

Double-bagger: (US) An ugly or contemptible person.

Double-dip: (US) To take more money from a job than one has earned.

Double-eyed: (UK) Untrustworthy.

Double-fisted: (US) 1) Strong; tough. 2) Oversized.

Doubler: 1) (UK) A severe blow. 2) (New Zealand) A double measure of spirits. 3) (Australian) A passenger on a bicycle.

Doubloon: (UK) Money.

Douchebag: (US) An awful person.

Dough: Money.

Doughboy: (UK) 1) A heavy blow or punch. 2) An American soldier. 3) (US) An Army private.

Doughnut: (UK) 1) An idiot. 2) A roundabout.

Doughy over: (Australian) To be in love with someone.

Doughy: (UK) 1) A baker. 2) Foolish.

Dout: (UK) A cigarette end.

Dover: (Australian) A clasp knife.

Dove-tart: (UK) Pigeon pie.

Down among the dead men: (UK) To be drunk or intoxicated.

Down and dirty: (US) Corrupt; deceitful; to employ unfair tactics.

Down the block: (UK) Solitary confinement.

Down the carsey: (UK) Lost; wasted.

Down the chute: (UK) To be ruined; to result in failure.

Down the drain: To be ruined; to result in failure.

Down the flush: (UK) To be ruined; to result in failure.

Down the pan: (UK) To be ruined; to result in failure.

Down the plughole: (UK) To be ruined; to result in failure.

Down the river: (UK) 1) To be betrayed. 2) To be imprisoned.

Down the road: (UK) To be imprisoned.

Down the tubes: To be ruined; to result in failure.

Down to Larkin: (UK) Free; without charge.

Down with the dust: (UK) To deposit the necessary money.

Down: (US) To feel depressed or sad.

Downer: Something that lowers one's mood.

Downhill: (UK) The second half of a prison sentence.

Downhome: (US) Unsophisticated; homely.

Downy: (UK) Cunning; sly; wary.

doypov: (Internet/text) Depends on your point of view.

Dozy: (UK) A slow-witted person.

dprsd: (Internet/text) Depressed.

DQ: (US) Dairy Queen.

dqmot: (Internet/text) Don't quote me on this.

dqydj: (Internet/text) Don't quit your day job.

drOOd: (Internet/text) Druid.

Drabbie: (UK) Someone who is puritanical.

Drack: (Australian) 1) An unattractive person, especially a woman. 2) Rubbish.

Dracks: (UK) Playing cards.

Drag ass: (US) To move slowly or reluctantly.

Drag: (US) 1) A negative situation; something unpleasant. 2) To criticize or disparage someone.

Dragging: (UK) To steal from cars.

Draggy: (UK) Slow-paced or boring; to feel like something lasts much longer than it does.

Dragon: (UK) An ugly or domineering woman.

Dragster: (US) A customized car used for drag racing.

Dragstrip: (US) A stretch of road used for drag racing.

Drainpipes: (UK) Tight trousers with straight, narrow legs.

Drama queen: Someone who is overly dramatic or hysterical about trifling matters.

Dratsab: (UK) A contemptible person.

Draw the crow: (Australian) To come off worst in a situation.

Draw: (UK) 1) Tobacco. 2) A winning bet.

drc: (Internet/text) Don't really care.

Dreadnought: (UK) A heavyweight boxer.

Dreamboat: (UK) A very attractive person.

Dreck: (UK) Rubbish; worthless.

Dregs: (UK) A contemptible person.

Dribbler: (UK) An incontinent man.

Driff: (UK) To leave; to escape.

Drill: To have sex.

Drink: 1) (UK) A small bribe or tip. 2) (US) A large body of water.

Drinker: (UK) A pub or club that opens out of hours.

Drinking vouchers: (UK) Money.

Drink-link: (UK) An ATM machine.

Drip: A boring or insipid person.

Dripping: (UK) To be weak or irresolute.

Drive crazy: (US) To cause someone much frustration.

drm: (Internet/text) Dream.

Droid: (US) A thoughtless or unimaginative person.

Drome: (UK) Aerodrome.

Drone: A dull, seemingly lifeless person.

Drongo: (Australian/New Zealand) A fool; a dim-witted person.

Droob: (Australian) An idiot; a pathetic person.

Drood: (Internet/text) Druid.

Drooly: (UK) Very attractive or appetizing.

Drop a bollock: (UK) To make a mistake.

Drop a brick: (UK) To make a mistake.

Drop a bundle: (UK) To lose a large amount of money.

Drop a clanger: (UK) To make a mistake, especially a faux pas.

Drop a pup: (Australian) To give birth.

Drop knowledge: (US) To share one's information or knowledge.

Drop of nonsense: (UK) A strong drink.

Drop off the perch: (UK) To die.

Drop off the twig: (UK) To die.

Drop one out: (UK) To exclude someone.

Drop one's bundle: (Australian/New Zealand) To panic; to give up hope.

Drop one's daks: (Australian) To take off one's trousers.

Drop out: To withdraw from school; to prematurely end one's enrolment in something.

Drop trou: (US) To take down one's trousers.

Drop: 1) A covert delivery. 2) To knock a person down. 3) To give or tell. 4) (Australian) A fall of the wicket in a game of cricket.

Dropdead gorgeous: A very attractive woman.

Drop-kick: (Australian) A worthless or miserable person.

Drop-out: Someone who withdraws from school; a person who prematurely ends their enrolment in something.

Dropped on: (UK) Reprimanded; scolded.

Dropper: (UK) Someone who deliberately passes counterfeit money.

Droppies: (UK) People who are self-employed.

Dropsy: (UK) A bribe or tip.

Drugstore cowboy: (US) A local male who regularly shows off.

Drum: 1) (UK) A house or home. 2) A road or street. 3) (Australian) A tip or piece of information. 4) A brothel.

Drummer: (UK) A door-to-door salesperson. 2) A burglar. 3) A vagrant. 4) (Australian/New Zealand) The slowest shearer in a team.

Drumming: (UK) Selling products door-to-door. 2) Housebreaking.

Drumsticks: (UK) Legs.

Drunk as a duck: (UK) To be a little drunk.

Drunk as an emperor: (UK) To be very drunk or intoxicated.

dsided: (Internet/text) Decided.

dsu: (Internet/text) Don't screw up.

dta: (Internet/text) Don't trust anyone.

dtb: (Internet/text) Don't text back.

dtg: (Internet/text) Days to go.

dth: (Internet/text) Down to hang.

dtl: (Internet/text) Damn the luck.

dtp: (Internet/text) Don't type please.

dtrt: (Internet/text) Do the right thing.

dts: (Internet/text) Don't think so.

dttm: (Internet/text) Don't talk to me.

du2h: (Internet/text) Damn you to hell.

Dubbed up: (UK) To be imprisoned.

Dubber: (UK) A thief who specializes in lockpicking.

Dubbo: (Australian) A fool; an idiot.

Duchess: (UK) A woman, especially one's wife.

Duck egg: (UK) A score of zero.

Duck shoot: (US) A task that is very easy to accomplish.

Duck soup: (US) Something that is easy to accomplish.

Duck: (UK) A batsman's score of zero in cricket.

Duck's arse: (UK) A miser.

Duck's breakfast: (UK) A drink of water.

Duckburg: (US) A rural town.

Ducky: (UK) Cute; charming.

ducy: (Internet/text) Do you see why?

Duds: Clothes; general effects.

Duff up: (UK) To beat someone badly.

Duff: 1) (UK) Useless; low quality. 2) (Australian) Fake; to make old or stolen goods appear new.

Duffluf: (UK) A fool; an idiot.

Dufus: (US) An idiot; a gauche person.

dugi: (Internet/text) Do you get it?

Dugout: (UK) A retired officer or civil servant who is recalled to employment.

dugt: (Internet/text) Did you get that?

DUI: (Internet/text) Driving under the influence.

duk: (Internet/text) Did you know?

Duke it up (also "duke it out"): (UK) A fight; a brawl.

Duke on it: (UK) To shake hands.

Dukes: (UK) Fists.

Dullsville: (UK) A place or situation that is boring.

dulm: (Internet/text) Do you like me?

dum: (Internet/text) Dumb.

Dumb cluck: (UK) A foolish person.

Dumbass: (US) An idiot.

Dumbbell: (US/Canadian) An idiot.

Dumb-head: (UK) A dim-witted person.

Dumbo: (UK) An idiot.

Dum-dum: (UK) An idiot.

Dummy up: (UK) To stay silent; to hold your tongue.

Dummy: An idiot; a fool. 2) Someone or something that is fake or misleading.

Dump on: 1) To criticize or denigrate. 2) To abuse.

Dump: A dirty or run-down place. 2) To defecate; to put something down roughly. 3) Excrement.

Dumpling: (UK) An idiot; a fool.

Dumps: (UK) Money that is returned to a losing player in a friendly game of cards.

dun: (Internet/text) Don't.

Dunkie: (UK) 1) A girl. 2) A condom.

Dunking: (UK) To have sex.

dunna: (Internet/text) I don't know.

Dunnee (also "dunny"): (Australian) A toilet; an outhouse.

dunno: (Internet/text) I don't know.

Dunny: (Australian) A toilet.

Dunop: (UK) A pound sterling.

dupe: (Internet/text) A duplicate.

Durry: (Australian) A cigarette.

Dust bunny: (US) A ball of dust and fluff in an uncleaned part of the room.

Dust kitty: (UK) A ball of dust and fluff in an uncleaned part of the room.

Dust one's jacket: (UK) To give someone a flogging.

Dust: 1) (UK) To run away quickly. 2) (US) To kill someone.

Dustbin: (UK) A person or animal that will always eat anything.

Dust-up: (UK) A fight; a brawl.

Dusty: (UK) 1) An old person. 2) A dustman.

Dutch beer: (UK) Flat, dull-tasting beer.

Dutch courage: (US) The confidence gained by alcohol.

dutma: (Internet/text) Don't you text me again.

dw: (Internet/text) Don't worry.

dwai: (Internet/text) Don't worry about it.

dwbh: (Internet/text) Don't worry, be happy.

dwbi: (Internet/text) Don't worry about it.

Dweeb: (UK) A nerdy or gauche person.

Dwell up: (UK) To stop; to wait.

dwi: (Internet/text) Deal with it.

dwmt: (Internet/text) Don't waste my time.

dwn: (Internet/text) Down.

dwt: (Internet/text) Don't wanna talk.

dwud: (Internet/text) Do what you do.

dya: (Internet/text) Do you?

dyac: (Internet/text) Damn you auto correct.

dyk: (Internet/text) Did you know?

dylh: (Internet/text) Do you like him?

dylm: (Internet/text) Do you love me?

dym: (Internet/text) Do you mind?

dymm: (Internet/text) Do you miss me?

Dynamite: 1) (UK) Astonishing news. 2) (US) High quality.

dynk: (Internet/text) Do you not know?
dynm: (Internet/text) Do you know me?
dyt: (Internet/text) Don't you think?
dyw: (Internet/text) Don't you worry.

— E —

e.g.: (Internet/text) Example.

e4u2s: (Internet/text) Easy for you to say.

Each way: (UK/Australian) Bisexual.

Eager beaver: Someone who likes to work and stay busy; a person who is enthusiastic to get started with something as soon as possible.

Eagle-hawk: (Australian) To pluck wool from a dead sheep.

Earache: (UK) Constant chatter, grouching, or nagging.

Ear-banger: (UK) A person who talks incessantly.

Earbash: (UK) To talk incessantly.

Ear-basher: (UK) A person who talks incessantly.

Ear-bender: (UK) A person who talks incessantly.

Early bird: Someone who arrives early, especially to enjoy some benefit from doing so.

Earn a crust: (UK/Australian/New Zealand) To earn a living.

Earner: (UK) A scheme or situation that brings financial benefits.

Earwig: (UK) 1) To eavesdrop. 2) An eavesdropper.

Earwigging: 1) (Irish/UK) To eavesdrop. 2) (UK) A reprimand; a scolding. 3) Constant chattering, grouching, or nagging.

Easing: (UK) Relaxing.

Easter egg: (US) A child who is born nine months after a summer romance.

Easy meat: (UK) 1) Someone who is easy to take advantage of. 2) Something that is easy to accomplish or acquire.

Easy rider: 1) A motorcyclist. 2) Someone who seems to succeed without putting in any effort.

Easy-peasy: (UK) Something that is very easy to accomplish.

Eat crow: (UK) To accept an insult without responding.

Eat dirt: (UK) To accept an insult without responding.

Eat it (also "eat the loss"): (US) To accept a loss or failure.

Eat my shorts: (US) A phrase that expresses defiance or scorn.

Eat the head off: (Irish) To be very angry with someone.

Eating irons: (UK) Cutlery.

ebbom: (Internet/text) Engage brain before opening mouth.

ecf: (Internet/text) Error carried forward.

Eckies: (UK) Expenses.

Eclipse: (UK) A very foolish person.

Edge city: (UK) A scary, exciting, or anxiety-inducing situation.

Eedyat: (Internet/text) Idiot.

Eefil: (UK) Life.

Eefink: (UK) A knife.

Eefoc: (UK) Coffee.

Eejit: (Irish/Scottish) Idiot.

efct: (Internet/text) Effect.

Eff and blind: (UK) To swear; to use rude language.

eg: (Internet/text) Evil grin.

Egg on: To encourage or provoke someone.

Egg: (US) To throw raw eggs at something or someone.

Egghead: A very studious person who usually lacks some social skills.

Eggy: (UK) Annoyed; irritated.

Ego massage: (UK) Flattering encouragement or reassurance.

Ego pricing: (UK) Placing too high a price on something based on one's own assumption of its value.

Ego trip: (US) To think highly of oneself.

ehlp: (Internet/text) Help.

Eighteen carat: (UK) First class.

Eighteen wheeler: (US) A truck with 18 wheels.

eil: (Internet/text) Explode into laughter.

Ejecta: (US/military) Missile debris.

El primo: (US) Top quality; the best.

el!t: (Internet/text) Elite.

Elbow bender: (UK) A habitual drinker.

Elbow grease: Hard work; physical effort.

Elbow in: To force oneself into a situation or role.

Elbow room: Space to maneuver; enough space to feel comfortable.

Elbow: (UK) To dismiss someone; to dispose of something. 2) A pickpocket's accomplice.

Elevator music: Background music.

Elevator surfing: (US) To jump from the top of one elevator shaft to another.

Eliminate: To murder someone, especially in a targeted operation.

Ella: (UK) Ale; beer.

ello: (Internet/text) Hello.

elo: (Internet/text) Hello.

em: (Internet/text) Them.

Embalmed: (UK) To be drunk or intoxicated.

Embrocation: (UK) An alcoholic drink.

emm: (Internet/text) Email me.

Emmet: (UK) 1) A tourist. 2) An unwelcome stranger.

emo: (Internet/text) Emotional.

Empty calories: (US) Food that is usually high in calories but which has very little or no nutritional value.

Empty nester: (US) Someone whose children have grown up and left the hose.

enat: (Internet/text) Every now and then.

Enby: Non-binary gender identity.

Endless sleep: (UK) Death.

Endsville: (US) 1) The best. 2) The worst.

Enemy: (UK) One's wife.

Enforcer: (UK) A sledgehammer.

England's last hope: (UK) An unheroic person.

enit: (Internet/text) Isn't it?

enof: (Internet/text) Enough.

Enough: (US) Stop.

enuf: (Internet/text) Enough.

enuff: (Internet/text) Enough.

eob: (Internet/text) End of business.

eoc: (Internet/text) End of conversation.

eod: (Internet/text) End of day.

eof: (Internet/text) End of file.

e-ok: (Internet/text) Electronically okay.

eom: (Internet/text) End of message.

eos: (Internet/text) End of story.

eot: (Internet/text) End of transmission.

eotw: (Internet/text) End of the world.

epa: (Internet/text) Emergency parent alert.

Equaliser: A handgun; a weapon.

Equipment: Genitals.

Erase: (UK) To murder, especially in a targeted operation.

ere: (Internet/text) Here.

Erk: (UK) An incompetent or boring person.

Ersatz: (US) Imitation.

esbm: (Internet/text) Everyone sucks but me.

esc: (Internet/text) Escape.

ESL: (Internet/text) English second language.

ETA: (Internet/text) Estimated time of arrival.

etmda: (Internet/text) Explain it to my dumb ass.

etp: (Internet/text) Eager to please.

ev1: (Internet/text) Everyone.

eva: (Internet/text) Ever.

Eve with a lid on: (US) Apple pie.

Even up the score: (US) To balance out any one-sided advantages.

Even-stevens: (UK) A fair outcome, especially financially.

Event: (US/military) A nuclear incident.

Every1: (Internet/text) Everyone.

Evil: (US) Impressive; admirable.

evn: (Internet/text) Even.

Evo: (Australian) Evening.

evr: (Internet/text) Ever.

evry: (Internet/text) Every.

evry1: (Internet/text) Everyone.

ex-bf: (Internet/text) Ex-boyfriend.

Excess baggage: (UK) A person or thing that is unnecessary; an encumbrance.

Exchange spit: (UK) To kiss.

Excremental: (UK) Rubbish.

Execs: Executives.

Execution day: (UK) Washing day.

Exes: (UK) Expenses.

ex-gf: (Internet/text) Ex-girlfriend.

Exotics: (US) Custom-made or imported cars.

exp: (Internet/text) Experience.

Extra: (UK) Excellent.

Extract the Michael: (UK) To mock; to ridicule.

Extract the urine: (UK) To mock; to ridicule.

Exy: (Australian) Expensive.

ey: (Internet/text) Hey.

Eye in the sky: (UK) A surveillance aircraft, such as a helicopter.

Eyeballer: (US) A know-it-all who always tells other people what to do and how to do it.

Eye-opener: (US) 1) A strong drink, especially an alcoholic one. 2) An intense experience.

Eye-popper: (US) Something amazing.

Eyes a winking: (UK) Something that is very easy or simple.

Eye-trouble: (New Zealand) Staring.

Eyewash: (UK) 1) Nonsense; rubbish. 2) Cheap liquor.

Eyewater: (US) Illegally distilled whisky.

eyez: (Internet/text) Eyes.

ez (also "ezi"): (Internet/text) Easy.

f&e: (Internet/text) Forever and ever.

f@: (Internet/text) Fat.

f2f: (Internet/text) Face to face.

f2m: (Internet/text) Female-to-male (gender transition).

f2p: (Internet/text) Free to play.

f2t: (Internet/text) Free to talk.

f4c3: (Internet/text) Face.

f4eaa: (Internet/text) Friends forever and always.

f4f: (Internet/text) Female for female.

f4m: (Internet/text) Female for male.

f8: (Internet/text) Fate.

f9: (Internet/text) Fine.

faa: (Internet/text) Forever and always.

fab: (Internet/text) Fabulous.

Fab: (UK) Brilliant; great.

Face furniture: (UK) Spectacles.

Face the music: To accept the consequences of one's actions, especially negative ones.

Face-ache: (UK) A person who looks miserable.

Faced: (US) 1) To be drunk or intoxicated. 2) To be snubbed.

Facey: (Australian) Facebook.

Factory: (UK) A police station.

Fade: (US) 1) To leave; to go away. 2) To meet or cover a bet.

Faff about: (UK) To spend one's time on an ineffectual activity.

Faffing: (Irish) 1) To waste time. 2) To do an activity ineffectually.

Fag: 1) (UK) A cigarette. 2) (US/derogatory) An offensive slur for a homosexual.

Fag-end: (UK) A cigarette butt.

fah: (Internet/text) Funny as hell.

faic: (Internet/text) For all I care.

Fair dinkum: (Australian) Honest; equitable; fair.

Fair go: (Australian) An appeal for someone to be fair or reasonable.

Fair play!: (Irish) An expression of congratulations (e.g., "Well done!").

Fair shake: (US) A fair or reasonable deal.

Fairy tale: (UK) An unbelievable story or excuse.

Fairy: (UK/US/derogatory) An offensive term for an effeminate man or homosexual.

Fall for: 1) To develop a crush on someone. 2) To be tricked.

Fall guy: (US) A scapegoat; someone who is set up to take the blame for something.

Fall out: For one's relationship to deteriorate with someone else.

fam: (Internet/text) Family.

Famble: (UK) A hand.

Family jewels: (UK) The male genitals.

Family tree: (UK) The lavatory.

Family: A mafia organization.

Fancy Dan: (UK) A man who looks the part but can't provide results.

Fancy man: (UK) A woman's lover.

Fancy piece: (UK) A mistress.

Fancy woman: (UK) A mistress.

Fangoggling: (UK) Furtively looking at nude women.

Fankle: (Internet/text) The area between one's foot and ankle.

Fanny about: (UK) To waste time on ineffectual activities.

Fanny Adams: (UK) 1) Nothing at all. 2) A very small amount.

Fantod: (UK) A state of anxiety or excitement.

fao: (Internet/text) For attention of.

Fapping: (Internet/text) Masturbating.

FAQ: (Internet/text) Frequently asked question.

Fare-dodger: (UK) A person who uses public transport without paying the fare.

Far-out: 1) Awesome; impressive. 2) Strange; avant-garde.

Fart around: To mess around; to waste time on idle activities.

Fashion victim: A person who follows the latest trends and fads slavishly.

fashizzle: (Internet/text) For sure.

Fast food: (US) Food that is made and served quickly, such as hamburgers.

Fast talk: (UK) Impassioned but deceptive talk.

Fat cat: A wealthy businessperson or politician; someone who enjoys the privileges of their high position.

Fat farm: A health farm or diet center.

Fathead: (UK) An idiot; a fool.

Fatso: An overweight person.

fav: (Internet/text) Favorite.

fave: (Internet/text) Favorite.

Fawney: (UK) A ring.

FB: (Internet/text) Facebook.

fbtw: (Internet/text) Fine, be that way.

fcfs: (Internet/text) First come, first served.

fcol: (Internet/text) For crying out loud.

fe: (Internet/text) Fatal error.

feat: (Internet/text) Featuring.

Features: (UK) A person's face.

Feck: (Irish) A variant of "fuck."

Feck off: (Irish) Fuck off.

Fed up: To feel frustrated.

Fed, the: (US) The FBI.

Feed the fishes: (UK) 1) To be seasick. 2) To drown.

Feed the worms: To die and be buried.

Feel one's oats: (UK) To be conceited.

Feel someone's collar: (UK) To arrest or take someone into custody.

Femme: (UK) A feminine lesbian.

Fence: A person who deals in stolen goods.

Fencer-bender: (US) 1) A minor traffic accident. 2) A person who stages an accident in order to get financial compensation.

Fencing: The buying and selling of stolen goods.

fer: (Internet/text) For.

Fess up: (US) To confess.

Fetch up: (UK) To vomit.

ff: (Internet/text) Friendly fire.

ffa: (Internet/text) Free for all.

ffcl: (Internet/text) Falling from chair laughing.

ffl: (Internet/text) Friend for life.

ffr: (Internet/text) For future reference.

fft: (Internet/text) Food for thought.

fgs: (Internet/text) For God's sake.

fi9: (Internet/text) Fine.

Fiddle face: (UK) Someone who looks miserable.

Fiddle: (UK) To cheat; to tamper with something.

Fidget: (UK) A secret.

Fierce: (Irish) Excellent; amazing.

fifo: (Internet/text) First in, first out.

Fifty winks: (UK) Death.

fify: (Internet/text) Fixed it for you.

File: (UK) 1) A shrewd or skillful person. 2) A pickpocket. 3) To pickpocket.

Fill in: (UK) To attack and injure someone badly.

fill me in: Tell me what happened.

Filleted: (UK) To be very disappointed.

Filth: (UK) The police.

Filthy: (UK) Very wealthy.

fimh: (Internet/text) Forever in my heart.

Fin: 1) (UK) A hand. 2) A five-pound note. 3) (US) A five-dollar bill.

Finagle: (US) To organize something through hard work or manipulation.

Finagling: (UK) Cunning maneuvers or manipulations.

Financial: (Australian) Well off; wealthy.

Find: (UK) To steal.

Fine thing: (Irish) An attractive person.

Finesse someone: (US) To deceive or outmaneuver someone.

Finest: The police.

Finger: (UK) To inform on someone.

Fingers: (UK) A pickpocket.

fio: (Internet/text) Figure it out.

Fire away: (US) An expression that tells the listener to ask any questions they have.

Fireball: (UK) Someone who is full of energy.

Fired up: (UK) 1) To be very drunk or intoxicated. 2) To be enthusiastic or excited. 3) To be angry.

Fireproof: (UK) A person who is safe from blame and trouble.

Firm: (UK) A gang; a criminal organization.

Firming: (UK) A beating given by a criminal gang.

First base: (UK) Kissing (romantically).

First lot: (UK) The Great War.

Fish: To seek out information.

Fisherman: (UK) A con artist.

Fishermans: (UK) Jealousy.

Fishing expedition: An attempt to covertly gather information.

Fishing fleet: (UK) A group of women in search of partners.

Fishing: (UK) An attempt to covertly gather information.

Fishtank: (UK) A cell or reception room for temporarily holding prisoners.

Fishy: (UK) Suspicious; questionable.

Fist magnet: (UK) A contemptible person.

Fisticuffs: (UK) A brawl; a physical fight.

Fit to be tied: (UK) To be very angry or upset.

Fit up: (UK) To frame someone.

Fit: (UK) A physically attractive person.

fitb: (Internet/text) Fill in the blank.

Five bellies: (UK) An obese person.

Five furlong job: (UK) A person who never lasts very long at something.

Five pinter: (UK) An unattractive woman.

Five-finger discount: (US) Stolen, especially from a store.

Fiver: (UK) Five pounds.

Fix: To get revenge on someone. 2) Crooked dealings.

Fixer: Someone who organizes and settles matters, especially by underhanded means.

Fizzer: (Australian) Someone or something that is disappointing.

Fizzhouse: (UK) A pub that doesn't sell proper ale.

Fizzle: (US) To lose energy; to gradually stop working.

fka: (Internet/text) Formerly known as.

Flag unfurled: (UK) The world.

Flag: (UK) A fourpenny piece.

Flagged: (US) 1) Reprimanded. 2) Identified, especially wrongdoing.

Flak: (UK) Criticism; aggression.

Flake: 1) (US) An eccentric or unreliable person. 2) (Australian) Shark meat.

Flaked out: (UK) Exhausted; collapsed.

Flako: (UK) To be drunk or intoxicated.

Flaky: (US) Unreliable; undependable.

Flam: (UK) A lie.

Flamer: (Internet/text) Someone who posts angry or offensive comments online.

Flames: (Internet/text) Angry or offensive comments.

Flaming: (UK) Posting rude or offensive comments online.

Flan: (UK) To hit someone with a custard pie.

Flanker: (UK) A confidence trick.

Flannel: (UK) Nonsense; rubbish.

Flap one's lips: (US) To speak; to chatter.

Flapdoodle: (UK) Nonsense; foolish talk.

Flaphead: (UK) Someone who combs their hair over the top of their head to hide their baldness.

Flapping track: (UK) An unlicensed greyhound track.

Flarge: (UK) Camouflage.

Flash Harry: (UK) A show-off; a braggart.

Flash on: (UK) To be inspired by something.

Flash the ash: (UK) To offer someone a cigarette.

Flash your dover: (Australian) To cut up food with a clasp knife.

Flash: 1) A glimpse of something. 2) To expose one's private parts in public.

Flasher: (UK) Someone who exposes their private parts in public.

Flat: (UK) 1) Penniless. 2) A credit card.

Flats: (UK) Playing cards.

Flavor of the month: The latest fad; something that is currently popular or trendy but which won't last very long.

Flea bite: (UK) Someone who is small and annoying.

Flea's footpath: (UK) A parting in one's hair.

Fleabag: (US) A disreputable person or place.

Fleapit: (US) A cheap, seedy cinema.

Fleece: To charge an exorbitant amount.

Flexible friend: (UK) A credit card.

Flexible: (UK) Bisexual.

Flick: A movie; a motion picture.

Flicking: (UK) Very.

Flicks 'n' chips: (UK) A night out.

Flicks: (UK) The cinema.

Flim-flam: (UK) A confidence trick involving a tall story.

Flimp: (UK) To steal.

Flimsy: (UK) 1) A banknote, especially a counterfeit one.

Fling: 1) (UK) A bribe or illicit payment. 2) A romantic affair.

Flip one's lid: To lose one's temper.

Flip out: (US) To fall into a rage.

Flip someone off (also "flip the bird"): (US) To give someone the middle finger.

Flip: An expression of mild annoyance.

Flip-flop: (US) To change one's mind.

Flipping: Very.

floabt: (Internet/text) For lack of a better term.

Floater: (Australian) A meat pie floating in soup.

Floaters: (UK) 1) Spots in the air in front of one's eyes. 2) Foreign bodies in a beer.

Floating: (UK) To be drunk or intoxicated.

Flob: (UK) To spit.

Flog a dead horse: To waste one's energy on a lost cause; to persist in trying to change an unalterable situation.

Flog: (UK) To sell something.

Floored: (UK) To be very drunk or intoxicated.

Floozie (also "floozy"): A disreputable or promiscuous woman.

Flop: (US/Canadian) A place to sleep.

Flophouse: (US) A cheap lodging house, especially one used by the homeless.

Florin: (UK) Defecation.

Flossy: (US/Canadian) Showy; gaudy.

Flour grader: (UK) A pasty-faced person.

Flower child: (US) A hippy who was young during the 1960s and who typically wore flowers as part of their pro-peace identity.

Fluff: (UK) 1) To make a mistake. 2) Women.

Fluffing: (UK) Very.

Fluke: A lucky success; something that happens by chance.

Flunk: (US) To fail at something.

Flush: (UK) A public toilet.

Flusher: (UK) A lavatory attendant.

Fluthered: (Irish) To be drunk or intoxicated.

Flutter: (UK) To place a wager.

Fly a kite: (UK) To issue a worthless cheque.

Fly by night: (UK) An untrustworthy person.

Fly: 1) (US) Cool; stylish. 2) (UK) A police officer. 3) Quick-witted.

Flybow: (UK) A contemptible person.

Flyer: (UK) A person who commits suicide by jumping from a building.

Flying: (UK) 1) To be intoxicated. 2) To be on a winning streak.

Fly-pitching: (UK) Selling goods at an unauthorized place.

Fly-posting: (UK) Putting up posters or flyers in unauthorized places.

Fly-tipping: (UK) Dumping rubbish at unauthorized places.

fmao: (Internet/text) Freezing my ass off.

fmi: (Internet/text) For my information.

fn: (Internet/text) First name.

fnar: (Internet/text) For no apparent reason.

fnpr: (Internet/text) For no particular reason.

fny: (Internet/text) Funny.

fo shizzle: (Internet/text) For sure.

fo sho: (Internet/text) For sure.

foaf: (Internet/text) Friend of a friend.

fob: (Internet/text/derogatory) Fresh off the boat.

focl: (Internet/text) Falling off chair laughing.

Fodder: (UK) Food.

fofl: (Internet/text) Fall on the floor laughing.

Foghorn: (UK) A person who speaks loudly.

Folderol: (UK) Complications; a fuss.

Folding stuff: (UK) Money, especially notes.

folo: (Internet/text) Follow.

foms: (Internet/text) Fell off my seat.

fone: (Internet/text) Phone.

foo: (Internet/text) Fool.

foocl: (Internet/text) Falls out of chair laughing.

Foodie: A cooking enthusiast; someone who loves food.

Fooding: (Internet/text) The act of acquiring food.

Fool around (with): 1) To have a casual physical relationship with someone. 2) To try or experiment with something casually.

Footling: (UK) Trivial; insignificant.

Footy: (UK) Football; soccer.

Foozling: (UK) 1) Clumsy; botched. 2) Trivial; insignificant.

For real: (US) 1) Honestly. 2) Seriously; in earnest.

For sheeze: (Internet/text) For sure.

For starters: To begin with; in the first place.

For sure: (US) Certainly; yes.

For the hell of it: For no good reason.

Foreign: (UK) Outside of one's own jurisdiction.

Forget about it: (US) Don't worry about it.

Fork out: To pay money, especially reluctantly.

Fork over: To hand something over, especially reluctantly.

Fork: (UK) A pickpocket.

Forks: (UK) Fingers.

Form: (UK) 1) A criminal record. 2) Luck.

Forty snoozewinks: (UK) A short sleep.

Forty winks: Sleep.

foshizzle: (Internet/text) For sure.

fosho: (Internet/text) For sure.

foss: (Internet/text) Free, opensource software.

fotcl: (Internet/text) Fell off the chair laughing.

fotm: (Internet/text) Flavor of the month.

Four flush: (US/Canadian) A bluff.

Four flusher: (US/Canadian) Someone who bluffs or tries to be deceptive.

Four-letter man: (UK) An unpleasant man.

Four-letter word: (US) A swear word.

Four-on-the-floor: (UK) Extremely; excessively.

Fourpenny all off: (UK) A short haircut.

Fourpenny one: (UK) A blow; a punch.

Fourpenny: (UK) A blow, especially a punch.

Fox: (UK) An attractive woman.

Foxy: (UK) Sexy; attractive.

fp: (Internet/text) First post.

FPS: 1) (Gaming) First-person shooter. 2) (Computer) Frames per second.

fr: (Internet/text) For real.

Fractured: (UK) Poor; lacking money.

Frag: (Gaming) Kill.

Frail: (US) A woman.

Frame: To deliberately incriminate an innocent person.

Frame-up: (UK) 1) A conspiracy to incriminate an innocent person. 2) A scheme to engineer a dishonest result.

Frantic: (US) Something exciting.

Freak: 1) An enthusiast. 2) To become hysterical.

Freaking: (US) Very.

Freak-out: To be extremely agitated; to lose one's cool.

Freaky: (UK) Strange; weird; unsettling.

Fred Karno's Army: (UK) FA group of incompetent people.

Free lunch: (US) Something you gain for free.

Freebie: (UK) Something you gain for free.

Freeloader: (UK) Someone who always depends on the charity of others to cover their wants and needs.

Freemans: (UK) Something obtained for free.

Freeze: (Computer) For a system or program to be unresponsive.

Freighted up: (UK) To be financially secure.

fren: (Internet/text) Friend.

French kiss: (UK) A kiss that involves tongue contact.

French letter: (UK) A condom.

French screwdriver: (UK) A hammer.

frens: (Internet/text) Friends.

Fresh fish: (UK) A newcomer; someone who is inexperienced.

Fresh meat: A newcomer; someone who is inexperienced.

Fresh: 1) (UK) An unpleasant smell. 2) (US) Stylish; good.

Fresher: (UK) A first-year undergraduate.

Freshwater trout: (US) Attractive women.

Fret: (US) To worry about something.

frgt: (Internet/text) Forgot.

fri: (Internet/text) Friday.

Fried egg: (UK/Australian) Leg.

Fried: (UK) To be drunk or intoxicated.

Friggin: (Internet/text) Freaking.

Frightener: (UK) Someone whose role is to be intimidating.

Frighteners: (UK) Threats of violence.

Frill: (US) A girl or woman.

Frit: (UK) Afraid; scared.

frk: (Internet/text) Freak.

frm: (Internet/text) From.

frnd: (Internet/text) Friend.

Frogspawn: (UK) Semolina or tapioca pudding.

From here to blooms: (UK) A long distance.

From out front: (US) From the beginning; from the outset.

From soup to afters: (UK) From start to finish.

From soup to cheeseboard: (UK) From start to finish.

From trap to line: (UK) Start to finish.

Front it: (UK) To face up to something or someone.

Front off: (UK) To face up to something or someone.

Front out: (UK) To face up to something or someone.

Front: 1) Cheek; impudence. 2) A business that uses a legitimate cover to hide its illegal practices.

Frost: (UK) 1) To snub someone. 2) To anger or irritate someone. 3) A failure.

Fruitcake: (UK) An eccentric or crazy person.

fs: (Internet/text) For sure.

fsho: (Internet/text) For sure.

fsm: (Internet/text) Flying spaghetti monster.

fsr: (Internet/text) For some reason.

fst: (Internet/text) Fast.

ft2t: (Internet/text) From time to time.

fta: (Internet/text) From the article.

ftbfs: (Computer) Failed to build from source.

ftf (also "F2F"): (Internet/text) Face to face.

ftfy: (Internet/text) Fixed that for you.

ftio: (Internet/text) Fun time is over.

ftlog: (Internet/text) For the love of god.

ftlt: (Internet/text) For the last time.

ftmp: (Internet/text) For the most part.

FTP: (Computer) File transfer protocol.

ftr: (Internet/text) For the record.

fttp: (Internet/text) For the time being.

ftw: (Internet/text) For the win.

fud: (Internet/text) Fear, uncertainty and doubt.

Fuddle: (UK) A drunk or muddled state.

Fuddy-duddy: (UK) An old-fashioned person.

Fug: (UK) A foul-smelling atmosphere, especially inside a room.

Fugle: (UK) To cheat or deceive.

fugly: (Internet/text) Very ugly.

fuhget: (Internet/text) Forget.

Fulham: (UK) A loaded die.

Full as a boot: (Australian) To be drunk.

Full monty: (UK) The full amount.

Full of beans: (UK) To be lively.

Full of it: (US) To say things that aren't true.

Full of oneself: (US) To be conceited or arrogant.

Full: (US/Australian) To be drunk.

fulla: (Internet/text) Full of.

Fully rigged: (UK) Dressed up.

Fumble: (UK) To have a clumsy or ineffectual sexual experience.

Funbags: (UK/Australian) Breasts.

Funee: (Internet/text) Funny.

Fungus: (UK) A beard; facial hair.

Funk: 1) (UK) A state of anxiety or fright. 2) A coward. 3) (US) A heavy, foul-smelling odor.

Funky: (US) 1) A heavy, foul-smelling odor. 2) Fashionable; trendy. 3) Lively.

Funny bones: (UK) A humorous person.

Funny business: Less-than-honest activity; suspicious or underhanded dealings.

Funny farm: (UK) A mental hospital.

Funny money: (UK) 1) Counterfeit money. 2) Worthless denominations. 3) Foreign currency.

Funny: (UK) Strange; weird; unusual.

Furphy: (Australian) A rumor or made-up story.

Fuzz, the: (UK) The police.

Fuzz: Facial hair that hasn't thickened into a beard.

fwb: (Internet/text) Friends with benefits.

fwd: (Internet/text) Forward.

fwiw: (Internet/text) For what it's worth.

fwm: (Internet/text) Fine with me.

fwob: (Internet/text) Friends with occasional benefits.

fwp: (Internet/text) First World problems.

fxe: (Internet/text) Foxy.

fxp: (Computer) File exchange protocol.

fya: (Internet/text) For your attention.

fye: (Internet/text) For your entertainment.

fyeo: (Internet/text) For your eyes only.

fyi: (Internet/text) For your information.

fyk: (Internet/text) For your knowledge.

fyp: (Internet/text) Fixed your post.

g: (Internet/text) Grin.

g/f: (Internet/text) Girlfriend.

g/g: (Internet/text) Got to go.

g/o: (Internet/text) Get out.

G: (US) 1) A friend or acquaintance. 2) A grand (e.g., one thousand). 3) A gram, especially in reference to drugs.

G'day: (Australian) Good day (i.e., "Hello!").

g'nite: (Internet/text) Good night.

g0: (Internet/text) Go.

g00g13: (Internet/text) Google.

g1: (Internet/text) Good one.

g2/-/: (Internet/text) Go to hell.

g2: (Internet/text) Go to.

g2bg: (Internet/text) Got to be going.

g2bl8: (Internet/text) Going to be late.

g2cu: (Internet/text) Glad to see you.

g2e: (Internet/text) Got to eat.

g2g (also "gtg"): (Internet/text) Got to go.

g2gb: (Internet/text) Got to go, bye.

g2ge: (Internet/text) Got to go eat.

g2gn: (Internet/text) Got to go now.

g2gs: (Internet/text) Got to go, sorry.

g2h: (Internet/text) Go to hell.

g2k: (Internet/text) Good to know.

g2p: (Internet/text) Got to pee.

g4u (also "g4y"): (Internet/text) Good for you.

g8: (Internet/text) Gate.

g9: (Internet/text) Good night.

ga: (Internet/text) Go ahead.

Gab: Talking; chattering.

Gabby Hayes: (UK) A very talkative person.

Gabby: (UK) To be talkative.

Gabfest: (US) A lot of chatter; long conversations.

Gable: (UK) The head.

Gadgie: (UK) An old or senile person.

Gaff: (UK) 1) A house or flat. 2) To cheat; to deceive. 3) Nonsense.

Gaffer: 1) A boss; a foreman. 2) The chief electrician on a film set.

gafi: (Internet/text) Get away from it.

Gafiate: (US) To relax on vacation.

gafm: (Internet/text) Get away from me.

Gag me with a spoon: (US) To be repulsed or sickened by something.

Gag rule: (US) A restriction on a debate or discussion of an issue within government.

Gaga: Crazy; senile.

Gagga: (UK) A wig.

Gagger: (US) A repulsive person or situation.

Gagging: (UK) To be very thirsty.

Gaggle: A group of aircraft.

gagp: (Internet/text) Go and get pissed.

gaj: (Internet/text) Get a job.

gal: (Internet/text) Get a life.

Gal: (US) A girl.

Galah: (Australian) A fool; a loudmouth.

Gall: Impudence; cheekiness.

Gallus: (Scottish) Bold; audacious.

Galoot: (UK) A clumsy or coarse person.

Galvo: (Australian) Galvanized iron.

Gam cases: (UK) 1) Trousers. 2) Tights or stockings.

Game bird: (UK) A promiscuous woman.

Gamer: (UK) Someone who plays a lot of video games.

Gammon: (UK) A deception.

Gammy: (UK) Injured; painful; lame.

Gamp: (UK) An umbrella.

Gams: (UK) Legs.

Gander, take/have a: (UK) To take an inquisitive look at something.

Gangbanger: (US) A member of a street gang.

Gangbusters: (US) Something that is outstanding or impressive.

Gangsta: (Internet/text) Gangster.

Gank: 1) (Internet/text) Kill, especially with a firearm. 2) (Video games) To gang up on a defenseless player.

Gannet: (UK) Someone who is gluttonous or greedy.

gaoep: (Internet/text) Generally accepted office etiquette principles.

Gap: (UK) The mouth.

Garbage down: (US) To devour food quickly and hungrily.

Garbage fees: (US) Expensive fees that are charged by lenders at the closing of a property's sale.

Garbage time: (US) The time left to play in a game when the outcome is already clear.

Garbo: (Australian) A dustman.

Garbonzas: (US) Breasts.

Gargle: (UK/Irish) An alcoholic drink.

Gargled: (UK) To be drunk or intoxicated.

Garmento: (US) Someone who works in the fashion industry.

Garnish: (UK) To extort money from someone.

Garret: (UK) The head.

Garretty: (UK) 1) Crazy; mad. 2) Angry.

Gas guzzler: (US) An uneconomical car (i.e., one that consumes a lot of gas).

Gas meter thief: (UK) A small-time criminal.

Gas: 1) (UK) An amusing or entertaining person or thing.2) (US) Flatulence.

Gasbag: (UK) A verbose, long-winded person.

Gasper: (UK) A cigarette, especially a cheap one.

Gassed: (UK) To be drunk or intoxicated.

Gasser: 1) (UK) Something amusing or entertaining. 2) (US) A depressing person or experience.

Gassing: (UK) Boasting.

Gat: (US) A pistol or revolver.

Gate arrest: (UK) Arresting someone as they leave prison for another offence.

Gate fever: (UK) The anxiety prisoners feel near the end of their sentence.

Gate: (US) A suffix that indicates a scandal or cover-up (such as Watergate or Irangate).

Gavel-to-gavel: (US) From the opening of a session of Congress to its adjournment.

Gawd: (Internet/text) God.

Gazump: (UK) To raise the selling price of a property after an agreement has been reached but before contracts have been formalized.

Gazunda: 1) (UK) A chamber pot. 2) (US) To negotiate a cheaper price on a property after striking a deal.

Gazungas: (UK) Breasts.

gb: (Internet/text) Go back.

gb2: (Internet/text) Go back to.

GBA: (Gaming) Game Boy Advance.

gbu: (Internet/text) God bless you.

gby: (Internet/text) Goodbye.

gd&r: (Internet/text) Grins, ducks, and runs.

gd: (Internet/text) Good.

gd4u: (Internet/text) Good for you.

gday: (Internet/text) Good day.

gdby: (Internet/text) Goodbye.

gded: (Internet/text) Grounded.

gdgd: (Internet/text) Good, good.

gdi: (Internet/text) God damn it.

gdr: (Internet/text) Grinning, ducking, running.

Gear: (UK) 1) Clothes or accessories. 2) Good-quality merchandise. 3) Excellent; first rate. 4) Stolen property.

Gee up: (UK) 1) A practical joke. 2) To encourage someone.

Gee-gee: (UK) A horse.

Geek out: (US) To be overenthusiastic about someone or something.

Geek: Someone who is intelligent but lacking in social skills or fashion sense.

Geewillies: (UK) Nervousness; anxiety.

Geezebag: (US) An old person.

Geezer: An old person.

Gel: (UK) A girl.

Gelt: (UK) Money; funds.

Gem: Someone or something that is special.

gemo: (Internet/text) Gay emo.

Gen: (UK) Information; facts.

Gendarmes: (UK) The police.

Generously cut: (UK) Clothing that is loose-fitting for large or overweight people.

Genial: (UK) Good.

Gentleman actor: (UK) A bland but attractive actor or actress.

Germ: (UK) An irritating or unpleasant person.

Gerry: (UK) An old person (short for "geriatric").

Get a bang: (US) To be amused or excited.

Get a body: (US) To kill somebody.

Get a clue: A phrase of frustration that suggests the listener doesn't understand the situation.

Get a creep on: (UK) To go faster.

Get a fix on: To make a reasoned decision.

Get a foot in the door: To get a chance to do something that will lead to further opportunities.

Get a grip: 1) To get one's emotions under control. 2) To understand the situation.

Get a handle on: 1) To get a situation under control. 2) To understand something.

Get a hustle on: (UK) To hurry up.

Get a job: (US) To do something useful.

Get a life: An order for the listener to find something meaningful to do with themselves (used as an insult).

Get a load of: (US) Look at.

Get a move on: (UK) Hurry up.

Get a rat: (Australian/New Zealand) Crazy; eccentric.

Get a rift on: (UK) To hurry up.

Get a rush on: (UK) To hurry up.

Get a rush: (US) To become excited or intoxicated.

Get a wiggle on: (UK) To hurry up.

Get a word in edgeways: To find an opportunity to speak when someone else is talking nonstop.

Get all bent out of shape: (US) To lose one's temper about something.

Get all that out of your mouth: (UK) Stop lying.

Get an edge: (US) Get an advantage.

Get at: (UK) To bribe or threaten.

Get away with murder: To avoid punishment despite certain guilt.

Get axed: (Surfing) To be thrown by a wave.

Get back on one's feet: To recover after an illness or serious problem.

Get back to one's roots: To return to one's personal heritage.

Get behind: To approve of or support someone or something.

Get benched: (US) To be removed from play during a game.

Get biffed: (Surfing) To be knocked around by a wave.

Get big air: (Surfing) To launch oneself high into the air above a wave.

Get busy: (UK) To rob someone.

Get by: To have just enough money to support oneself.

Get canned: (US) To be fired from one's job.

Get cold feet: To lose one's nerve at the last moment.

Get cracking: (US) To hurry; to get busy.

Get creamed: (Surfing) To be dumped roughly by a wave.

Get down to brass tacks: To focus on what is essential.

Get down: (US) To start something in earnest.

Get go: The beginning.

Get going: To leave; to depart.

Get hitched: (US) To get married.

Get in on the act: (UK) To participate in something, especially to reap a profit.

Get in the game: (UK) To become aware of a situation.

Get into bed: To agree to liaise closely with someone or merge with another business.

Get it through one's head: To finally understand something.

Get it together: (UK) 1) To get organized. 2) To collect one's cool.

Get knotted: (UK) Go away.

Get laid: To have sex.

Get loose: (UK) To relax; to have fun.

Get lucky: To have sex.

Get lunched: (Surfing) To get dumped by a wave.

Get moded: (US) To be humiliated.

Get naked: (US) To have fun.

Get no change out of: (UK) To be unsuccessful in trying to get information from somebody.

Get off easy: To face no serious consequences.

Get off on the wrong foot: To form a relationship that starts out badly.

Get off on: (UK) To enjoy something greatly, almost like a form of arousal.

Get off one's back: To stop nagging someone.

Get off the ground: To make a successful start at some venture.

Get off with your bad self: (US) To be pleased with oneself.

Get off: 1) (UK) Stop bothering. 2) (US) To be aroused by something.

Get on one's tits: (UK) To irritate or annoy.

Get on one's wick: (UK) To irritate or annoy.

Get on someone's case: (US) To harass or pester someone.

Get on someone's goat: To irritate or annoy someone.

Get on the ball: To try harder; to pay more attention.

Get on with (it): To get something over with sooner rather than later, especially something unpleasant.

Get one's act together: To change one's behavior or performance for the better.

Get one's arse in gear: (UK) To get organized and be proactive, especially after a period of idleness.

Get one's end away: (UK) To have sex.

Get one's feet wet: To do something for the first time.

Get one's head together: To collect oneself and change one's behavior or performance for the better.

Get one's jollies: (UK) To derive enjoyment from something.

Get one's knickers in a twist: (UK) To be unduly agitated or worried.

Get one's leg over: (UK) To have sex.

Get one's oats: (UK) To have sex.

Get one's rear in gear: (UK) To hurry; to stop being idle.

Get one's rocks off: To have sex.

Get out of here: (US) An expression of disbelief (similar to "No way!").

Get out of my face: Go away.

Get out of one's hair: To remove a nuisance.

Get over: (US) To accept something difficult or unpleasant.

Get paid: A successful robbery.

Get pounded: (Surfing) To be dumped by a wave.

Get rats: (Australian/New Zealand) Crazy or eccentric.

Get real: An expression that tells the listener to be serious or realistic.

Get sacked: To be fired from a job.

Get shot of: To get rid of something.

Get small: (US) 1) To disappear. 2) To hide.

Get someone up: (UK) 1) To bribe someone. 2) To outmaneuver someone.

Get someone's goat: To irritate or anger someone.

Get stiffed: 1) To be conned; to be overcharged. 2) To not receive one's due payment.

Get stuffed: An insult telling the listener to go away or leave the speaker alone.

Get the axe: To be fired from a job.

Get the ball rolling: To begin something; to take the initial steps to do something.

Get the glory: (UK) To become religious.

Get the goods on: (US) To find evidence of somebody's guilt.

Get the hang of: (US) To learn how to do something, especially after initial difficulties.

Get the hook: To remove a performer from the stage when they are performing badly.

Get the hump: (UK) To become ill-tempered; to be offended.

Get the lead out: (US) To hurry.

Get the message: To understand what someone is trying to communicate, especially when the real meaning is being implied.

Get the needle: (UK) To become ill-tempered or vindictive.

Get the picture: To understand the full situation.

Get the rap: To be blamed for something.

Get the run: (Australian) To be fired from a job.

Get the shaft: (US) To be put in a bad position.

Get the show on the road: To begin something.

Get through to: To make someone understand something, especially when they are reluctant to do so.

Get to the bottom: To uncover the full truth of a situation.

Get to the heart: To determine the most important aspect of something.

Get under someone's skin: To be irritating or aggravating.

Get up one's nose: (UK) To irritate or annoy.

Get what's coming: To get what one deserves, especially a negative consequence for wrongdoing.

Get wind of: To hear about something.

Get with it: (US) 1) To be receptive to new ideas or styles. 2) To pay attention to what is happening around oneself.

Get with the program: (US) To conform to expectations.

getcha: (Internet/text) Get you.

geto: (Internet/text) Ghetto.

Get-together: A large gathering of people.

get-up-and-go: (US) Energy; motivation.

gewd: (Internet/text) Good.

gf: (Internet/text) Girlfriend.

gfak: (Internet/text) Go fly a kite (e.g., "Go away!" or "Get lost!").

gfe: (Internet/text) Girlfriend experience.

gfe2e: (Internet/text) Grinning from ear to ear.

gfl: (Internet/text) Grounded for life.

gfm: (Internet/text) God forgive me.

gfx: (Internet/text) Graphics.

gfy: (Internet/text) Good for you.

gg: (Gaming) Good game.

gga: (Gaming) Good game all.

ggal: (Internet/text) Go get a life.

ggg: (Internet/text) Go, go, go!

ggi: (Internet/text) Go Google it.

ggnore: (Gaming) Good game, no rematch.

ggp: (Internet/text) Gotta go pee.

ggs: (Gaming) Good games.

ggwp: (Gaming) Good game, well played.

gh: (Internet/text) Good half.

Gherkin: (UK) An idiot; a fool.

Ghetto box: (US) A large portable radio and cassette (or CD) player.

Ghettoblaster: (US) A large portable radio and cassette (or CD) player.

Ghost of a chance: (UK) For something to be very unlikely.

Ghost speech: (US) A legislator's speech that isn't delivered in person but is entered into the Congressional Record as though it had been.

Gib: (UK) Trouble; problems.

Giblets: (UK) Innards; guts.

Gift of the gab: (UK) To be talkative; to make conversation easily.

Gifted: (UK) To be talented at something.

Gig: 1) A live performance by a musician or entertainer. 2) (Computer) Gigabyte.

Giggle house: (Australian) A mental hospital.

Giggle juice: (UK) An alcoholic drink.

Giggle water: (UK) An alcoholic drink.

gigig: (Internet/text) Get it, got it, good.

Gig-lamps: (UK) Spectacles.

gigo: (Internet/text) Garbage in, garbage out.

Gilligan: (Surfing) An idiot.

gim: (Internet/text) Google Instant Messenger.

gimme: (Internet/text) Give me.

Gimmer: (UK) An elderly person.

gimmie: (Internet/text) Give me.

Gin lane: (UK) The throat.

Ginch: (UK) 1) Excellence; elegance. 2) Style.

Ginchy: (UK) Excellent; elegant. 2) Smart; skillful.

Gink: (US) An idiot; a contemptible person.

Ginormous: Massive; enormous.

Ginzy trading: (US) The unscrupulous practice of giving customers different prices on the same buy-and-sell order.

Gip: (UK) Vomit.

Gippy: (UK) Nausea.

Girl: A weak or effeminate man.

gis: (Internet/text) Google image search.

Gismo: 1) A device or gadget. 2) A gadget whose name one doesn't know or remember.

Git: (UK) An annoying or contemptible person.

gitar: (Internet/text) Guitar.

giv: (Internet/text) Give.

Give a hand: To provide assistance.

Give a person rats: (UK) To berate or rebuke someone.

Give a sample: (UK) To urinate.

Give an oral sacrifice at the altar of the porcelain god: (US) To vomit.

Give chase: To pursue; to run after someone or something.

Give cuts: (US) To allow someone to go ahead of you in a queue.

Give five: (US) To greet someone by hand.

Give ground: (US)To retreat.

Give it a burl: (Australian) To give something a try.

Give it a lash: (Irish) To give something a try.

Give it a shot: To attempt something, particularly without any pressure regarding the outcome.

Give it large: (UK) 1) To intimidate someone, especially verbally. 2) To boast.

Give it some boot: (UK) To accelerate.

Give it some cog: (UK) To accelerate.

Give it some stick: (UK) To add some pressure or force to achieve something.

Give it some welly: (UK) To accelerate.

Give it some: (UK) To apply some effort into achieving something.

Give one a taste of plum: (UK) To wound or kill with gunfire.

Give one's eyetooth for: (UK) To be willing to give something of great value in order to receive something one desires.

Give one's right arm: To be willing to give something of great value in order to receive something one desires.

Give skin: (US) To slap hands with someone, especially in greeting or celebration.

Give someone a piece of one's mind: 1) To chastise or rebuke someone. 2) To share what one really thinks without sugar-coating it.

Give someone a serve: (Australian) To reprimand or be critical of someone.

Give someone a wedgie: To pull someone's underwear up so that it wedges between their buttocks.

Give someone curry: (Australian) To assault someone, either verbally or physically.

Give someone five: (US) To slap hands with someone in greeting or celebration.

Give someone the air: (US) To dismiss or reject someone.

Give someone the arse: (Australian) 1) To get rid of something. 2) To jilt someone.

Give someone the cold shoulder: To be unfriendly towards someone; to purposely ignore someone.

Give the air: (UK) To get rid of something; to dismiss someone

Give the devil his due: To be fair to someone.

Give the finger: (US) A rude gesture made by sticking up one's middle finger while keeping the others down.

Give the rinky-dink: To cheat or deceive someone.

Give the shaft: (US) To put someone in a bad position.

Give the slip: To escape; to purposely lose a pursuer or evade the authorities.

Give them heaps: (Australian/sports) To compete spiritedly against an opposing team.

Give up the digits: (US) To share one's phone number.

Give up the ghost: To expire; to break down.

Give up the ship: (UK) To surrender or give up.

Given out with the rations: (Military) A medal awarded automatically without regard of merit.

Giving out: (Irish) Scolding; chastising.

giyf: (Internet/text) Google is your friend.

gj: (Internet/text) Good job.

gjp: (Internet/text) Good job, partner.

gjsu: (Internet/text) God, just shut up.

gjt: (Gaming) Good job, team.

gl hf: (Internet/text) Good luck; have fun.

gl&hf: (Internet/text) Good luck and have fun.

gl: (Internet/text) Good luck.

gla: (Internet/text) Good luck, all.

Gladhand: (US) To greet people superficially.

Glam: Glamorous.

Glar: (UK) Paint.

Glarney: (UK) A marble.

Glasgow kiss: (UK) A headbutt.

Glasgow magistrate: (Scottish) A herring.

Glass arm: (US/baseball) A pitcher's arm that is easily injured or strained.

Glass jaw: (US) 1) A coward. 2) A boxer's tendency to get knocked down by a punch to the jaw.

Glass of lunch: (UK) An alcoholic drink for lunch (without food).

Glass someone: (UK) To strike someone with a bottle or glass.

Glass: Diamonds; jewels.

Glasshouse: (UK) An army prison.

Gleamer: (UK) Excellent.

glf: (Internet/text) Group looking for.

glhf: (Internet/text) Good luck, have fun.

Glim: (UK) A light; a candle.

Glitch: An unforeseen error or malfunction.

Glitterati: (UK) Stylish and fashion-focused celebrities.

Glitz: (UK) Gaudiness; extravagant but superficial showiness.

Glitzy: (UK) Gaudy; flashy but superficial.

glln: (Internet/text) Got laid last night.

glnhf: (Internet/text) Good luck and have fun.

Glob: (Computers) Using wildcards in file names.

Gloopy: Sticky; gooey; viscous.

Glop: (UK) 1) To drink alcohol. 2) A thick liquid. 3) Unappetizing food.

glty: (Internet/text) Good luck this year.

glu2: (Internet/text) Good luck to you too.

Glue foot: (Surfing) A surfer who seldom loses their footing.

Gluebag: (UK) Someone who is mentally unstable.

Glug: (UK) To take a drink of alcohol.

glux: (Internet/text) Good luck.

glwt: (Internet/text) Good luck with that.

GM: Game master (someone who runs a role-playing tabletop game).

gm: (Internet/text) Good morning.

gma: (Internet/text) Grandma.

gmab: (Internet/text) Give me a break.

G-man: (US) An FBI agent.

gmao: (Internet/text) Giggling my ass off.

gmod: (Internet/text) Global moderator.

gmta: (Internet/text) Great minds think alike.

gmtyt: (Internet/text) Good morning to you too.

gmv: (Internet/text) Got my vote.

gmybs: (Internet/text) Give me your best shot.

gn: (Internet/text) Good night.

gn8: (Internet/text) Good night.

Gnarlatious: (Surfing) Awesome; great.

Gnarly: (US) Extreme, either in a good or bad way.

gnasd: (Internet/text) Good night and sweet dreams.

Gnasher snatcher: (UK) A dentist.

Gnashers: (UK) Teeth.

Gnat's piss: (UK) A weak alcoholic drink.

gndn: (Internet/text) Goes nowhere, does nothing.

gnfpwlbn: (Internet/text) Good news for people who love bad news.

gng: (Internet/text) Going.

gng2: (Internet/text) Going to.

gnight: (Internet/text) Good night.

gnite: (Internet/text) Good night.

gno: (Internet/text) Going to do.

gnst: (Internet/text) Good night, sleep tight.

gnstdltbbb: (Internet/text) Good night, sleep tight, don't let the bed bugs bite.

Go a bundle on: (UK) To like something or someone a lot.

Go all the way: (UK) To have sex.

Go ape: (US) 1) To go wild 2) To be very angry.

Go apeshit: (US) 1) To rage; to become very angry. 2) To act wildly.

GOAT: (Internet/text) Greatest of all time.

Go ballistic: To be very angry; to rage.

Go belly up: 1) To die. 2) To fail. 3) For a business to go bankrupt.

Go Borneo: (US) 1) To get drunk. 2) To behave wildly.

Go bung: (Australian/New Zealand) To fail; to die.

Go bush: (Australian) To go native.

Go crook at: (Australian/New Zealand) To scold or rebuke someone.

Go down: 1) (UK) To go to prison. 2) (US) For something to happen. 3) To perform oral sex. 4) To shoulder the blame or responsibility for something bad.

Go figure: An expression of puzzlement (e.g., "Who would have thought?").

Go for a burn: (Australian) To drive fast; to speed.

Go for a burton: (UK) 1) To be broken or useless. 2) To be lost. 3) To die.

Go for broke: To risk everything in a final attempt at success.

Go for it: To attempt something difficult.

Go for the doctor: (Australian) To put forth a big effort; to move very fast.

Go gaga: To be very excited about something.

Go great guns: To act with great power or force.

Go into one: (UK) To lose one's temper.

Go into: (UK) To borrow.

Go it: To do something energetically.

Go regulars: (UK) To share profits.

Go scratch: (UK) An expression of refusal.

Go spare: (UK) To lose one's temper; to be very angry.

Go straight: To renounce a life of crime.

Go the full distance: To be arrested, convicted, and imprisoned.

Go the limit: (UK) To have sex.

Go through: (UK) To have sex.

Go to hell in a handcart: (UK) For a situation to deteriorate quickly and terribly.

Go to pot: (UK) For a situation or object to deteriorate.

Go upstairs: (UK) To drink spirits in a pub.

Go walkabout: (UK) To daydream; to lose one's focus.

Go: (UK) 1) An incident. 2) A glass of spirits.

Go-ahead: (UK) Progressive; forward thinking.

Goalie: (UK) An ace in a deck of cards.

Goalkeeper: (UK) An ace in a deck of cards.

Goat: (UK) A miserable old man.

GOAT: (US) Greatest of all time.

Gob iron: (UK) A harmonica; a mouth organ.

Gob: (UK) 1) A person's mouth. 2) To spit. 3) Saliva; spittle.

Gobbledygook: Nonsense.

Gobslutch: (UK) A slovenly person.

Gobsmacked: (UK) Dumbfounded; astonished; to be rendered speechless.

Gobsmacking: (UK) Astonishing.

God squad: (UK) A group of religious people.

Godawful: (UK) Terrible; awful.

God-botherer: (UK) An annoyingly pious person.

Goer: (UK) Something that is mechanically sound.

Gofer: An employee or assistant who takes care of menial tasks.

Go-getter: (US) Someone who works hard and with initiative.

Goggle: (UK) To stare at someone or something.

Gogglebox: (UK) A television.

Goggles: (UK) Spectacles.

Goggy: (UK) A misfit.

goi: (Internet/text) Get over it.

goia: (Internet/text) Get over it already.

goin: (Internet/text) Going.

Going-over: (UK) A beating.

gok: (Internet/text) God only knows.

gokid: (Internet/text) Got observers, keep it decent.

gokw: (Internet/text) God only knows why.

gol: (Internet/text) Giggle out loud.

Gold brick: (US) An idle person; someone who shirks their responsibilities.

Gold fish: (US) Sliced peaches.

Gold-card: (US) To act ostentatiously.

Golden ager: (US) An elderly person.

Golden coffin: (US) A benefits package that is paid to an executive's heirs upon his or her death.

Golden gater: (US) A terrible script.

Golden grease: (US) 1) A bribe. 2) A fee.

Golden handcuffs: A package of benefits that are offered to employees to keep them locked in their jobs.

Golden oldie: (UK) Something old but classic.

Golden syrup: (UK) An obvious wig.

Golden: (US) Excellent; perfect.

Golgotha: (UK) A meeting place for the heads of universities or other such institutes.

Gollier: (UK) A lump of phlegm.

Gollopagoose: (UK) A glutton.

Gom: (UK) A gormless-looking person.

gomb: (Internet/text) Get off my back.

goml: (Internet/text) Get out of my life.

gona: (Internet/text) Gonna.

Gone for a Burton: (UK) To be missing or broken.

Gone Goose: (US) Someone or something that is beyond help.

Gone Gosling: (US) Someone or something that is beyond help.

Gone native: (UK) A police officer turned criminal.

Gone west: (UK) 1) Passed; dead. 2) Failed.

Gone: (UK) An exhilarated state.

Gonef: (UK) A thief.

Goner: (UK) Someone or something that is beyond saving.

Gong: (UK) A medal, especially from the military.

Gongoozler: (UK) Someone who stares at something for a long time.

Gonies: (UK) The testicles.

Gonna: (Internet/text) Going to.

Gonnof: (UK) A thief.

Gonoph: (UK) A thief; a pickpocket; a con artist.

Gonzo: (UK) 1) An idiot; a fool. 2) To be drunk or intoxicated. 3) (US) Strange; crazy.

Goob: (US) An unpopular or socially awkward person.

Goobatron: (UK) An idiot; a fool.

Goober: (US) A naive or foolish person.

Good 'un: (UK) A decent person.

Good breeding: (UK) To have good manners.

Good egg: A decent, fair-minded person.

Good guy: (US) A decent person who treats others well.

Good hands: To be good at catching things with one's hands.

Good oil: (Australian) Information, or a suggestion, that is considered good or reliable.

Good on ya: (Australian) "Good for you!"

Good time Charlie: (UK) A promiscuous man.

Good-time Jane: (UK) A promiscuous woman.

Good to go: (US) For something to be ready.

good9: (Internet/text) Good night.

Goodefella: (US) A member of an organized crime gang, especially the Mafia.

Good-fellow: (UK) A pleasant, sociable person.

Goody-goody: An annoyingly virtuous person.

Goody-two-shoes: An annoyingly virtuous person.

Goof around: To play around; to shirk one's responsibilities.

Goof off: (US) To neglect one's responsibilities.

Goof on: (US) To laugh at or make fun of something or someone.

Goof up: (US) To make a mistake.

Goof: 1) A blunder; a mistake. 2) Someone who makes careless mistakes.

Goofball: (US) A silly person.

Goof-off: (US) 1) A lazy or negligent person. 2) To neglect one's responsibilities.

Goofy foot: (Surfing) A person who surfs with their right foot forward.

Goofy: Stupid; silly.

Goog: (Australian) An egg.

Googie: (Australian) An egg.

Goo-goo: An adoring look, especially a romantic one.

Googs: (US) Spectacles.

Googy: (UK) An egg.

Googy-egg: (Australian) An egg.

gooh: (Internet/text) Get out of here!

Gooliboos: (UK) The testicles.

Goolies: (Australian) Stones; pebbles.

Goolies: (UK) The testicles.

Goombah: (US) A member of an organized crime gang.

goomh: (Internet/text) Get out of my head.

Goon squad: A group of thugs who are sent to intimidate someone.

Goon: 1) A thug. 2) A dim-witted person.

Goony: (US) A foolish person.

Goop: (UK) 1) A fool. 2) (US/Canadian) A rude person.

Goopy: (UK) 1) Foolish. 2) Unfortunate.

Goose egg: (UK) A score of zero.

Goose: To condemn someone by hissing at them.

Goosy: (UK) Nervous; skittish.

Gorbals kiss: (UK) A headbutt.

Gorilla: 1) (UK) A hired thug, used for their physical strength. 2) (US) A very successful movie.

gork: (Internet/text) God only really knows.

Goss: (UK) Gossip; chatter.

Got it going on: 1) To be attractive. 2) To be successful.

Got to hand it to: To give credit to someone.

gotc: (Internet/text) Get on the computer.

gotcha: (Internet/text) Got you.

Gotta: (Internet/text) Got to.

Gouge: (US) To intimidate; to damage. 2) To overcharge.

Gouger: (Irish) A thug or hoodlum.

Gourd: (US) The head.

Governor: (UK) A boss or someone in a leadership position.

GoW: (Gaming) 1) Gears of War. 2) God of War.

Gowl: (Irish) Idiot.

goya: (Internet/text) Get off your ass.

gp: (Internet/text) Good point.

gpb: (Internet/text) Gotta pee bad.

gpwm: (Internet/text) Good point well made.

gr8 (also "gr8t"): (Internet/text) Great.

Grab a granny: (UK) For a young man to seduce an older woman.

Grab: (UK) 1) Overtime. 2) A bag.

Grabbers: (UK) The hands.

Graft: (UK) 1) Work; a job. 2) To engage in dishonest schemes to make money. 3) Bribery.

Grafter: (UK) 1) A worker. 2) A fraudulent street trader; a petty criminal.

Grand Central Station: (US) A very crowded place.

Grand: (UK) 1) One thousand dollars or pounds. 2) Excellent; awesome. 3) (Irish) Fine; all right; okay.

Grandstand: (US) To show off to an audience.

Granny lane: (UK) The inside lane of a motorway.

Granny: (UK) A prim old woman.

Grape-cat: (US) Someone who drinks a lot of wine.

Grapefruits: (UK) Breasts.

Grapes: (UK) Hemorrhoids.

Grasp at straws: To make a flimsy, desperate argument that isn't substantiated by facts.

Grass: (UK) 1) An informer. 2) To inform on someone.

Grassroots: Ordinary people.

Grats (also "gratz"): (Internet/text) Congratulations.

Gravel train: (US) A sugar bowl.

Graveyard shift: Work that takes place during the night.

Graveyard: (UK) The mouth.

Gravy train: To earn excessively well from one's job.

Gray area: (US) An ethically, morally, or legally dubious issue or matter.

Graze: (UK) To eat while standing or working.

Grease burger: (UK) A cheap, low-quality hamburger.

Grease monkey: A mechanic.

Grease one's chops: (US) To eat.

Grease one's palm: To bribe; to tip.

Greaser: (UK) 1) A mechanic. 2) A long-haired biker. 3) An unpleasant, obsequious person.

Grease-trap: (US) A lunch counter.

Grease-up: (UK) A meal consisting of fried food, especially for breakfast.

Greasy chin: (UK) Dinner.

Greasy spoon: (UK) A cheap cafe.

Great guns: Extremely fast; something done vigorously.

Great unwashed: (UK) The masses; ordinary people.

Greedy guts: (UK) A glutton; someone who always wants more.

Greeking: (UK) Cheating at a card game.

Green crystal job: (UK) To be over the drinking limit for driving.

Green fingers: Someone with a natural talent for gardening.

Green light: Official approval (especially to begin a project or production).

Green marketing: Advertising efforts to promote an environmentally friendly product or initiative.

Green monster: (Surfing) A massive wave.

Green product: A product that is environmentally friendly.

Green room: 1) A room where performers or guests wait before going on stage. 2) (Surfing) Inside the tube of a wave.

Green seal: (US) A label on a product that marks it is environmentally friendly.

Green stuff: (UK) Money; cash.

Green thumb: Someone with a natural talent for gardening.

Green welly: (UK) The upper-middle class.

Green: 1) A naive or unsophisticated person. 2) Money; cash. 3) A clean energy source or non-polluting technology.

Greenacre: (UK) An accident.

Greenback green: (US) A person who is willing to spend money on environmental issues and non-polluting products.

Greenback: (US) Paper money notes from a dollar upwards.

Greener: (UK) Someone who is naive.

Greenhorn: (US) An inexperienced person; someone who is unsophisticated.

Greenie: (UK) A naive or unsophisticated person.

Greenlock: (US) Traffic congestion around national parks and forests during the tourist season.

Greenmail: (UK) Money paid by a company to foil an attempted takeover.

Greenwashing: (UK) Extensive public relations efforts to promote a product or company as being environmentally friendly.

Green-welly brigade: (UK) Wealthy townsfolk who visit the country on weekends.

Grem: (Australian) A novice or unskilled surfer.

Gremlin: 1) (UK) An error or malfunction in how something operates. 2) (Surfing) Someone who is still learning to surf.

Gremmie: (Surfing/Australian) Someone who is still learning to surf.

Grey area: (UK) An ethically, morally, or legally dubious issue or matter.
Grey ghost: (US) A legislator's top aide.
Grey market: (UK) A retail enterprise that operates in a legally dubious manner.
Grey matter: (UK) The brain.
Greybeard: (UK) An old or elderly man.
Greyhound: (UK) A miniskirt.
Grey-mare: (UK) A wife.
grfx: (Internet/text) Graphics.
Grief: Trouble; an aggravation or hassle.
Griefy: (UK) Depressing or bothersome.
Griff: (UK) News or information.
Grifter: (US) Someone who scams or takes advantage of people for their own gain (typically financial).
Grill: 1) Interrogate. 2) A person's face.
grillz: (Internet/text) Metal teeth.
Grind to a halt: To come to a complete stop.
Grind: To work excessively hard at something. 2) (Gaming) To keep repeating a task in order to level up one's character.
Grindage: (UK) Food.
Grinder: 1) (UK) A sportsperson who exerts a lot of pressure on their opponent. 2) (Surfing) A large wave.
Grinders: (UK) The teeth.
Grip: (UK) A stagehand or film-set technician.
Gristle grabber: (UK) A dishonest or deceitful person.
Grit: Courage or determination; the ability to persevere.
Gritch: (UK) To moan or complain about something.
Grizz: (UK) A gray beard.
grl: (Internet/text) Girl.
grmbl: (Internet/text) Grumble.
Grockle: (UK) An unwelcome outsider (such as a tourist or visitor).
Grody: (US) Being of poor or shabby quality.
Grog: (UK) An alcoholic drink; beer.
Groin: (UK) A diamond ring.
Grok: (UK) To understand.

Grolley: (UK) A quick look or glance.

Grommet: (UK) 1) An unnamable object. 2) A woman who is regarded as a sex object.

Gronk: (UK) To fix a machine that is jammed with something.

Gronked: (UK) For something to be dysfunctional.

Groover: (UK) 1) Someone who is fashionable person. 2) A tedious or overly studious person.

Groovy: Fashionable; funky; fun.

Gross out: (US) To disgust or revolt someone.

Gross player: (US) An actor so successful that they command a percentage of a movie's gross income.

Gross: (UK) Gross indecency.

Grot: (UK) Rubbish or dirt.

Grotbag: (UK) An unkempt or unpleasant person.

Grotty: (UK) 1) Unpleasant or foul. 2) Being of poor quality or in bad condition.

Ground zero: (US/military) The location of a nuclear missile strike.

Ground: (UK) The region under a particular police station's jurisdiction.

Grounded: To be confined to home, especially as a punishment by one's parents.

Groupie: A passionate (usually female) fan of a celebrity, especially a musician, who seeks out regular contact with them.

Grouse: (Australian/New Zealand) Great; excellent.

Growzy: (UK) A slow computer.

grrl: (Internet/text) Girl.

grtg: (Internet/text) Getting ready to go.

Grub: (UK) Food (typically of a plain/simple variety).

Grudge match: When two opponents have history with each other, with one side looking to rectify a past defeat.

Gruey: (UK) Unpleasant or foul.

Grungey/grungy: Grimy or scruffy; dirty.

Grunt work: (US) Hard, often tedious, work (especially manual labor).

Grunt: (US/military) An infantry soldier or US marine.

Grunter: (UK) 1) A pig. 2) An ignorant or slovenly person. 3) A policeman.

Gruntled: (UK) Satisfied or gratified (the opposite of disgruntled).

Grunts: (US) Food.

grvy: (Internet/text) Groovy.

gsd: (Internet/text) Getting shit done.

gsfg: (Internet/text) Go search fucking Google.

gsi: (Internet/text) Go suck it.

gsoh: (Internet/text) Good sense of humor.

gsta: (Internet/text) Gangster.

gt: (Internet/text) Get.

GTA: (Gaming) Grand Theft Auto.

gtb: (Internet/text) Go to bed.

gtfa: (Internet/text) Go the fuck away.

gtfo: (Internet/text) Get the fuck out.

gtfoi: (Internet/text) Get the fuck over it.

gtfu: (Internet/text) Grow the fuck up.

gtg: (Internet/text) Got to go.

gtgb: (Internet/text) Got to go, bye.

gtgn: (Internet/text) Got to go now.

gtgp: (Internet/text) Got to go pee.

gtgtb: (Internet/text) Got to go to bed.

gth: (Internet/text) Go to hell.

gtho: (Internet/text) Get the hell out.

gthu: (Internet/text) Grow the heck up.

gtk: (Internet/text) Good to know.

gtm: (Internet/text) Giggling to myself.

gtn: (Internet/text) Getting.

gtp: (Internet/text) Got to pee.

gtr: (Internet/text) Got to run.

gts: (Internet/text) Going to school.

gtsy: (Internet/text) Good to see you.

gttp: (Internet/text) Get to the point.

gtty: (Internet/text) Good talking to you.

gu: (Internet/text) Grow up.

gu2i: (Internet/text) Get used to it.

Gubbins: (UK) Paraphernalia.

Gucci gulch: (US) The lobbying community in Washington, D.C.

Guck: (UK) A sticky (usually unpleasant) substance.

gud (also "gudd"): (Internet/text) Good.

Gudgeon: (UK) Someone who is easy to fool or deceive.

Guerrilla marketing: (UK) A marketing strategy whereby samples of a product are distributed in order to quickly gauge consumer response.

Guff: (UK) 1) Nonsense. 2) Flatulence; breaking wind. 3) A messy, sticky substance.

GUI: (Computer) Graphical user interface.

Guiver: (UK) A young man who is well-dressed and arrogant.

Gumballs: (US) The flashing lights on a police car.

Gumby: (UK) A foolish or dull person.

Gummy: (UK) A toothless person.

Gump: (UK) A foolish person.

Gumshoe: (US/Canadian) A detective or someone who moves about stealthily.

Gun for: (US) To make a concerted effort to obtain or achieve something.

Gun shy: (US) To be overly cautious.

Gun: (Australian/New Zealand) An expert.

Gunge: (UK) A sticky, often grimy, substance.

Gung-ho: To be overly enthusiastic or assertive.

Gunk: (UK) 1) A sticky, often grimy, substance; rubbish. 2) A misfit.

Guns: (US) Muscles (especially describing someone's arms).

Gunship: (UK) An unmarked police car.

Guppy: (UK) An environmental yuppie.

Gurgle: (UK) An alcoholic drink.

Gurgler: (UK/Australian) A toilet.

gurl: (Internet/text) Girl.

gurlz: (Internet/text) Girls.

guru: (Internet/text) An expert.

Gut reaction: One's immediate response; instinct.

Gut: The belly/stomach; a paunch.

Gut-rot: (UK) 1) Low-quality alcoholic drinks or food. 2) A stomach ache.

Gutsache: (UK) A miserable person; someone who complains a lot.

Gutsy: To be brave; bold, or courageous.

Gutted: (UK) To be disappointed, upset, or shocked.

Gutty: (UK) To be brave, bold or determined.

Guv: (UK) A man.

Guvnor: (UK) A boss or leader.

Guy: A man or person.

Guzunder: (UK) A chamber pot.

Guzzle: 1) To drink quickly or in large amounts. 2) (UK) Beer.

Guzzled: (UK) Intoxicated or drunk.

gw: (Internet/text) Good work.

gwork: (Internet/text) Good work.

Gwot: (UK) An intolerable person.

gws: (Internet/text) Get well soon.

gyal: (Internet/text) Girl.

Gym rat: (US) A person who spends all their time at the gym.

Gyp: (UK) To cheat or swindle.

Gyppy tummy: (UK) Diarrhea.

Gyver: (UK) A young man who is well-dressed and arrogant.

— H —

h&k (also "h+k"): (Internet/text) Hugs and kisses.

h*r: (Internet/text) Homestar runner.

h.a.: (UK) Home address.

h.o: (Internet/text) Hold on.

h/e: (Internet/text) However.

h/o: (Internet/text) Hold on.

h/u: (Internet/text) Hold up.

h/w: (Internet/text) Homework.

h@x0r: (Internet/text) Hacker.

h2gtb: (Internet/text) Have to go to the bathroom.

h2o: (Internet/text) Water.

h2sys: (Internet/text) Hope to see you soon.

h3y: (Internet/text) Hey.

h4x: (Internet/text) Hacks.

h4x0r: (Internet/text) Hacker.

h8: (Internet/text) Hate.

h80r: (Internet/text) Hater.

h82sit: (Internet/text) Hate to say it.

h83r: (Internet/text) Hater.

h8ed: (Internet/text) Hated.

h8er (also "h8r"): (Internet/text) Hater.

h8red: (Internet/text) Hatred.

h8s: (Internet/text) Hates.

h8t (also "h8te"): (Internet/text) Hate.

h8t0r (also "h8t3r"): (Internet/text) Hater.

h8ter (also "h8tr"): (Internet/text) Hater.

h8u: (Internet/text) I hate you.

Habit: (UK) An addiction.

habt: (Internet/text) How about this.

Hack into: To bypass a program's security.

Hack it: To succeed at something; to manage at a task or in a position (often used negatively; e.g., "He can't hack it as a manager.").

Hack off: (UK) To irritate or annoy.

Hack: 1) A dull person who lacks originality; someone who acts more competent than they really are. 2) A journalist.

Hacked: (UK) Irritated or annoyed.

Hacked-off: (UK) Irritated or annoyed.

Hackette: (UK) A female journalist.

Had over: (UK) To be tricked or deceived.

hafta: (Internet/text) Have to.

hagd: (Internet/text) Have a good day.

hagl: (Internet/text) Have a great life.

hagn: (Internet/text) Have a good night.

hago: (Internet/text) Have a good one.

hags: (Internet/text) Have a great summer.

hai: (Internet/text) Hello.

Hail Mary: (US/American football) A long pass into the end zone, thrown in the last few seconds of play.

Hair of the dog: An alcoholic drink to help relieve a hangover.

Hairball: (US) A contemptible person.

Haircut: (UK) A short prison sentence.

Hairless: (UK) To be very angry; to be in a rage.

Hair-up: (UK) A fight between women.

Hairy: A difficult, complicated, or dangerous situation.

hait: (Internet/text) Hate.

hak: (Internet/text) Here's a kiss.

hakas: (Internet/text) Have a kick-ass summer.

Half a stretch: (UK) A prison sentence of six months.

Half a surprise: (UK) A black eye.

Half and halfer: (UK) A bisexual person.

Half of marge: (UK) A police sergeant.

Half pint: (UK) A child or short person.

Half-assed: (US/ Canadian) To do something lazily or incompetently.

Half-cut: (UK) To be drunk or intoxicated.

Half-shaved: (US) To be slightly intoxicated or drunk.

Half-soaked: (UK) Foolish; idiotic.
Halfway there: (UK) The number forty-five.
Ham fat: (US) Someone or something that is mediocre.
Ham: An unconvincing or incompetent actor.
Ham-fisted: Clumsy; inept.
Hammered: To be very drunk or intoxicated.
Hams: (US) Legs (of a person).
han: (Internet/text) How about now.
Hancocks: (UK) Half an hour.
Hand like a foot: (UK) Poor handwriting.
Handbags at twenty paces: (UK) A fight in which neither person is really trying to cause injury.
Handbags: (UK) A fight between two women.
Handcuffs: (US) An engagement or wedding ring.
Handful: (UK) A prison sentence of five years.
Handle: (UK) A person's name, title, or nickname.
Handles: (US) Rings of fat that hang around the stomach.
Hand-me-downs: Second-hand clothes.
Handshake: (UK) A tip; a bribe.
Hands-off: To allow others to do their work without micromanaging them.
Handsome: (UK) Excellent or impressive.
Hands-on: (US) To be personally involved; to be an active part of something.
Handy: To be useful or convenient.
Hang a Louie: (US) Make a left turn.
Hang a Ralph: (UK) Make a right turn.
Hang five: (US/surfing) To surf with the toes of one foot curled over the front of the board.
Hang it up: (US) To stop doing something.
Hang loose: (US) To relax.
Hang one on: (UK) To hit or punch.
Hang out: To relax; to spend time with friends.
Hang ten: (US/surfing) To surf with the toes of both feet curled over the front of the board.
Hang the rap on: (US) To charge someone with circumstantial evidence.

Hang-up: Emotional or psychological baggage.

Hanky-panky: (UK) Sexual activity.

Happening: (UK) Exciting, trendy, or fashionable.

Happy bollocks: (UK) A miserable man.

Happy hour: A time at a bar or restaurant when prices are lowered.

Happy juice: (UK) An alcoholic drink.

Happy pratt: (UK) A miserable woman.

Hard case: 1) Someone who is tough or uncompromising. 2) (New Zealand) A quick-witted person.

Hard cheese: (UK) Bad luck.

Hard dog: (US) An attack dog.

Hard nut: 1) (UK) Someone who is tough or uncompromising. 2) (Australian) A horse that is difficult to break.

Hard out: (New Zealand) An expression to convey strong agreement.

Hard stuff: (UK) A strong alcoholic drink.

Hard words: To speak harshly or bluntly.

Hard: (UK) To be tough or uncompromising.

Hard-arse: (UK) A tough or uncompromising person.

Hard-arsed: (UK) To be tough or uncompromising.

Hard-baked: (UK) Constipated.

Hardball: (US) A tough and competitive situation.

Hardbody: (US) A fit, attractive person, especially a body-builder.

Hard-faced: (UK) Shameless or brazen.

Hard-hat: (US) A construction worker.

Hard-on: (UK) An erection.

Hardrock: (UK) A tough or uncompromising person.

Hard-up for: (US) To be desperate to get something.

Hard-up: (UK) To be lacking money.

Harp: (UK) A harmonica.

Harpic: (UK) To be crazy or deranged.

Harry-starkers: (UK) To be completely naked.

Has-been: A former celebrity; someone who has lost their fame or following.

Hat holder: (UK) A person's head.

Hat peg: (UK) A person's head.

Hat rack: (UK) A person's head.

Hatch: (UK) A person's throat (often used in the phrase "down the hatch", when about to drink something quickly).

hau: (Internet/text) How are you?

Haul ass: (US) To move quickly; to speed.

hav: (Internet/text) Have.

Have a ball: To enjoy yourself; to have fun.

Have a cow: To be angry; to lose one's temper.

Have a down on: (UK) To dislike something.

Have a liver: (UK) To be grumpy.

Have a pop at: (UK) To insult something or someone.

Have a scene: (UK) To have sexual relations with someone; to have an affair.

Have a snout on someone: (Australian) To bear a grudge against someone.

Have a word with: (UK) To beat up someone.

Have all your buttons: (UK) To be intelligent; to be clever.

Have it away on one's toes: (UK) To run away; to escape.

Have it away: (UK) 1) To run away; to escape. 2) To have sexual intercourse.

Have it good: (US) To be in an enviable position, particularly financially or at work.

Have it in: (UK) To have sexual intercourse.

Have it off: (UK) 1) To have sexual intercourse. 2) To fight. 3) To be successful at something.

Have it on one's toes: (UK) To run away; to escape.

Have it on the thumb: (UK) To hitchhike.

Have it through the slips: (UK) To escape a situation without being caught.

Have it together: To have your affairs in order; to be well-organized; to be sensible or mentally/emotionally/financially stable.

Have it: To lose one's temper or patience (typically used in the pattern, "I have had it with his poor attitude!").

Have one's ass in a sling: (US) To be in trouble.

Have over: (UK) To deceive or cheat; to swindle.

Have some bollocks: (UK) To be brave or bold.

Have someone over: (UK) To deceive or cheat; to swindle.

Have the decorators in: (UK) To be menstruating.

Have the goods on: To have incriminating information about someone or something.

Have the hots (for someone): To be attracted to someone.

Have the painters in: (UK) To be menstruating.

Having the craic: (Irish) To be out having fun.

havnt: (Internet/text) Haven't.

hawf: (Internet/text) Husband and wife forever.

Hawk: 1) (UK) To spit. 2) (US) To vomit.

hawt: (Internet/text) Hot.

hawtie: (Internet/text) Hottie.

hax (also "H4X"): (Internet/text) Hacks.

hax0r (also "haxer"): (Internet/text) Hacker.

hax0red: (Internet/text) Hacked.

hax0rz (also "haxorz"): (Internet/text) Hackers.

hayd: (Internet/text) How are you doing?

Hazing: (US) Teasing or bullying, especially as a form of initiation.

hb: (Internet/text) Hurry back.

hb4b: (Internet/text) Hoes before bros.

hbd: (Internet/text) Happy birthday.

hbu: (Internet/text) How about you?

hbuf: (Internet/text) How about your family?

hby: (Internet/text) How about you?

hc: (Internet/text) 1) How come? 2) Head cannon (details about a story or character that are not official but which the reader or viewer chooses to believe).

hcbt1: (Internet/text) He could be the one.

hcib: (Internet/text) How can it be?

H-dropper: (UK) A Cockney person.

hdu: (Internet/text) How dare you.

Head honcho: The top person in charge; the person with the most authority.

Head job: (UK) A crazy person.

Head rake: (UK) A comb.

Head trip: (US) Someone who has an inflated opinion of themselves.

Head: 1) The boss or leader of an organization or company. 2) A toilet.

Headbang: To shake one's head wildly to loud (typically aggressive-sounding) music.

Headcase: (UK) A crazy or delusional person.

Headlamps: (UK) Female breasts.

Headshrinker: (UK) A psychiatrist.

Heads-up: A warning or word of caution.

Heap: (UK) An old or worn-out vehicle.

Heat: (US) The police.

Heater: (US) A pistol; a gun.

Heave: (US) To vomit.

Heave-ho: (UK) A dismissal; to be rejected or fired.

Heaves: (UK) Vomiting.

Heavy bevvy: (UK) Strong beer; a heavy drinking session.

Heavy: 1) A hired thug; a person whose role is to be violent or physically intimidating. 2) Something that is emotionally or mentally taxing.

Heebie-jeebies: Anxiety; nervousness; to be creeped out or scared.

Heel: (US) An unpleasant person.

heh: (Internet/text) A chuckle; laughter.

Heinie: (US) A person's buttocks.

Hell: An intolerable situation.

Hell's waiting room: (UK) An awful place.

Hella: (US) Very.

Hellacious: (US) Awful; intolerable.

Hellery: (Canadian) Mischievous or reckless behavior.

Helmet: (UK) The glans of the penis.

Hen night: A pre-wedding celebration for the bride-to-be and (typically) her female friends and family.

Hen: (Scottish) A girl or woman.

Hep cat: (US) A person who is hip and knowledgeable.

Hep: (US) Stylish; knowledgeable.

Het: Heterosexual.

heya: (Internet/text) Hey.

heyt: (Internet/text) Hate.

heyya: (Internet/text) Hello.

hf: (Internet/text) Have fun.

hfwt: (Internet/text) Have fun with that.

hght: (Internet/text) Height.

hhyb: (Internet/text) How have you been?

hi2u: (Internet/text) Hello.

hi2u2: (Internet/text) Hello to you too.

Hick: (US) Someone who lives in a rural location and whose education is limited.

Hickey: A love bite.

Hicksville: (US) A rural place populated by people with limited education and narrow world views.

Hide the sausage: (UK) To have sex.

High five: To slap hands with someone, typically in celebration.

High roller: Someone who spends money extravagantly, often when gambling.

High stepper: (UK) Someone who is trendy and fashion conscious.

High: To be intoxicated, typically through drug use.

High-hat: (US) To act condescendingly.

High-tech: (US) Technologically advanced; electronics that are very modern.

hiik: (Internet/text) Hell if I know.

Hijack: (Internet/text) To divert the topic of somebody else's discussion.

Hike: (UK) A departure; a journey.

Himbo: A male airhead; the male equivalent of a bimbo.

Hinky: (US) Dubious; suspicious.

Hip: (US) 1) Trendy; in style. 2) Knowledgeable.

Hippy: Someone whose rejection of traditional social values is often paralleled by drug use and the concept of free love and peace.

Hipster: A trendy, progressive, unconventional person, often in a way that is regarded as overly deliberate.

His nibs: (UK) A title that refers to an authority figure.

History: A threat of impending disaster.

Hit it: To start something (especially to start playing music).

Hit man: An assassin.

Hit on (someone): To flirt with someone.

Hit the bricks: To leave; to begin a journey.

Hit the hay: To go to bed.

Hit the post: (UK) To be unlucky.

Hit the road: To leave; to begin a journey.

Hit the sack: To go to bed.

Hit the spot: (US) To eat or drink something satisfying.

Hit: 1) Drug use. 2) An assassination. 3) A visit to a website.

Hitch: To marry.

Hitched: Married.

hith: (Internet/text) How in the hell?

Hitter: (UK) 1) A successful person. 2) An assassin.

hiya: (Internet/text) Hello.

hld: (Internet/text) Hold.

hldn (also "hldon"): (Internet/text) Hold on.

hll: (Internet/text) Hell.

hlm: (Internet/text) He loves me.

hlo: (Internet/text) Hello.

hlp: (Internet/text) Help.

hly: (Internet/text) Holy.

hmb: (Internet/text) Hold me back.

hml: (Internet/text) Hate my life.

hmp: (Internet/text) Help me, please.

hmu: (Internet/text) Hit me up.

hmul: (Internet/text) Hit me up later.

hmus: (Internet/text) Hit me up sometime.

hmw: (Internet/text) Homework.

hmwk: (Internet/text) Homework.

ho: (Internet/text) Hold on.

Hoachin': (Scottish) To be very busy.

hoas: (Internet/text) Hang on a second.

Hobo: (US) A vagrant.

Hockshop: (UK) A pawnbroker.

Hog: 1) Someone who is greedy. 2) A motorbike, typically a Harley-Davidson.

Hoggins: (UK) Sexual gratification.

Hogsnorton: (UK) A glutton.

Hog-tied: (US) To be incapacitated.

Hog-wild: (US) To act wildly.

Hog-wimpering: (UK) 1) Helpless. 2) To be intoxicated or drunk.

hoh: (Internet/text) Head of household.

Ho-hum: Dull or wearisome.

Hoist: (UK) To steal, particularly describing petty theft (such as pickpocketing).

Hoister: (UK) A thief, especially a shoplifter or pickpocket.

Hoity-toity: Arrogant; haughty.

Hokey: Corny; contrived; overly sentimental.

Hokum: 1) Nonsense. 2) Hackneyed; overly sentimental.

Hold up: (US) Wait.

Hold your noise: (UK) An order to be quiet.

Holding folding: (UK) To have money on one's person.

Holding: (UK) To have money on one's person.

Hole in one's own shoe: (UK) To be the cause of one's own misery.

Hole in the wall: (UK) An ATM.

Holed below the water line: (UK) To be impotent.

Holler: (UK) To share information with the police.

Hols: (UK) Holidays.

Holy cow: (US) Wow!

Holy Joe: (UK) A religious man.

Holy water: (UK) Whiskey and water.

Home run: (US) Sexual intercourse.

Homeboy: (US) A close friend who lives in your area.

Homely: Plain-looking.

Homer: (US) Sexual intercourse (from "home run").

Homework: (UK) An attractive woman.

Homie: (US) A close friend who lives in your area.

Honey: A term of endearment (such as "darling" or "sweetheart").

Honk up: 1) To vomit. 2) To spread a terrible smell.

Honk: (UK) 1) To vomit. 2) To smell terrible.

Honked: (UK) To be drunk or intoxicated.

Honker: (UK) A nose, especially in reference to one that is large.

Honking down: (UK) To be raining hard.

Honking: (UK) 1) To be drunk or intoxicated. 2) Foul-smelling.

Hood: (US) 1) A low-income neighborhood. 2) A gangster.

Hooey: Nonsense.

Hoof it: 1) To go by foot. 2) To leave in a hurry.

Hoof: (UK) A foot.

Hoofer: (UK) A dancer.

Hoofing: (UK) Dancing.

Hooha: (UK) A commotion; a ruckus.

Hook it: (UK) To leave in a hurry; to run away.

Hook up: A casual or short romantic/sexual encounter.

Hook: (UK) To steal.

Hooked: To be addicted to something.

Hooker: A prostitute.

Hooking: Prostitution.

Hooky Street: (UK) A trading area for stolen goods.

Hooky: (US) Truancy; skipping out on school or work.

Hoolie: (UK) A noisy party or celebration.

Hoolivan: (UK) A police van that is used in riots involving hooligans.

Hoon: (Australian) A disreputable person, especially a wild youth.

Hoop out: (US) To play basketball.

Hoopla: 1) A commotion; a ruckus. 2) Nonsense.

Hoops: (US) Basketball.

Hooray Henry: (UK) An unruly young man of upper-middle-class standing.

Hooray: (UK) An unruly young man of upper-middle-class standing.

Hoot: (Australian/New Zealand) Money.

Hootchie cootchie: (US) 1) Sexual activity. 2) Erotic dancing.

Hooter: (UK) A nose, especially one that is large.

Hooters: (US) A woman's (large) breasts.

Hoover: (US) To eat or drink quickly.

Hop a babe: (US) To have sex with a woman.

Hop into: (Australian/New Zealand) 1) To initiate a task. 2) To attack someone.

Hop it: (UK) To go away; to leave (often quickly).

Hop the wag: (UK) To play truant.

Hop: (Australian) A cop; a police officer.

Hophead: (UK) A beer drinker.

Hopped-up: (US) To be intoxicated.

Hopper: (US) A toilet bowl.

Hoppy: (UK) A beer drinker.

Hops: (UK) Beer.

Horace: (UK) The penis.

Horizontal dancing: Sexual intercourse.

Horizontal refreshment: (UK) Sexual intercourse.

Horizontal relaxation: (Australian/New Zealand) Sexual intercourse.

Horizontal worker: (US) A prostitute.

Horizontals: (UK) Sexual intercourse.

Hork: (US) 1) To steal. 2) To spit. 3) To vomit.

Horlicks: (UK) A mess.

Hormone fix: (US) Sexual activity.

Hormone: (US) A sexually aggressive person.

Horn in: (US) To interrupt; to interfere.

Horn movie: (UK) A pornographic film.

Horn: (US) A telephone.

Hornbug: (US) A person who is obsessed with sex.

Horndog: (US) A person who is obsessed with sex.

Hornet: (UK) An ill-tempered person.

Hornets: (US) Bullets.

Hornety: (UK) Angry.

Hornswoggle: (UK) To deceive or cheat; to swindle.

Horny: To be sexually aroused; to be lustful.

Horrors: (UK) A state of depression or anxiety.

Horrorshow: Something that is horrifying.

Horse around: To mess around; to play about.

Horse feathers: (US) Nonsense.

Horse piddle: (UK) A hospital.

Horse's ass: (US) A fool; an ignoramus.

Horseshit: Nonsense; rubbish.

Horsey set: (UK) Wealthy people from the countryside.

Hose: (US) 1) To cheat. 2) To defeat soundly.

Hosehead: (US) An idiot; a fool.

Hoser: (US) 1) A fraud; a cheat. 2) A womanizer.

Hot cack: (Australian) The latest news.

Hot pants: (US) Brief shorts.

Hot potato: A controversial or awkward issue.

Hot roller: (US) A stolen car.

Hot seat: (US) 1) The electric chair. 2) The position of someone who bears a lot of responsibility.

Hot shit: (US) Something or someone that is impressive.

Hot tamale: (US) An attractive person, typically a woman.

Hot to trot: (UK) To be eager to have sex.

Hot: 1) To be sexually attractive. 2) Stolen goods. 3) To be under enemy fire.

Hot-dog: (US) To perform impressively.

Hotel: (UK) A police station.

Hotpot: (Australian) A strongly backed horse.

Hots (to have the hots for): To be sexually attracted to someone.

Hottie: 1) (UK/Australian) A hot-water bottle. 2) (US) An attractive woman.

Hotting: (UK) Stealing cars for entertainment.

Houdini: (UK) To escape; to disappear.

Hound: (UK) 1) A contemptible person. 2) A male thug.

How's your father: (UK) 1) A bad state of affairs. 2) A placeholder for something nameless or for which the name has slipped one's mind.

howdey: (Internet/text) Hello.

Howl: An outburst of laughter.

howz: (Internet/text) How's (i.e., "how is").

hpy: (Internet/text) Happy.

hpybdy: (Internet/text) Happy birthday.

hr: (Internet/text) Hour.

hre: (Internet/text) Here.

hrs: (Internet/text) Hours.

hru: (Internet/text) How are you?

hrud: (Internet/text) How are you doing?

hruf: (Internet/text) How are you, friend?

hs: (Gaming) Headshot.

hsd: (Internet/text) High school dropout.

hsik: (Internet/text) How should I know?

ht: (Internet/text) Heard through.

htf: (Internet/text) How the fuck?

htfu: (Internet/text) Hurry the fuck up.

htg: (Internet/text) Have to go.

hth: (Internet/text) Hope that/this helps.

hthu: (Internet/text) Hurry the hell up.

htr: (Internet/text) Hater.

hu: (Internet/text) Hey you.

Hubby: Husband.

hud: (Internet/text) Heads up display.

Huey: (UK) A helicopter.

Huff: To inhale a drug.

Huffy: To be irritable or in a bad mood.

Hug the porcelain wishing well: (US) To vomit in the toilet.

huggle: (Internet/text) Hug and cuddle.

Hughies: (UK) Green vegetables.

hugz: (Internet/text) Hugs.

Hum: 1) (UK) To smell unpleasant. 2) (Australian) To scrounge for something.

Humdinger: Something or someone remarkable or impressive.

Hum-hole: (UK) The mouth.

Hump: (UK) To have sexual intercourse.

Humped-up: (UK) To be in a bad mood; to be irritated or angry.

Hun: (US) A term of endearment (short for "honey").

Hunchfront: (UK) A woman with very large breasts.

Hung up on: To remain fixated on something; to be unable to stop thinking about something or someone.

Hung up: To be delayed or impeded in some way.

Hung: For a man to be physically well-endowed.

Hungry Horace: (UK) A person who is always hungry.

Hunk: An attractive man.

Hunker down: To ignore distractions and focus hard on doing something.

Hunky-dory: To be fine; to be satisfactory.

Hurl: (Australian/South African) To vomit.

Hurry up van: (UK) A police car.

Hustle your bustle: (UK) Hurry up.

Hustle: To solicit business; to generate work.

Hustler: A person who swindles people by deliberately performing badly at something in order to drive up the betting price.

hv (also "hve"): (Internet/text) Have.

hvnt: (Internet/text) Haven't.

hw: (Internet/text) Homework.

hwg: (Internet/text) Here we go.

hwga: (Internet/text) Here we go again.

hwik: (Internet/text) How would I know?

hwk: (Internet/text) Homework.

hwu: (Internet/text) Hey, what's up?

hwz: (Internet/text) How is (it going)?

hy: (Internet/text) Hell yeah.

hyb: (Internet/text) How you been?

hyg: (Internet/text) Here you go.

Hype: 1) To promote something; to generate excitement about something. 2) The excitement that precedes an event of some sort.

Hyped up: To be very excited for something.

Hyper: To behave energetically or manically; to be agitated.

i <3 u: (Internet/text) I love you.
i8: (Internet/text) All right.
i8u: (Internet/text) I hate you.
iab: (Internet/text) I am bored.
iag: (Internet/text) It's all good.
iai: (Internet/text) I am interested.
ianabs: (Internet/text) I am not a brain surgeon.
ianal: (Internet/text) I am not a lawyer.
ianalb: (Internet/text) I am not a lawyer, but.
ianars: (Internet/text) I am not a rocket scientist.
ians: (Internet/text) I am not sure.
ianyl: (Internet/text) I am not your lawyer.
iap: (Internet/text) I am pissed.
iasb: (Internet/text) I am so bored.
iatb: (Internet/text) I am the best.
iavb: (Internet/text) I am very bored.
iaw: (Internet/text) In another window.
iawtc: (Internet/text) I agree with this comment.
iawtp: (Internet/text) I agree with this post.
iawy: (Internet/text) I agree with you.
ib: (Internet/text) I'm back.
ibbl: (Internet/text) I'll be back later.
ibcd: (Internet/text) Idiot between chair and desk.
ibt: (Internet/text) I'll be there.
ibtl: (Internet/text) In before the lock (i.e., posting one's comment in anticipation of the thread being locked soon by moderators).
ibw: (Internet/text) I'll be waiting.
ic (also "i c"): (Internet/text) I see.
icb: (Internet/text) I can't believe.
icbi: (Internet/text) I can't believe it.

icbt: (Internet/text) I can't believe that.

icbu: (Internet/text) I can't believe you.

iccl: (Internet/text) I couldn't care less.

Ice cold: (Australian) A beer.

Ice maiden: (UK) An aloof woman.

Ice man: (US) A professional killer; a hit man.

Ice: 1) Diamonds. 2) To kill.

Iceberg: (US) To have an aloof or reserved manner.

Icebox: A solitary confinement cell.

icic: (Internet/text) I see, I see.

icr: (Internet/text) I can't remember.

icty: (Internet/text) I can't tell you.

icu: (Internet/text) I see you.

icudk: (Internet/text) In case you didn't know.

icw: (Internet/text) I care why? (i.e., "Why should I care about that?").

id1ot: (Internet/text) Idiot.

idac: (Internet/text) I don't actually care.

idak: (Internet/text) I don't actually know.

idby: (Internet/text) I don't believe you.

idc: (Internet/text) I don't care.

Idea-pot: (US) The mind.

idec: (Internet/text) I don't even care.

idek: (Internet/text) I don't even know.

idfc: (Internet/text) I don't fucking care.

idfk: (Internet/text) I don't fucking know.

idgac: (Internet/text) I don't give a crap.

idgad: (Internet/text) I don't give a damn.

idgaf: (Internet/text) I don't give a fuck.

idgas: (Internet/text) I don't give a shit.

idgi: (Internet/text) I don't get it.

Idiot board: (UK) An autocue.

Idiot box: (UK) A television.

Idiot's lantern: (UK) A television.

idjit: (Internet/text) Idiot.

idk: (Internet/text) I don't know.

idkbibt: (Internet/text) I don't know but I've been told.

idke: (Internet/text) I don't know either.

idkh: (Internet/text) I don't know how.

idkw: (Internet/text) I don't know why.

idkyb: (Internet/text) I don't know why but.

idl: (Internet/text) I don't like.

idli: (Internet/text) I don't like it.

idlu (also "idly"): (Internet/text) I don't like you.

idm: (Internet/text) I don't mind.

idn: (Internet/text) I don't know.

idnk: (Internet/text) I don't know.

idno: (Internet/text) I don't know.

idop: (Internet/text) It depends on price.

idr: (Internet/text) I don't remember.

idrc: (Internet/text) I don't really care.

idrk: (Internet/text) I don't really know.

idsw: (Internet/text) I don't see why.

idts: (Internet/text) I don't think so.

idu: (Internet/text) I don't understand.

idwk: (Internet/text) I don't wanna know.

idwtg: (Internet/text) I don't want to go.

idyat: (Internet/text) Idiot.

ifwis: (Internet/text) I forgot what I said.

ig: (Internet/text) I guess.

ig2g: (Internet/text) I've got to go.

igg: (Internet/text) I've got to go.

ight: (Internet/text) All right.

igs: (Internet/text) I guess so.

igt: (Internet/text) I got this.

igtg: (Internet/text) I've got to go.

igu: (Internet/text) I give up.

igyb: (Internet/text) I got your back.

ih: (Internet/text) It happens.

ih2p: (Internet/text) I'll have to pass.

ih8: (Internet/text) I hate.

ih8tu (also "ih8u"): (Internet/text) I hate you.

ihml: (Internet/text) I hate my life.

ihnc: (Internet/text) I have no clue.

ihni: (Internet/text) I have no idea.

iht: (Internet/text) I heard that.

ihu (also "ihy"): (Internet/text) I hate you.

ihya: (Internet/text) I hate you all.

ihysm: (Internet/text) I hate you so much.

iight: (Internet/text) All right.

iiok: (Internet/text) Is it okay?

iirc: (Internet/text) If I recall correctly.

iiuc: (Internet/text) If I understand correctly.

iiwii: (Internet/text) It is what it is.

ij: (Internet/text) Inside joke.

ijaf: (Internet/text) It's just a fact.

ijdk: (Internet/text) I just don't know.

ijdl: (Internet/text) I just died laughing.

ijit: (Internet/text) Idiot.

ijk: (Internet/text) I'm just kidding.

ijp: (Internet/text) Internet job posting.

ijr: (Internet/text) I just remembered.

ijs: (Internet/text) I'm just saying.

ik: (Internet/text) I know.

iki: (Internet/text) I know it.

ikic: (Internet/text) I know I can.

ikm: (Internet/text) I know, man.

ikt: (Internet/text) I knew that.

ili: (Internet/text) I love it.

Illin': (US) 1) Foolish; bad; uncool. 2) Unhealthy.

ilml: (Internet/text) I love my life.

ilms: (Internet/text) I love myself.

ilu: (Internet/text) I love you.

ilu2: (Internet/text) I love you too.

ilul: (Internet/text) I love you loads.

ilum: (Internet/text) I love you more.

ilusm: (Internet/text) I love you so much.
iluvu: (Internet/text) I love you.
iluvya: (Internet/text) I love you.
ilvu: (Internet/text) I love you.
ily: (Internet/text) I love you.
ily2: (Internet/text) I love you too.
ily4e (also "ily4ev"): (Internet/text) I love you forever.
ilyaas: (Internet/text) I love you as a sister.
ilyal: (Internet/text) I like you a lot.
ilyf: (Internet/text) I'll love you forever.
ilylab: (Internet/text) I love you like a brother.
ilylabf: (Internet/text) I love you like a best friend.
ilylas: (Internet/text) I love you like a sister.
ilylc: (Internet/text) I love you like crazy.
ilym: (Internet/text) I love you more.
ilysm: (Internet/text) I love you so much.
ilyt: (Internet/text) I love you too.
IM: (Internet/text) Instant message.
ima: (Internet/text) I am a.
imao: (Internet/text) In my arrogant opinion.
imb: (Internet/text) I am back.
Imbo: (Australian) An imbecile; a fool.
imh: (Internet/text) I am here.
imhe: (Internet/text) In my humble experience.
imho: (Internet/text) In my humble opinion.
imma: (Internet/text) I'm going to.
imnl: (Internet/text) I'm not laughing.
imo: (Internet/text) In my opinion.
impo: (Internet/text) In my personal opinion.
Import: (Canadian) A foreign member of a sports team.
impov: (Internet/text) In my point of view.
imsb: (Internet/text) I am so bored.
imsry: (Internet/text) I am sorry.
imts: (Internet/text) I meant to say.
imu: (Internet/text) I miss you.

imvho: (Internet/text) In my very humble opinion.

imy: (Internet/text) I miss you.

imy2: (Internet/text) I miss you too.

imya: (Internet/text) I miss you already.

In a deuce: (UK) In a pair.

In a heap: (Irish) To be drunk or intoxicated.

In a hoop: (Irish) To be drunk or intoxicated.

In a jiffy: To do something quickly.

In a pig's arse: (UK) A strong refusal or dismissal.

In a pig's eye: (UK) A strong refusal or dismissal.

In and out: (UK) Sexual intercourse.

In bed with: To be in partnership with someone.

In bits: (Irish) A person or situation that is in a bad or confused state.

In bother: (UK) To be in trouble.

In Carey Street: (UK) To be in financial difficulties; to be bankrupt.

In collar: (UK) To be employed.

In costume: (US) In uniform (especially regarding the police).

In deep shit: To be in serious trouble.

In dock: (UK) To be incapacitated; to be sick.

In Dutch: (UK) To be in trouble.

In hock: (UK) Pawned.

In like Flynn: (UK) To be in an advantageous position.

In line for: To be next; to be very likely to receive something, such as a promotion.

In lumber: (UK) To be in trouble.

In no time flat: Very quickly.

In one piece: Without injury; without damage.

In one's pocket: To have someone's loyalty, often through blackmail or bribery.

In rag order: (Irish) To be drunk or intoxicated.

In ribbons: (Irish) To be drunk or intoxicated.

In schtuk (also "shtook" or "shtuk"): (UK) To be in trouble.

In shit street: (UK) To be in trouble.

In Swell Street: (UK) To be wealthy.

In the alley: (US) To serve something as a side dish.

In the bag: To be sure of achieving a certain outcome.

In the chair: (UK) Someone whose turn it is to pay.

In the closet: To conceal one's sexuality or gender identity.

In the club: (UK) To be pregnant.

In the doghouse: To be in trouble with someone.

In the Flynn: (UK) To be in an advantageous position.

In the frame: (UK) To be identified as a suspect.

In the groove: To be working well at something; to find a good rhythm in doing something.

In the loop: To receive information that others do not.

In the money: (US) To have a lot of money, especially if obtained quickly.

In the raw: (UK) Naked; nude.

In the shit: (UK) To be in trouble.

In the soup: (UK) To be in trouble.

In the trap: (UK) To be ready and waiting to go.

In the works: For a project, plan, or idea to be in active development.

In your eye: (UK) A strong refusal or dismissal.

In: Trendy; fashionable; part of the current fad.

in2: (Internet/text) Into.

In-and-out man: (UK) An opportunistic thief.

inb4: (Internet/text) In before.

inbd: (Internet/text) It's no big deal.

incld: (Internet/text) Include.

incrse: (Internet/text) Increase.

ind2p: (Internet/text) I need to pee.

Index: (US) A person's face.

Indie kid: (US) A young person who loves indie music.

Indie: (Internet/text) Independent.

inef: (Internet/text) It's not even funny.

inet: (Internet/text) Internet.

inh: (Internet/text) I need help.

inhwh: (Internet/text) I need homework help.

init: (Internet/text) Isn't it.

Inked: (UK) To be drunk or intoxicated.

Inky: (UK) To be drunk or intoxicated.

inmp: (Internet/text) It's not my problem.
innit: (Internet/text) Isn't it?
ino: (Internet/text) I know.
In-out: (UK) Sexual intercourse.
Inside job: A crime committed by someone who belongs to that place or business.
Inside: (UK) In prison.
instakill: (Internet/text/gaming) Instant kill.
Intel: (Internet/text) Intelligence.
Intelligence department: (UK) The head.
Intense: (US) Good; favorable.
Interior decorating: (UK) Sexual intercourse.
Interweb: (Internet/text) The internet.
Into: An interest in something (e.g., "What music are you into?").
invu: (Internet/text) I envy you.
ioh: (Internet/text) I'm out of here.
iois: (Internet/text) Indicators of interest.
iokiya: (Internet/text) It's ok if you are.
iomw: (Internet/text) I'm on my way.
ionno: (Internet/text) I don't know.
iono: (Internet/text) I don't know.
iotd: (Internet/text) Image of the day.
iou: (Internet/text) I owe you.
iow: (Internet/text) In other words.
ioyk: (Internet/text) If only you knew.
IP: (Internet/text) Internet protocol.
irc: (Internet/text) Internet relay chat.
irdc: (Internet/text) I really don't care.
irdk: (Internet/text) I really don't know.
irhy: (Internet/text) I really hate you.
Irish screwdriver: (UK) A hammer.
irl: (Internet/text) In real life.
irly: (Internet/text) I really like/love you.
Irons: (UK) Cutlery.
irt: (Internet/text) In reply to.

irtf: (Internet/text) I'll return the favor.

is2g: (Internet/text) I swear to god.

Isaacs: (UK) An overweight person.

Isadora: (UK) A long scarf.

isb: (Internet/text) I'm so bored.

isbya: (Internet/text) I'm sorry but you asked.

isdc: (Internet/text) I so don't care.

isg: (Internet/text) I speak geek.

ishii: (Internet/text) I see how it is.

isj: (Internet/text) Inside joke.

iso: (Internet/text) In search of.

iss: (Internet/text) I'm so sorry.

istg: (Internet/text) I swear to god.

istr: (Internet/text) I seem to remember.

It's your funeral: (US) An expression with which the speaker conveys their indifference regarding an unpleasant outcome that is likely to face the listener.

ita: (Internet/text) I totally agree.

itc: (Internet/text) In that case.

Itchy: (UK) To be eager or restless.

itd: (Internet/text) In the dark.

ite: (Internet/text) All right.

Item: People who are in a romantic relationship with each other.

itk: (Internet/text) In the know.

itn: (Internet/text) I think not.

itt: (Internet/text) In this thread.

itym: (Internet/text) I think you mean.

itys: (Internet/text) I told you so.

itz: (Internet/text) It's.

itzk: (Internet/text) It's ok.

Ivan: (UK) A Russian person.

ive: (Internet/text) I have.

Ivories: (UK) 1) Piano keys. 2) Teeth. 3) Dice.

Ivory snatcher: (UK) A dentist.

Ivory thief: (UK) A dentist.

Ivy: (UK) A foolish woman.
iw2mu: (Internet/text) I want to meet you.
iwaa: (Internet/text) It was an accident.
iwc: (Internet/text) In which case.
iwg: (Internet/text) It was good.
iwjk: (Internet/text) I was just kidding.
iwk: (Internet/text) I wouldn't know.
iwtk: (Internet/text) I want to know.
iyam: (Internet/text) If you ask me.
iyc: (Internet/text) If you can.
iyd: (Internet/text) In your dreams.
iyo: (Internet/text) In your opinion.
iyss: (Internet/text) If you say so.
iywt: (Internet/text) If you want to.
iz: (Internet/text) Is.

j/a: (Internet/text) Just asking.

j/c: (Internet/text) Just curious.

j/j: (Internet/text) Just joking.

j/k: (Internet/text) Just kidding.

j/p: (Internet/text) Just playing.

j/s: (Internet/text) Just saying.

j/t: (Internet/text) Just talking.

j/w: (Internet/text) Just wondering.

j00: (Internet/text) You.

j00r: (Internet/text) Your.

j2bs: (Internet/text) Just to be sure.

j2f: (Internet/text) Just too funny.

j2luk (also "j2lyk"): (Internet/text) Just to let you know.

j4f: (Internet/text) Just for fun.

j4g: (Internet/text) Just for grins.

j4l: (Internet/text) Just for laughs.

j4u: (Internet/text) Just for you.

Jack and Jill: (UK) A male and female police officer who are partners.

Jack of dibs: (UK) A generous man.

Jack of legs: (UK) A tall man.

Jack of no trades: (UK) A useless man; a man who is incapable of anything.

Jack of tall tales: (UK) A liar.

Jack off: (UK) To masturbate.

Jack shit: Nothing.

Jack straw: (UK) A man without substance.

Jack the lad: (UK) A brash, cocky young man.

Jack up: 1) (UK) To organize something, especially at short notice. 2) To raise the price of something, often exorbitantly.

Jack: 1) Nothing. 2) (Australian) Fed up; tired.

Jackanory: (UK) 1) A tall tale; a lie. 2) An informant.

Jacked off: (UK) To be angry or ill-tempered.
Jacked-up: (US) To be agitated or overly excited.
Jacket: (US) A personal file, record, or dossier.
Jack-in-a-box: (UK) An unborn child.
Jacking: (UK) Gossip; idle talk.
Jack-in-the-box: (UK) A venereal disease.
Jacks, the: (Irish) The toilet.
Jag: (UK) 1) Intoxication or inebriation. 2) A bout of unrestrained activity.
Jagged: (UK) Intoxication or inebriation.
Jail bird: A prisoner.
Jailbait: An attractive person who is just below the legal age of consent.
Jake: (Australian/New Zealand) Satisfactory; fine.
Jalopy: (UK) An old, dilapidated car.
Jam rag: (UK) A sanitary towel.
Jam raid: (UK) Menstruation.
Jam sandwich: (UK) A police car.
Jam: 1) Something good or desirable. 2) To perform music; to play music in a group or band.
Jammed: (UK) To be intoxicated.
Jammies: (UK) Pajamas.
Jammy: (UK) 1) Something good or desirable. 2) (Irish) Lucky.
Jam-packed: At capacity; full of people.
Jane Doe: (UK) An unnamed woman.
Jane Q: (UK) An average woman.
Jane: (UK) 1) A girl or woman. 2) A women's restroom. 3) A female prostitute.
Jangle: (UK) Gossip; idle talk; chatter.
Jangled: (UK) Nervous; anxious; on edge.
Jar: (UK) A pint of beer.
Jarmies: (UK) Pajamas.
Jarred up: (UK) To be drunk or intoxicated.
Jarred: (UK) To be drunk or intoxicated.
jas: (Internet/text) Just a second.
Jasper: (UK) A wasp.
Java: (US) Coffee.

Jaw: (UK) Incessant chatter.

Jawdropper: (UK) Something that is shocking.

Jawing: (UK) Rowdy or abusive talk.

Jaywalk: (US) To cross the street illegally.

Jazz house: (UK) A pub that plays loud music.

Jazz up: (UK) To decorate something in a lively way; to make something more visually appealing.

Jazz: 1) To tease or goad. 2) General or unspecified things.

Jazzed: Excited.

Jazzy: (UK) Showy; flashy.

jbu: (Internet/text) Just between us.

j-c: (Internet/text) Just chilling.

jc: (Internet/text) Just curious.

jcath: (Internet/text) Just chilling at the house.

jdi: (Internet/text) Just do it.

jebus: (Internet/text) Jesus.

Jeebies: (US) Unsettling thoughts; nameless horrors.

Jeetled: (Irish) Exhausted; tired.

Jeez: An exclamation of surprise or frustration (short for "Jesus").

Jelly (US): Jealous.

Jelly-belly: (UK) An obese person.

Jellybone: (UK) Telephone.

Jenny: (UK) A generator.

Jerk off: To masturbate (in reference to males).

Jerk someone around: To break an agreement with someone; to change plans with someone on short notice.

Jerk: A horrible person; a bully.

Jerkoff: (US) An unpleasant, arrogant man.

Jerkwater: (US/Canadian) Inferior; unimportant; insignificant.

Jerry Diddle: (UK) Illegal business.

Jerry: (UK) A German person.

Jessie: (Scottish/UK) An effeminate or timid man.

Jesus boots: (UK) Thong-type sandals.

Jesus freak: A born-again Christian; a fervent Christian.

jf: (Internet/text) Just fooling.

jfc: (Internet/text) Jesus fucking Christ.

jff: (Internet/text) Just for fun.

jfg: (Internet/text) Just for giggles.

jfgi: (Internet/text) Just fucking Google it.

jfi: (Internet/text) Just forget it.

jfj: (Internet/text) Jump for joy.

jfl: (Internet/text) Just for laughs.

jfn: (Internet/text) Just for now.

jftr: (Internet/text) Just for the record.

jfu: (Internet/text) Just for you.

jh: (Internet/text) Just hanging.

jho: (Internet/text) Just hanging out.

jic: (Internet/text) Just in case.

Jiffy: (UK) A short time; a moment (e.g., "in a jiffy").

Jig it: (UK) An easy win.

Jig: 1) A lie; a scam. 2) (Australian) To play truant.

Jig-a-jig: (UK) Sexual intercourse.

Jiggered: (UK) 1) Exhausted. 2) Astounded; astonished.

Jill: (UK) A policewoman.

Jillion: A massive number or amount.

Jillock: (UK) A foolish person.

Jim-dandy: (US) First-rate; excellent.

Jimjams: (UK) Pajamas.

Jingle: 1) (UK) Money. 2) (US) A telephone call.

Jingle-jangle: (US) Money.

Jinx: To cause bad luck.

jit: (Internet/text) Just in time.

Jitters: Nervousness; anxiety.

Jittery: (US) To feel anxious or afraid.

Jive: (US) 1) Words; language. 2) Jokes. 3) Deceptive talk.

Jive-ass: (US) Dishonest; deceitful.

jj/k: (Internet/text) Just joking.

jj: (Internet/text) Just joking.

jja: (Internet/text) Just joking around.

jk: (Internet/text) Just kidding.

jka: (Internet/text) Just kidding around.

jking: (Internet/text) Joking.

jklol: (Internet/text) Just kidding, laughing out loud.

jkn: (Internet/text) Joking.

jks (also "jkz"): (Internet/text) Jokes.

jlma: (Internet/text) Just leave me alone.

jlt: (Internet/text) Just like that.

jm: (Internet/text) Just messing.

jma: (Internet/text) Just messing around.

jml: (Internet/text) Just my luck.

jmo: (Internet/text) Just my opinion.

jms: (Internet/text) Just making sure.

Job and finish: (UK) To work until the job is finished.

Job someone: (UK) To beat someone.

Job: A crime, especially an organized one.

Jobbed: (UK) To be convicted of someone else's crime. 2) To be punched. 3) Finished; completed.

Jobbie (also "jobby"): (UK) 1) To defecate. 3) Excrement; feces.

Jobsworth: (UK) Someone who is very pedantic, particularly about work details.

Jock: (US) An athlete or sportsperson.

Joe Bloggs: (UK) An average or unremarkable man.

Joe Blow: (UK) An average or unremarkable man.

Joe Public: (UK) The general public.

Joe Schmo: (US) 1) An average or unremarkable man. 2) A man who is duped by a scam.

Joe Six-Pack: (UK) An average, beer-drinking man.

Joe Soap: (UK) 1) An unintelligent man. 2) A male stooge or scapegoat. 3) (New Zealand) An average or unremarkable man.

Joe: 1) (UK) A man who is duped by a scam. 2) (US/Canadian) An average man. 3) Coffee.

Joes: (Australian) Depression.

Joey the plum: (UK) 1) A fool. 2) Someone who is duped by a scam.

Joey: (UK) 1) A fool. 2) Someone who is duped by a scam. 3) (Australian) An effeminate man. 4) A young kangaroo, wallaby, or possum. 5) A baby.

John Doe: (US) An unnamed man; an anonymous party in a legal action.

John Hancock: (US) One's signature.

John Q Citizen: (US) An average man.

John Roscoe: (US) A pistol; a revolver.

John Thomas: (UK) The penis.

John: (UK) 1) The restroom. 2) A prostitute's client.

Johnny Raw: (UK) A novice or amateur; a new recruit.

Johnny: (UK) A condom.

Johnny-come-lately: (UK) A newcomer or late arrival to a group.

Johnnydom: (UK) A condom.

Johnny-no-stars: (UK) An unintelligent man.

Johnson: The penis.

Joint: 1) A bar or nightclub. 2) A marijuana cigarette.

Jollies: (UK) Pleasure; enjoyment.

Jollop: (UK) A large serving or portion of something.

Jolly along: (UK) To encourage someone.

Jolly-up: (UK) A lively party; a drinking session.

jom: (Internet/text) Just one minuite.

jooc: (Internet/text) Just out of curiosity.

Josh: (UK) To tease someone playfully; good-natured banter.

Josser: 1) (UK) A fool; a simpleton. 2) (Australian) A clergyman.

Journo: (UK) A journalist.

Joystick: (UK) The penis.

Jozzer: (UK) The penis.

jp: (Internet/text) Just playing.

js: (Internet/text) Just saying.

jsuk: (Internet/text) Just so you know.

jsyk: (Internet/text) Just so you know.

jtbs: (Internet/text) Just to be sure.

jtc: (Internet/text) Join the club.

jtluk: (Internet/text) Just to let you know.

jtlyk: (Internet/text) Just to let you know.

jtol: (Internet/text) Just thinking out loud.

jtty: (Internet/text) Just to tell you.

Jubbies: (UK) A woman's breasts.

Judy: (UK) 1) A girl; a woman. 2) A prostitute.

Jug handles: (UK) Large ears.

Jug up: (UK) 1) To imprison someone. 2) To drink, especially alcohol.

Jug: (UK) 1) A prison. 2) To imprison. 3) To drink, especially alcohol. 4) A pint of beer.

Jugged: (UK) 1) Imprisoned. 2) To be drunk or intoxicated.

Juggins: (UK) 1) A foolish person. 2) A dupe; someone who has been swindled.

Jughead: (UK) An idiot; a fool.

Jugs: (Australian/UK) A woman's breasts.

Juice joint: (US) A bar.

Juice up: (US) To make something more lively; to decorate something in a more appealing way.

Juice: 1) Electrical or battery power. 2) Gossip; interesting news.

Juiced up: (US) To be drunk or intoxicated.

Juiced: (US) To be drunk or intoxicated.

Juicer: (US) An alcoholic.

Juicy: (UK) An attractive woman.

Jumbly: (UK) A jumble sale.

Jumbo: (UK) A large, slow-witted person.

Jump bail: To flee from sentencing while out on bail.

Jump on: To attempt to have the initiative in a situation.

Jump salty: (US) To become angry; to lose one's temper quickly.

Jump someone's bones: (US) To have sexual intercourse.

Jump the gun: To act too quickly.

Jump: (US) To mug or attack someone.

Jumper: Someone who is threatening to commit suicide by jumping from a height.

Jumping the couch: (Internet/text) To be behaving strangely.

Jump-up: (UK) Theft from the back of a truck.

Jungly: (UK) Messy; jumbled; lacking a sense of order.

Junk food: Food with little to no nutritional value.

Junk mail: Unsolicited advertising that arrives by mail.

Junker: (US) A run-down car.

Junkie (also "junky"): A drug addict.

Juvie: 1) A juvenile delinquent. 2) Juvenile detention.
jw: (Internet/text) Just wondering.
jw2k: (Internet/text) Just wanted to know.
jwas: (Internet/text) Just wait a second.
jwing: (Internet/text) Just wondering.

— K —

K.O.: (Internet/text) Knock out.

k: (Internet/text) Okay.

K: One thousand (e.g., 1K is the same as 1 000).

k3wl: (Internet/text) Cool.

ka: (Internet/text) Kickass.

Ka-ching: A sound effect used to convey something that is financially profitable.

kah: (Internet/text) Kisses and hugs.

Kangaroo court: (US) An unofficial court formed by a group of people in order to pass judgment on someone.

Kangaroo it: (Australian) To squat.

Kangaroos in the top paddock: (Australian) To be crazy or eccentric.

Kaplonker: (UK) A crowbar.

Kaput: (UK) Broken or beyond further use.

kay: (Internet/text) Okay.

Kazoo: (US) The buttocks.

Keel over: 1) To collapse from sickness. 2) To die abruptly of natural causes.

Keen as mustard: (UK) To be very enthusiastic.

Keen: (US/Canadian) Very good.

Keeno: (UK) An enthusiast.

Keep a stiff upper lip: To remain brave and steadfast.

Keep a straight face: To stop oneself from laughing or showing one's emotions.

Keep an eye on: To observe or pay attention to someone or something over time.

Keep cave: To keep watch; to remain vigilant.

Keep cool: To stay calm and composed.

Keep dog-eye: (UK) To keep watch; to remain vigilant.

Keep on keeping on: (US) To persevere.

Keep on trucking: (US) To persevere; to carry on.

Keep one's ear to the ground: To stay well-informed about the latest information.

Keep one's end up: (UK) To do or pay one's share; to handle one's own responsibilities.

Keep one's hair on: (UK) To stay calm and composed; to stay in control.

Keep shtoom: (UK) To keep one's secrets; to stay quiet, especially when pressed for information.

Keep tabs on: To stay informed about something or someone.

Keep up with the Joneses: (US) To make an effort to match one's peers, especially in regards to financial appearances.

Kegged: (US) To be drunk or intoxicated.

Kegger: (US) A party with a keg of beer.

kek: (Internet/text) Laughter.

Kelt: (UK) Money.

Ken: 1) (Scottish) To know. 2) (US) A man who is dull and conventional.

Kennel: (US) A small, low-quality house or home.

Kevin: (UK) An unsophisticated, uncouth young man.

Kevinish: (UK) Unsophisticated; uncouth.

kewl: (Internet/text) Cool.

Kewpie doll: (UK) An excessively made-up girl or woman.

Key: Vital; essential.

Keyed up: Agitated; tense; on edge.

Keyholing: (UK) To busk outside of a building's main entrance.

KIA: (Internet/text) Killed in action.

kib: (Internet/text) Okay, I'm back.

kic: (Internet/text) Keep it clean.

Kick around: To discuss an idea.

Kick back: (US) 1) To relax. 2) A bribe.

Kick in the bollocks: (UK) To receive a shock.

Kick in: 1) (US) To make a contribution, especially financial. 2) (UK) To begin something.

Kick it: 1) To die. 2) (US) To relax with a friend.

Kick off: (US) 1) For trouble to break out. 2) To leave.

Kick on: (Australian) To persevere.

Kick out the jams: (US) To act without inhibitions.

Kick the bucket: To die.

Kick the habit: To break an addiction.

Kick: To break a habit or addiction.

Kicked to the curb: (US) To be rejected or dismissed.

Kicker: 1) (US/Canadian) A disadvantageous factor, especially hidden in a contract. 2) (US) A decisive factor. 3) Loan fees.

Kickers: (UK) Shoes; footwear.

Kickin': (US) 1) Alive. 2) Full of life.

Kicking: 1) (UK) A physical attack; a beating. 2) (US) Great; excellent.

Kicks: Enjoyment; amusement; fun.

Kiddo: A term of endearment for a young person.

Kidlet: (UK) A small child.

kig: (Internet/text) Keep it going.

Kill it: (US) To do something very well.

Kill that noise: (US) Shut up; be quiet.

Killer: (UK) 1) Very difficult. 2) Awesome; cool; impressive.

Kilt: (UK) A girl or woman.

kinda: (Internet/text) Kind of.

Kindy: (Australian) Kindergarten.

King hit: (Australian) An attack from behind; A knockout blow.

Kink: A mistake; a minor flaw.

Kinky boots: (UK) Knee-high leather boots.

Kip down: (UK) To go to sleep; to take a nap.

Kip: (UK) 1) To go to sleep; to take a nap.

Kipper season: (UK) A slow period of trade.

Kippered: (UK) Devastated; exhausted.

kir: (Internet/text) Kid in room.

kis: (Internet/text) Keep it simple.

kisa: (Internet/text) Knight in shining armor.

Kiss ass: (US) To act obsequiously.

Kiss of death: An act that condemns someone or something to certain death or failure.

Kiss off: (US/Canadian) To ignore or dismiss someone or something.

Kiss up: (US) To act obsequiously.

Kiss-ass: (US) An obsequious person.

Kisser: A person's mouth.

Kissing tackle: (UK) A person's mouth or lips.

Kit and caboodle: (UK) Everything as a whole; the entire amount.

kit: (Internet/text) Keep in touch.

Kit: (UK) Clothes.

Kite flyer: (UK) A person who issues dud cheques.

Kiting: (UK) Issuing dud cheques.

kiu: (Internet/text) Keep it up.

kiwf: (Internet/text) Kill it with fire.

Kiwi: A New Zealander.

KKK: Ku Klux Klan.

kl: (Internet/text) Cool.

Kleenex: (UK) A foolish person.

Klepto: A kleptomaniac.

Klink: (UK) Prison; jail.

Kludge: (UK) Something that is overcomplicated or cumbersome.

Klutz: (US/Canadian) A clumsy or blundering person.

Klutzy: (US/Canadian) To be clumsy or blundering.

kma: (Internet/text) Kiss my ass.

kmb: (Internet/text) Kiss my butt.

kmsl: (Internet/text) Killing myself laughing.

kmu: (Internet/text) Kinda miss you.

Knacker: 1) (UK) To exhaust or tire out. 2) (Irish) A contemptible person.

Knackered: (Irish/UK) 1) Exhausted; worn-out; weary. 2) Broken; beyond use.

Knee bender: (UK) A religious person.

Knee-jerk: A reflex or instinctual reaction.

Kneel before the porcelain throne: (US) To vomit in a toilet.

Knees up: (UK) A party or celebration, especially with dancing.

Knicker bandit ("panty thief" in US English): (UK) Someone who steals women's underclothes.

Knickers: (UK) Panties.

Knicker-wrecker: (UK) A man who seduces a lot of women; a man who is popular with women.

kno: (Internet/text) Know.

Knob-head: (UK) An idiot; a jerk.

Knob-twister: (Australian) A bookmaker.

Knock back: To finish a drink quickly.

Knock down: (Australian) To drink.

Knock into a cocked hat: (UK) To defeat or outperform.

Knock it off: A command for someone to stop doing something.

Knock it on the head: (UK) To stop doing something; to give up an activity.

Knock off: To kill somebody. 2) To leave work early. 3) A counterfeit object. 4) To stop doing something.

Knock out: (UK) To distribute or sell something.

Knock over: (UK) To rob; to burglarize.

Knock someone's block off: (UK) To punch or hit someone in the head.

Knock the tar out of: (US) To beat someone up.

Knock them bandy: (UK) To garner a positive response; to impress somebody.

Knock them cold: (US) To garner a positive response; to impress somebody.

Knock them dead: To garner a positive response; to impress somebody.

Knock them stiff: To garner a positive response; to impress somebody.

Knock up: To impregnate someone.

Knock: 1) To criticize; to insult or make fun of. 2) (UK) A sure thing; a certainty. 3) To impress.

Knock-about: (Australian) A vagrant.

Knock-around: (Australian) A vagrant.

Knockback: (UK) A rejection or dismissal.

Knocked out: (UK) To be very impressed.

Knocked up: 1) To be pregnant. 2) (Australian) Exhausted; weary.

Knocker: (UK) 1) A debtor. 2) A door-to-door salesperson.

Knockers: (UK) A woman's breasts.

Knockie: (UK) Sexual intercourse.

Knockie-knockie: (UK) Sexual intercourse.

Knocking on: (UK) To be growing old; to be getting on in years.

Knocking shop: (UK) A brothel.

Knockout: 1) Someone or something that is very impressive. 2) A great success. 3) A beautiful woman.

Knotted: (UK) A tied score.

Know one's onions: (UK) To be knowledgeable; to be proficient at one's task.

Know-it-all: Someone who acts like they know all the answers.

Knuckle sandwich: A punch, especially in to the mouth or face.

Knuckle: (UK) A fistfight.

Knucklehead: An idiot; a fool.

kol: (Internet/text) Kiss on lips.

Kook: An eccentric or strange person; someone who seems crazy.

Kooky: Eccentric; crazy; strange.

kool: (Internet/text) Cool.

kos: (Internet/text) Kid over shoulder.

Kosher: Legitimate; genuine.

kotc: (Internet/text) Kiss on the cheek.

Kotchel: (UK) A large quantity.

kotd: (Internet/text) Kicks of the day.

kotl: (Internet/text) Kiss on the lips.

kq: (Internet/text) Keep quiet.

kss: (Internet/text) Kiss.

kssd: (Internet/text) Kissed.

ksw: (Internet/text) Okay, so what?

kt: (Internet/text) Keep talking.

kthx: (Internet/text) Okay, thank you.

kuhl: (Internet/text) Cool.

kutgw: (Internet/text) Keep up the good work.

Kutu: (New Zealand) Body louse.

kuwl: (Internet/text) Cool.

Kvetch: To complain; to whine.

kwim: (Internet/text) Know what I mean?

kwis: (Internet/text) Know what I'm saying?

kwl: (Internet/text) Cool.

kyfc: (Internet/text) Keep your fingers crossed.

kyko: (Internet/text) Keep your knickers on.

l@u: (Internet/text) Laughing at you.

l2: (Internet/text) Learn to.

l2m: (Internet/text) Listening to music.

l2ms: (Internet/text) Laughing to myself.

l2p: (Internet/text) Learn to play.

l2r: (Internet/text) Learn to read.

l337: (Internet/text) Elite.

l33t: (Internet/text) Elite.

l8: (Internet/text) Late.

l8er (also "l8r"): (Internet/text) Later; see you soon.

La la land: Daydreaming; to be untethered from reality.

Lace into: (UK) 1) To attack someone. To criticize someone.

Lace: Adding an extra ingredient to a drink or narcotic.

Laced up: (UK) 1) Completed; finished. 2) Accomplished. 3) Inhibited; repressed.

Laddette: (UK) An uncouth young woman.

Laddish: (UK) Behaving like an uncouth young man.

laff: (Internet/text) Laugh.

lafs: (Internet/text) Love at first sight.

Lager lout: (UK) An uncouth male who drinks a lot.

Lagered up: (UK) To be drunk or intoxicated.

Lagged: (UK) To be drunk or intoxicated.

Lagging: (UK) A period in jail.

Laid back: Relaxed; unconcerned; easy-going.

Laid out: (US) To be drunk or intoxicated.

Lair: (Australian) A man who shows off, especially in a flashy way.

Lairy: 1) (UK) Rowdy; boisterous. 2) (Australian) Flashy; ostentatious.

lak: (Internet/text) Love and kisses.

lal: (Internet/text) Laughing a little.

Lala: (Australian) A toilet.

lalol: (Internet/text) Lots and lots of laughs.

lam: (Internet/text) Leave a message.

Lamb down: (Australian/New Zealand) To waste all one's money on alcohol.

Lame: (US) Uncool; boring; unfashionable.

Lame-ass: (US) An uncool or boring person.

Lamebrain: (UK) A foolish person.

Lamp along: (Irish) To move at a great pace.

LAN party: (Gaming) A gathering of people with computers to play video games together.

Lance: (UK) The penis.

Lancejack: (UK) A lance corporal.

Land one: To connect a strike; for one's aim to hit true.

Lard: (UK) An overweight person.

Lard-arse: (UK) An overweight person.

Lard-head: (UK) A foolish person.

Lardo: (UK) An overweight person.

Lardy: (UK) An overweight person.

Large: (UK) 1) Great; excellent. 2) One thousand.

LARP: (Internet/text) Live action role play.

Larrikin: (Australian/New Zealand) A hooligan.

Lash: (Australian) 1) Wild behavior. 2) An attempt at something.

Lashed: (UK) To be drunk or intoxicated.

Last shake of the bag: (UK) The youngest child in a family.

later: (US) Goodbye; see you soon.

lates: (Internet/text) Later; see you soon.

latn: (Internet/text) Laugh at the newbs.

latr: (Internet/text) Later; see you soon.

lau: (Internet/text) Laughing at you.

Laugh at the carpet: (US) To vomit.

Laugh at the lawn: (US) To vomit.

Laugh at your shoes: (US) To vomit.

Laughing boy: (UK) 1) A sullen person. 2) A person who is overly cheerful or optimistic.

Laughing gas: Nitrous oxide.

Laughing gear: (UK) A person's mouth.

Laughing juice: (UK) An alcoholic drink.

Laughing soup: (UK) An alcoholic drink.

Laughing water: (UK) An alcoholic drink.

Lav: (UK) A restroom (short for "lavatory").

lawd: (Internet/text) Lord.

lawl: (Internet/text) Laughing out loud.

Lawn: (UK) The hair on one's head.

Lay across the drink: (US) The continent of Europe, especially from America's perspective.

Lay an egg: (US/Canadian) A joke or performance that falls flat.

Lay by: (Australian) To reserve an item, especially by paying a deposit for it.

Lay down: To surrender; to give up.

Lay one on someone: (UK) To hit; to punch.

Lay out: To knock out one's opponent in a fight.

Lay rubber (also "burn rubber"): (US) To speed; to drive very fast.

Lay some pipe: (Australian) To have sexual intercourse.

Lay: 1) To have sexual intercourse. 2) A sexual partner.

Lazzy: (UK) An elastic.

lbh: (Internet/text) Let's be honest.

lbnr: (Internet/text) Laughing but not really.

lbo: (Internet/text) Laughing butt off.

lbvs: (Internet/text) Laughing but very serious.

ldr: (Internet/text) Long-distance relationship.

Lead in one's pencil: (UK) An expression that describes male virility.

Lead poisoning: (US) To be shot with bullets.

Leak air: (US) Idle chatter; to talk nonsense.

Leak: (UK) Urination; to urinate.

Lean and mean: (US) A small but threatening person.

Leather merchant: (UK) A pickpocket.

Leather: (UK) A wallet; a purse.

Leathering: (UK) A thorough beating.

Leave lunch: (US) To vomit.

Lech: A lecherous person.

Lechy: (UK) Lecherous.

lee7: (Internet/text) Elite.

Leech off: To profit or live off another person.

Leery: (UK) 1) Wary; cautious. 2) Untrustworthy, deceitful.

LEET (also "L33T" or "1337"): (Internet/text) Elite.

Left field: (US) Unexpected; out of nowhere.

Left footer: (UK) A catholic.

Leg bail: (UK) To escape from custody.

Leg it: To run; to sprint.

Leg-biter: A small child.

Legholders: (UK) Trousers; pants.

Legit: Legitimate.

Legless: (UK) To be very drunk.

Leg-man: A man who favors a woman's legs as her best physical feature.

Leg-opener: (UK) A strong alcoholic drink.

Leg-over: (UK) To have sexual intercourse.

Lekker: (South African) Enjoyable; good; fun.

lemme: (Internet/text) Let me.

Lemon: 1) A foolish person. 2) A bad product or result. 3) A sex scene, especially in fan fiction.

Lemons: (UK) Female breasts.

Lemony: (Australian) Irritable; angry; ill-tempered.

Lend a hand: To lend assistance.

Length: (UK) A prison sentence of six months.

LEO: (Internet/text) Law enforcement officer.

Lergi: (UK) An unspecified illness or disease.

Lesbo: (UK/US/Derogatory) Lesbian.

Let it all hang out: To act without restraint or inhibition.

Let it slide: (US) To be lenient; to be relaxed about something; to not enforce a punishment.

Let off: (UK) To fart.

Let rip: 1) To fart. 2) To unleash an outburst of abuse.

Letch: (UK) A lecherous person.

Lettuce: (UK) Money.

Lez: (UK/US/Derogatory) Lesbian.

lezbean: (Internet/text) Lesbian.

Lezbo: (Internet/text/Derogatory) Lesbian.

Lezzie: (UK/Derogatory) Lesbian.

lf: (Internet/text) Looking for.

lfnar: (Internet/text) Laughing for no apparent reason.

lfr: (Internet/text) Laughing for real.

LGBTQ: Lesbian, Gay, Bisexual, Transgender, Queer.

lgn: (Internet/text) Link goes nowhere.

lgo: (Internet/text) Life goes on.

lgot: (Internet/text) Let's go out tonight.

lia: (Internet/text) Life is awesome.

Libber: (UK) A feminist.

lic: (Internet/text) Like I care.

Lick: A short piece of music played on an electric guitar.

Lickety-split: (US) Very fast; in a hurry.

Lie down: (UK) 1) To surrender; to give up. 2) To abase oneself.

Lie low: To stay concealed or inactive, especially to avoid being found.

liec: (Internet/text) Like I even care.

liek: (Internet/text) Like.

Life and soul: A fun and lively person.

Life-preserver: (US) A ring doughnut.

Lifer: A prisoner serving life imprisonment.

Liffey water: (UK/Irish) Guinness beer.

lifo: (Internet/text) Last in, first out.

Lift: (UK) To steal; petty theft.

ligad: (Internet/text) Like I give a damn.

Light a shuck: (UK) To leave in a hurry.

Light fingers: A thief; a pickpocket; a shoplifter.

Lighten up: Relax; cheer up; take things less seriously.

Lighthouse: (UK) A drunk person's red nose.

Lights: (UK) Matches.

Like a butcher's daughter: (UK) To be sexually active.

Like cheese: (US) A strong odor.

Likely load: (UK) A cheeky or precocious youth.

lil: (Internet/text) Little.

Lily: (UK) An effeminate man.
lim: (Internet/text) Like it matters.
Limey: (US/Canadian) A British person.
limh: (Internet/text) Laughing in my head.
Limo: A limousine.
Limp-wristed: (UK) An effeminate or feeble man.
Line: A portion of cocaine to be ingested.
Lingo: Dialect; language; words.
Lint-brain: (US) A foolish person; an idiot.
Lint-head: (US) A foolish person; an idiot.
Lionel: (UK) The penis.
Lip: Backchat; impertinence.
Lippy: 1) (UK) Cheeky; impertinent. 2) (Australian) Lipstick.
Lipstick lesbian: A feminine lesbian.
Liquid laugh: (Australian) To vomit.
Liquid lunch: (UK) Drinking alcohol for lunch.
Liquor up: (US/Canadian) 1) To become drunk. 2) To cause someone to become drunk.
lirl: (Internet/text) Laughing in real life.
Listeners: (UK) The ears.
Listing to starboard: (UK) To be drunk or intoxicated.
Lit up: (UK) To be drunk or intoxicated.
Litter lout: (UK) A litterer; someone who leaves refuse in public places.
Litterbug: (US/Canadian) A litterer; someone who leaves refuse in public places.
Little bit: (UK) A niece.
Little black book: A book full of women's phone numbers; a record of one's romantic or sexual encounters.
Little boys' room: (UK) A bathroom for men.
Little girls' room: (UK) A bathroom for women.
Littleworth: (UK) Someone who is unimportant or insignificant.
liu: (Internet/text) Look it up.
Live-in lover: (UK) An unmarried cohabitee who is also a sexual partner.
Livener: (UK) An alcoholic drink.
Liverbird: (UK) A young woman from Liverpool.

Liverpool's at home: (UK) The menstrual cycle.

liyf: (Internet/text) Laughing in your face.

llc: (Internet/text) Laughing like crazy.

llh: (Internet/text) Laughing like hell.

llol: (Internet/text) Literally laughing out loud.

lma: (Internet/text) Leave me alone.

lmao: (Internet/text) Laughing my ass off.

lmap: (Internet/text) Leave me alone please.

lmbo: (Internet/text) Laughing my butt off.

lmg: (Internet/text) Let me guess.

lmk: (Internet/text) Let me know.

lml: (Internet/text) Love my life.

lmso: (Internet/text) Laughing my socks off.

lmtd: (Internet/text) Limited.

ln: (Internet/text) Last name; surname.

lnk: (Internet/text) Link.

Load up: (US) To take prohibited drugs.

Loaded: 2) To be drunk or intoxicated. 2) Wealthy.

Loads: (UK) A lot; a large amount.

Loaf: (UK) 1) A lazy person. 2) An elderly person.

Lob the gob: (Irish) To kiss.

Lob: (UK) To throw something away; to dispose of something.

Lobe: (UK) A boring, conformist person.

Lobster: (UK) Someone who is sunburnt.

Lock: (US) A certainty; a sure thing.

Lockjawed: (UK) To be drunk or intoxicated.

Loco: (US) Crazy; insane.

Locust: (UK) A person who will eat anything.

Lodger: (UK) A flea; a head louse.

lofl: (Internet/text) Laughing out fucking loud.

loflmao: (Internet/text) Laying on floor laughing my ass off.

Loft: (UK) A person's head.

Loghead: (UK) A fool; an idiot.

Log-rolling: (UK) A dubious or unofficial partnership for mutual benefit.

loi: (Internet/text) Laughing on the inside.

lol: (Internet/text) Laughing out loud.

lol@u: (Internet/text) Laughing out loud at you.

lol'd: (Internet/text) Laughed out loud.

lolaw: (Internet/text) Laughing out loud at work.

lolbs: (Internet/text) Laughing out loud but seriously.

lolci: (Internet/text) Laughing out loud, crying inside.

lolf: (Internet/text) Lots of love forever.

Lollies: (Australian) Lollipops.

Lolly: (Australian/New Zealand/UK) Money. 2) (UK) To inform on someone.

lolol: (Internet/text) Laughing out loud.

lolrotf: (Internet/text) Laughing out loud rolling on the floor.

lols: (Internet/text) Laughing out loud.

Loly water: (Australian) A soft drink.

lolz: (Internet/text) Laughing out loud.

Lombard: (UK) A rich but unpleasant person.

lomg: (Internet/text) Like, oh my god.

loml: (Internet/text) Love of my life.

London to a brick: (Australian) An expression that conveys the speaker's belief that something has a high probability of happening or being true.

Long drink of water: (UK) A tall, bland person.

Long firm: (UK) A fraud; a business that makes purchases on credit and then sells the products quickly before disappearing without settling the debt.

Long green: (US) Money.

Long haul: (US) A long period of time.

Long John: (UK) Silver coins.

Long pockets: (UK) A miser; someone who is stingy with money.

Long streak of misery: (UK) Someone who is tall, thin and morose.

Long Tom: (UK) A cannon.

Longbeard: (UK) An old person.

Loo: (UK) Lavatory.

Look sick: (UK) To be outclassed.

Looker: An attractive person or thing.

Looksy: (UK) To take a quick look; a gander.

loomm: (Internet/text) Laughing out of my mind.

Loon about: (UK) To act in an unrestrained or uninhibited way.

Loon out: (UK) To act in an unrestrained or uninhibited way.

Loon: (UK) A crazy or eccentric person.

Loony bin: (UK) A mental hospital.

Loony tunes: (UK) A crazy or eccentric person.

Loony: (UK) A crazy or eccentric person.

Looped: (US) To be intoxicated.

Loop-legged: (UK) To be drunk or intoxicated.

Loopy: (UK) Crazy; deranged; eccentric.

Loose cannon: (US) An uncontrolled person; someone who is unpredictable, often in dangerous or harmful ways.

Loose jaw: (UK) A gossip.

Loose screw: (UK) A crazy person.

Loose: (UK) 1) Relaxed; casual. 2) Promiscuous.

Loot: Money.

Lootworthy: (UK) A profitable investment.

Lord Muck: (UK) A snob; a haughty man.

Lord of the pies: (UK) An overweight person.

Lose it: To lose control; to snap and become enraged.

Lose one's bottle: (UK) To lose one's nerve.

Lose one's cookies: (US) To vomit.

Lose one's cool: (UK) To get angry; to lose one's composure.

Lose one's marbles: (US) To go crazy; to lose one's mind.

Lose one's rag: (UK) To lose one's temper; to lose one's composure.

Lose your lunch: (US) To vomit.

Loser: 1) An unfortunate or unsuccessful person. 2) An unfashionable or uncool person.

Lotion: (UK) An alcoholic drink.

loto: (Internet/text) Laughing on the outside.

Lotsa: (Internet/text) Lots of.

Lotta: (Internet/text) A lot of.

Loud: Gaudy; ostentatious.

Lounge lizard: (UK) A person who spends a lot of time at fashionable bars and lounges.

Louse house: (UK) A cheap hotel; shoddy lodgings.
Louse: (UK) A horrible person.
Lousy: (UK) An excessive amount of something. 2) Awful; unpleasant.
Louthouse: (UK) A pub that caters to a rough crowd.
Love bubbles: (UK) A woman's breasts.
Love bumps: (UK) A woman's breasts.
Love handles: (UK) The folds of flesh around a person's waist.
Love lumps: (UK) A woman's breasts.
Love: (UK) A term of endearment.
Loved up: (UK) To be in love; to be infatuated with someone or something.
Love-in-a-punt: (UK) Weak or watered-down beer.
Low light job: (UK) To need the toilet.
Low profile: To keep one's activities discreet, especially to avoid detection.
Low rent: (US) Cheap; inferior.
Low: (US) Underhanded behavior.
Low-ball: (US) To offer a low amount of money for a deal.
Low-down: (US) 1) Information. 2) The truth; relevant facts. 3) Mean and unfair.
Low-heel: (Australian) A prostitute.
Lowie: (Australian) A prostitute.
Lowlife: A disreputable person; a criminal.
Low-wheel: (Australian) A prostitute.
lozer: (Internet/text) Loser.
lpms: (Internet/text) Life pretty much sucks.
lq: (Internet/text) Laughing quietly.
lq2m: (Internet/text) Laughing quietly to myself.
lrh: (Internet/text) Laughing really hard.
lrt: (Internet/text) Last retweet.
lsfw: (Internet/text) Less safe for work.
lshic: (Internet/text) Laughing so hard I'm crying.
lsr: (Internet/text) Loser.
lt: (Internet/text) Long time.
ltl: (Internet/text) Let's talk later.
ltm: (Internet/text) Listen to me.
ltms: (Internet/text) Laughing to myself.

ltnc: (Internet/text) Long time no see.

ltns: (Internet/text) Long time no see.

ltr: (Internet/text) Later; see you later.

lu2: (Internet/text) Love you too.

lu4l: (Internet/text) Love you for life.

Lube: Lubrication.

Lubricate: (UK) To drink, especially alcohol.

Lubricated: (UK) To be drunk or intoxicated.

Luck out: (UK) To have good luck; to be lucky.

Lucky legs: (UK) Thin or skinny legs.

Lucy Lastic: (UK) A promiscuous woman (a play off "loose elastic").

Lug: (UK) A large, dim-witted man.

Luggage: (UK) Male genitals.

Lug-hole: (UK) The ear.

lul: (Internet/text) Love you lots.

lulab: (Internet/text) Love you like a brother.

lulas: (Internet/text) Love you like a sister.

lulz: (Internet/text) Laughing out loud.

Lumber: (UK) A fight; an altercation; a struggle.

Lumbered: (UK) To be burdened with something.

Lummock (also "lummox"): (UK) A large, dim-witted person.

Lump it: (UK) To suffer or endure something patiently.

Lump: (UK) An overweight person.

Lumps: (UK) A woman's breasts.

Lunatic soup: (UK) An alcoholic drink.

Lunchbox: (UK) The stomach; the belly.

Lunk: (UK) A large, dim-witted person.

Lunkhead: (UK) A large, dim-witted person.

Lurghi: (South African/UK) An unspecified illness or sickness.

Lurk: (Australian/New Zealand) A scheme or plan for success.

Lurker: (Internet/text) Someone who frequents a forum or thread but doesn't post comments or interact with anyone.

Lush roller: (UK) Someone who mugs drunk people.

Lush: (UK) 1) A heavy drinker. 2) Very attractive.

Lushed: (UK) To be drunk or intoxicated.

Lusher: (UK) A prostitute who targets drunk people.
lusm: (Internet/text) Love you so much.
Lusty: (UK) Sexually excited.
luv: (Internet/text) Love.
luver: (Internet/text) Lover.
luvuvm: (Internet/text) Love you very much.
lvl: (Gaming) Level.
lvr: (Internet/text) Lover.
lvya: (Internet/text) Love you.
ly: (Internet/text) Love you.
ly2: (Internet/text) Love you too.
lyaab: (Internet/text) Love you as a brother.
lyaaf: (Internet/text) Love you as a friend.
lyaas: (Internet/text) Love you as a sister.
lyao: (Internet/text) Laugh your ass off.
lybo: (Internet/text) Laugh your butt off.
lyl: (Internet/text) Love you lots.
lylab: (Internet/text) Love you like a brother.
lylal: (Internet/text) Love you lots and lots.
lylas: (Internet/text) Love you like a sister.
lylno: (Internet/text) Love you like no other.
lyls: (Internet/text) Love you lots.
lysm: (Internet/text) Love you so much.
lyt: (Internet/text) Love you too.
lyvm: (Internet/text) Love you very much.
lzr: (Internet/text) Loser.

m$: (Internet/text) Microsoft.

m&d: (Internet/text) Mom and dad.

m/b: (Internet/text) Maybe.

m/f: (Internet/text) Male or female.

m2: (Internet/text) Me too.

m2f: (Internet/text) Male-to-female (gender transition).

m3: (Internet/text) Me.

m473s (also "m473z"): (Internet/text) Mates; friends.

m8: (Internet/text) Mate; friend.

m84l: (Internet/text) Mate for life.

m8s: (Internet/text) Mates; friends.

m8t: (Internet/text) Mate; friend.

m9: (Internet/text) Mine.

Maccas: (Australian) McDonald's.

Macho: Manly; masculine in an overly assertive way.

Macintosh: (UK) Raincoat.

mah: (Internet/text) My.

mai: (Internet/text) My.

Make a killing: (US) To make a lot of money.

Make a pass at: (US) To flirt with someone.

Make it: (US) To be successful; to find success.

Make like shepherds: (UK) To leave.

Make out: 1) A kissing session. 2) Profit; outcome.

Manky: (Irish/UK) Dirty; soiled; grubby.

Marbles: (UK) One's wits or mental faculties.

Mare: (New Zealand) To be having a hard time.

Mark: The victim being targeted for a scam.

Mate: (Australian/UK) Friend.

Max out: (US) To reach a credit card's limit.

mb: (Internet/text) My bad.

mbf: (Internet/text) My best friend.

mbl8r: (Internet/text) Maybe later.

MC: (Internet/text) Master of ceremonies.

mcs: (Internet/text) My computer sucks.

me2: (Internet/text) Me too.

Mean: (US) Very good; awesome.

Meanie: (US) A mean person.

Meat and potatoes: (US) Basic needs; the bare essentials; the minimum requirements.

Meatspace: (Internet/text) The real world.

meh: (Internet/text) Unimpressive; uninspiring.

Mellow out: (US) Calm down; relax.

Melter: (Irish) Someone who is irritating or vexing.

Mental: (UK) 1) Crazy; insane. 2) Foolish.

Mess around: (US) To kiss or have sexual intercourse.

mgmt: (Internet/text) Management.

mhh: (Internet/text) My head hurts.

mhm: (Internet/text) Yes; sure.

mho: (Internet/text) My humble opinion.

MIA: (Internet/text) Missing in action.

mic: (Internet/text) Microphone.

Micro$oft: (Internet/text) Microsoft.

Miffed: (UK) Upset; peeved; moderately angry.

miid: (Internet/text) My internet is down.

Mileage: (US) The benefits or advantages that one is able to gain from something before it loses its usefulness.

milf: (Internet/text) Mom I'd like to fuck.

Milk run: (US) A flight or mission that is considered safe or routine.

Milk: To take full advantage of something; to profit from something for all the value it's possibly worth.

Million bucks: (US) To feel or look good.

min: (Internet/text) Minute.

Minge: (UK) Vagina.

Minger: (UK) 1) A person who smells bad. 2) An ugly person.

Mint: (UK) Good; excellent.

Minted: (UK) Wealthy; rich.

Minus craic: (Irish) A person or situation that is no fun at all.

miq: (Internet/text) Make it quick.

mir: (Internet/text) Mom in room.

misc: (Internet/text) Miscellaneous.

Miss the boat: To lose out on an opportunity.

Missus: (UK) Wife.

Mits: (UK) Hands.

miw: (Internet/text) Mom is watching.

Mix-up: (US) A mistake; an error.

mkay (also "m'kay"): (Internet/text) Okay.

mlc: (Internet/text) Midlife crisis.

mlia: (Internet/text) My life is amazing.

mmas: (Internet/text) Meet me after school.

mmk: (Internet/text) Um, okay.

mml: (Internet/text) Making me laugh.

mml8r: (Internet/text) Meet me later.

MMO: (Internet/text/gaming) Massively multiplayer online.

MMORPG: (Internet/text/gaming) Massively multiplayer online role-playing game.

mngr: (Internet/text) Manager.

mobo: (Internet/text) Motherboard.

Mod: (Internet/text) Moderator.

mof: (Internet/text) Matter of fact.

mofo: (Internet/text) Motherfucker.

Moggy: (UK) A cat.

Mojo: (US) Strength; power; influence; ability.

mol: (Internet/text) More or less.

Mole grip: (UK) Vice.

Mom and pop: (US) A small store, usually owned and run by a family.

mompl: (Internet/text) Moment, please.

Mong: (UK) An idiot; a fool.

Monged (out): (UK) To be drunk or intoxicated.

Monkey around: To fool around; to fiddle with something out of curiosity.

Mooch: 1) (UK) To loiter or wander about. 2) (US) To benefit off others; to take advantage of other people's generosity.

Moocher: (UK) Someone doesn't provide for themselves but rather takes advantage of other people's generosity.

Moolah: (US) Money.

Moon: (UK) To expose one's backside.

Moony: (UK) Crazy; eccentric; foolish.

Moose: (UK) An unattractive woman.

morf: (Internet/text) Male or female.

mos: (Internet/text) Mom over shoulder.

Mosey: (UK) Walk; amble.

Mosie: (UK/South African) Mosquito.

moss: (Internet/text) Member of the same sex.

motos: (Internet/text) Member of the opposite sex.

Mouth off: (US) To be cheeky; to speak disrespectfully.

Move: To sell; to be purchased.

Mozzie: (Australian/South African) A mosquito.

mpaw: (Internet/text) My parents are watching.

mph: (Internet/text) Miles per hour.

mpty: (Internet/text) More power to you.

msg: (Internet/text) Message.

msm: (Internet/text) Mainstream media.

msmd: (Internet/text) Monkey see, monkey do.

msngr: (Internet/text) Messenger.

mssg: (Internet/text) Message.

mtc: (Internet/text) More to come.

mtf: (Internet/text) More to Follow.

mtg: (Internet/text) Meeting.

mtl: (Internet/text) More than likely.

mu: (Internet/text) Miss you.

Muck about: (UK) Mess around; waste time.

Muck in: (UK) Share a task or assignment.

Muck raking: (UK) Digging up dirt.

Muck: (UK) Dirt; filth.

Mucker: (UK) Friend; mate; buddy.

Mud-slinging: To trade insults; verbal sparring.

Mug: (UK) 1) A person's face. 2) A naive or dim-witted person.

muh: (Internet/text) My.

mul: (Internet/text) Miss you lots.

Mullered: (UK) To be drunk or intoxicated.

Munted: (New Zealand) 1) To be broken. 2) To be drunk or intoxicated.

Munter: (UK) An unattractive woman.

Muppet: (UK) A fool; an idiot.

Mush: (UK) A person's face or mouth.

Mushie: (Australian) A mushroom.

Mushy: 1) Overly sentimental; overly sweet and romantic. 2) Soft and squishy.

musm: (Internet/text) Miss you so much.

Muso: (Australian/South African) A musician.

mutha: (Internet/text) Mother.

MVP: (Internet/text/game) Most valuable player.

mwah: (Internet/text) The sound of a kiss.

myaly: (Internet/text) Miss you and love you.

myob: (Internet/text) Mind your own business.

mysm: (Internet/text) Miss you so much.

Mystery meat: (US) Low-quality meat served in a cafeteria; processed meat that is hard to identify.

n/a: (Internet/text) Not applicable.

n/c: (Internet/text) No comment.

n/m: (Internet/text) Never mind.

n/n: (Internet/text) Nickname.

n/o: (Internet/text) No offense.

n00b: (Internet/text) Newbie.

n1: (Internet/text) Nice one.

n2: (Internet/text) Into.

n2b: (Internet/text) Not too bad.

n2bb: (Internet/text) Nice to be back.

n2bm: (Internet/text) Not to be mean.

n2br: (Internet/text) Not to be rude.

n2g: (Internet/text) Not too good.

n2m: (Internet/text) Not too much.

n2mu: (Internet/text) Not too much, you?

n2n: (Internet/text) Need to know.

n2p: (Internet/text) Need to pee.

N64: (Gaming) Nintendo 64

n8v: (Internet/text) Native.

na4w: (Internet/text) Not appropriate for work.

naa: (Internet/text) Not at all.

Nab: (UK) To arrest; to seize; to capture.

Nadgers: (UK) Testicles.

Nads: (UK) Testicles.

nafc: (Internet/text) Not appropriate for children.

Naff off: (UK) A rude phrase telling someone to go away or leave the speaker alone.

Naff: (UK) 1) Inferior; useless. 2) A useless person.

Naffed-off: (UK) Fed up; disgruntled.

Naffing: (UK) Very.

nafkam: (Internet/text) Not away from keyboard any more.

Nag pie: (UK) A marriage (a play off the word "magpie").

nah: (Internet/text) No.

Nail in one's own shoe: (UK) To be one's own worst enemy.

Nail: 1) To catch someone or gain incontrovertible proof against them. 2) To identify or establish something precisely. 3) (US) To have sexual intercourse. 4) To do something very well.

Nailed on: (UK) A certainty; a sure thing.

Nam: (US) Vietnam.

Namby: (UK) A timid, ineffectual person.

namh: (Internet/text) Not at my house.

Nana: (UK) 1) An idiot; a fool. 2) A person's head.

Nancy boy: (UK/Derogatory) 1) An effeminate male. 2) A male homosexual.

nao: (Internet/text) Not as often.

Napper: (UK) A person's head.

Narc: (US) A narcotics officer.

Narco: (US) A narcotics officer.

Nark it: (UK) A phrase telling someone to stop doing something.

Nark: (Australian/New Zealand/UK/US) A spy or informant. 2) (UK) Someone who complains a lot. 3) (Australian/New Zealand) A spoilsport; a killjoy.

Narked: (UK) Irritated; annoyed.

Narking dues: (UK) Punishment that arose from information that was given against that person.

Narks: (UK) The police.

Narky: (UK) Irritable; annoyed.

Nasho: (Australian) Conscription; national military service.

Nasty party: (UK) The Conservative party.

Nasty, the: (UK) Sexual intercourse.

natch: (Internet/text) Naturally.

natm: (Internet/text) Not at the moment.

Natty: (UK) Smartly dressed; fashionable.

Naughties: (UK) Sexual intercourse.

Naughty bits: (UK) A person's genitals.

Naughty: 1) (Australian/UK) A criminal act. 2) (Australian/New Zealand) Sexual intercourse.

Nause: (UK) 1) An unpleasant person. 2) A nuisance.

naw: (Internet/text) No.

Naw: (Scottish) No.

nb: (Internet/text) Not bad.

nbd: (Internet/text) No big deal.

nc: (Internet/text) Not cool.

ndit: (Internet/text) No details in thread.

ne: (Internet/text) Any.

ne1: (Internet/text) Anyone.

Neanderthal: (UK) An unintelligent but physically strong man.

Neat: (UK) Pleasing; good.

Nebbish: (UK) A pathetic or ineffectual person.

Nebech (also "nebesh"): (UK) A pathetic or ineffectual person.

Neck: (UK) Boldness; daring. 2) To make out; to kiss passionately.

Neck-oil: (UK) An alcoholic drink.

Ned: (Scottish) A rowdy, drunken person; a lout.

neday: (Internet/text) Any day.

nedn: (Internet/text) Any day now.

Needle match: (UK) A game or competition in which the opponents have a score or grievance to settle with each other.

Needle: (UK) To taunt; to tease; to irritate.

nefing: (Internet/text) Anything.

negl: (Internet/text) Not even going to lie.

nei: (Internet/text) Not enough information.

neida: (Internet/text) Any idea.

nekkid: (Internet/text) Naked.

Nellie: (UK) An ineffectual, timid man.

Nelly: (Australian) Cheap wine.

nemore: (Internet/text) Any more.

Neo-con: (US) Neo-conservative.

Nerf: (Gaming) To lower the effectiveness of a character, weapon, or skill.

Nerk: (UK) An unpleasant person.

Nerve: 1) Courage; confidence. 2) Impertinence; audacity.

Net: The internet.

nething: (Internet/text) Anything.

neva: (Internet/text) Never.

Neversweat: (UK) A lazy or idle person.

nevm: (Internet/text) Never mind.

nevr: (Internet/text) Never.

neway: (Internet/text) Anyway.

newb: (Internet/text/gaming) A newcomer, particularly a game.

newbie: (Internet/text/gaming) A newcomer, particularly a game.

newez: (Internet/text) Anyways.

Newted: (UK) To be drunk or intoxicated.

nf: (Internet/text) Not funny.

nfc: (Internet/text) No fucking clue.

nfi: (Internet/text) No fucking idea.

nfs: (Internet/text) Not for sale.

nfw: (Internet/text) No fucking way.

ng: (Internet/text) Nice game.

ngaf: (Internet/text) Nobody gives a fuck.

ngl: (Internet/text) Not gonna lie.

ni: (Internet/text) No idea.

nib: (Internet/text) New in box.

Nibbles: (UK) Snacks, especially at a party or bar.

Nice one: (Irish) An expression of approval or congratulations.

Nicely done: (UK) To be drunk or intoxicated.

Nick off: (UK) To play truant from work or school.

Nick: (UK/Scottish) 1) To steal. 2) To arrest; to capture.

Nickel and dime (someone): (US) Exhaust or weaken someone by continually charging them small amounts or making numerous small requests of them.

Nickel-and-dime: (US) 1) Small scale; unimportant. 2) Cheap.

nif: (Internet/text) Non-internet friend.

Niff: (UK) A bad smell.

Niffy: (UK) Smelly.

Nifty: (UK) 1) Convenient; useful. 2) Cool; stylish.

nimby: (Internet/text) Not in my backyard.

nin: (Internet/text) No, it's not.

Nine ways from breakfast: (UK) In a variety of ways.

Nine winks: (UK) A short nap.

Niner: 1) (UK) Someone serving a nine-year prison sentence. 2) (Australian) A woman who is nine months pregnant.

Nineteener: (Australian/New Zealand) An unlikable or dishonest person.

Nine-to-five: A full-time job; regular employment.

Nine-to-fiver: (UK) A full-time employee; an office worker.

Ninnified: (UK) Foolish; idiotic.

Ninny: (UK) A coward; a timid man.

nip: (Internet/text) Nothing in particular.

Nip: (UK) 1) To steal. 2) To snatch; to act swiftly.

Nip-in: (UK) A cafe or pub.

Nipper: (UK) A child; an adolescent.

Nipperhood: (UK) Childhood; adolescence.

nips: (Internet/text) Nipples.

Nit: (UK) An idiot; a fool.

nite: (Internet/text) Night; good night.

nitm: (Internet/text) Not in the mood.

Nitty: (UK) Silly; foolish.

Nitty-gritty: (UK) The small or fine details; the essential facts or most important practical aspects of something.

Nitwit: (UK) An idiot; a fool.

Nix: (UK) 1) Nothing. 2) Put an end to or cancel something.

Nixie: (UK) Nothing.

Nixies: (UK) Items for which one isn't charged.

nj: (Internet/text) Nice job.

nk: (Internet/text) No kidding.

nkt: (Internet/text) Never knew that.

nm: (Internet/text) Not much.

nmb: (Internet/text) Not my business.

nmbr: (Internet/text) Number.

nme: (Internet/text/gaming) Enemy.

nmf: (Internet/text) Not my fault.

nmjb: (Internet/text) Not much, just bored.

nmjc: (Internet/text) Not much, just chilling.

nmp: (Internet/text) Not my problem.

nmu: (Internet/text) Nothing much, you?

nmw: (Internet/text) No matter what.

nn: (Internet/text) Good night (from the phrase "night-night").

nn2r: (Internet/text) No need to respond.

nnaa: (Internet/text) No, not at all.

nnr: (Internet/text) No, not really.

nntr: (Internet/text) No need to reply.

No cow: (US) Without milk.

No dice: (US/Canadian) A refusal; for something not to go as hoped.

No drama: (Australian) No problem.

No go: A failure; for something not to go as hoped.

No show: (US) A person who doesn't appear for a meeting or appointment.

No spring chicken: (UK) Someone who is no longer in their youth.

No stress: (US) Don't worry; no problem.

No sweat: (US) 1) No problem. 2) Something that is easy to accomplish.

No way: 1) A denial of something being possible. 2) An exclamation of surprise at something actually happening.

No worries: (Australian) No problem.

no1: (Internet/text) No one.

Nob: (UK) A person's head.

Nobby: (UK) Fashionable; stylish; aristocratic.

Nod off: (UK) To fall asleep.

Noddy: (UK) A simpleton; a clumsy person.

nofi: (Internet/text) No flame intended.

Noggin: (UK) 1) A person's head. 2) An idiot; a fool.

Noghead: (UK) An idiot; a fool.

No-go: (US) A plan or idea that got canceled or which isn't going to happen.

Noise funnels: (UK) A person's ears.

nolm: (Internet/text) No one loves me.

nomw: (Internet/text) Not on my watch.

Non compos: (UK) To be very drunk or intoxicated.

Nong: (Australian) Am idiot; an incompetent person.

No-no: 1) Something inadvisable or prohibited. 2) A bad situation.

noob: (Internet/text/gaming) A newcomer, especially to a game.

noobie: (Internet/text/gaming) A newcomer, particularly a game.

Noodge: (UK) An irritating or ineffectual person.

Noodle: (UK) A person's head.

noodz: (Internet/text) Nude pictures.

Nookie (also "nooky") 1) (UK) Sexual intercourse. 2) (US) The vagina.

Nooner: (UK) An alcoholic drink at lunchtime.

Noov: (UK) Nouveau riche (people who have recently acquired wealth).

NOP: (Internet/text) Normal operating procedure.

norc: (Internet/text) No one really cares.

Norks: (Australian) A woman's breasts.

Nose candy: (US) Cocaine.

Nose itch of summer: (UK) Hay fever.

Nosh up: (UK) A large meal; a feast.

Nosh: (UK) 1) Food. 2) To eat.

Not a bean: (UK) To not have any money.

Not all there: To be a bit crazy or strange.

Not go nap on: (Australian) To hold someone or something in disfavor.

Not on your life: Under no conditions; impossible.

Not on: (UK) Unacceptable; objectionable.

Not right: (UK) Crazy; strange.

Not so hot: (US) Not good.

Not so much: (US) Not good, especially compared to something else.

Not the full quid: (Australian/New Zealand) A bit crazy; foolish.

Not to run a drum: (Australian) A racehorse that fails to perform as expected.

Not to worry: Don't worry.

Not worth a crumpet: (Australian) Totally worthless.

noty: (Internet/text) No thank you.

noub: (Internet/text) None of your business.

nowai: (Internet/text) No way.

Nowheresville: (UK) An isolated place, especially in a rural area.

Now-now girl: (Zimbabwean) A trendy or fashionable young woman.

noyb: (Internet/text) None of your business.

np: (Internet/text) No problem.

npa: (Internet/text) Not paying attention.

NPC: (Gaming) Non-playable character.

nph: (Internet/text) No problem here.

npi: (Internet/text) No pun intended.

nrn: (Internet/text) No response necessary.

nsfw: (Internet/text) Not safe for work.

nt: (Internet/text) Nice try.

ntb: (Internet/text) Not too bad.

NTD.: (UK) Not top drawer (referring to something being of low quality).

nthg: (Internet/text) Nothing.

ntk: (Internet/text) Need to know.

ntkb: (Internet/text) Need to know basis.

ntm: (Internet/text) Not too much.

ntmk: (Internet/text) Not to my knowledge.

ntmu: (Internet/text) Nice to meet you.

ntmy: (Internet/text) Nice to meet you.

ntn: (Internet/text) Nothing.

ntrly: (Internet/text) Not really.

nts: (Internet/text) Note to self.

ntt: (Internet/text) Need to talk.

ntta: (Internet/text) Nothing to talk about.

ntty: (Internet/text) Nice talking to you.

ntw: (Internet/text) Not to worry.

nty: (Internet/text) No thank you.

Nubbing: (UK) Sexual intercourse.

Nuclear, to go: (US) To become enraged; to become very angry.

Nuddy: (Australian) Naked.

nuff: (Internet/text) Enough.

Nuke: (US) To attack with a nuclear bomb; to destroy something completely.

Nuker: (UK) A microwave oven.

Nukes: (US) Nuclear weapons.

Number one: 1) The best. 2) Urination.

Number two: Defecation.

Number: To identify someone; to understand something about someone, especially how they operate (i.e., "to have their number").

Number-cruncher: (UK) 1) A calculator. 2) A person who handles calculations, such as an accountant.

Number-crunching: (UK) Doing complex calculations.

Numb-nuts: An idiot; a fool.

Numbskull: An idiot; a fool.

Numero uno: Someone or something that is the best of its class.

Numpty: (UK) An idiot; a fool.

Nut house: (UK) A mental hospital.

Nut job: A crazy or eccentric person.

Nut: 1) A crazy or eccentric person. 2) A person's head.

Nutcase: (UK) A crazy or reckless person.

Nuthouse: (UK) A mental hospital.

Nuts and bolts: The fundamental or practical aspects of something.

Nuts: 1) Crazy; insane; reckless. 2) Testicles.

Nut-sack: The scrotum.

Nutter: (UK) A crazy person.

Nutty: (UK) Crazy; eccentric.

nvm: (Internet/text) Never mind.

nvr: (Internet/text) Never.

nw: (Internet/text) No way.

nwb: (Internet/text) A newcomer; a newb.

nwih: (Internet/text) No way in hell.

nws: (Internet/text) Not work safe.

nwy: (Internet/text) No way.

nxt: (Internet/text) Next.

ny1: (Internet/text) Anyone.

nyf: (Internet/text) Not your fault.

Nympho: A promiscuous woman.

nyp: (Internet/text) Not your problem.

nywy: (Internet/text) Anyway.

— O —

o&o: (Internet/text) Over and out.

o/y: (Internet/text) Oh yeah.

oaoa: (Internet/text) Over and over again.

oar: (Internet/text) On a roll.

Oatsy: (UK) Spirited; bold; assertive.

obtw: (Internet/text) Oh, by the way.

obv: (Internet/text) Obviously.

OC: (Internet/text) Original character (primarily used in fan fiction).

ocgg: (Internet/text) Oh crap, got to go.

Ocker: (Australian) An unsophisticated or uncouth person.

Ockerina: (Australian) An unsophisticated or uncouth person.

Octopus: (UK) A man who is very handsy with woman.

OD: Overdose.

Oddball: (UK) A strange or eccentric person.

Oddbod: (UK) A strange or eccentric person.

Odd-lot: (UK) A police car.

Odds against: To be unlikely to happen or succeed.

Odds and sods: (UK) Bits and pieces; miscellaneous items.

Odds it: (UK) To take a chance.

Odds on: (UK) To be likely to happen or succeed.

of10: (Internet/text) Often.

ofc: (Internet/text) Of course.

Off one's block: (UK) To be crazy or eccentric.

Off one's box: (UK) To be drunk or intoxicated.

Off one's chump: (UK) To be crazy or eccentric.

Off one's crust: (UK) To be crazy or eccentric.

Off one's face: (Australian) To be drunk or intoxicated.

Off one's head: (UK) To be crazy or deranged.

Off one's nut: (UK) To be crazy or reckless.

Off one's rocker: (UK) To be crazy or deranged.

Off one's scone: (Australian) To be angry; to be crazy.

Off one's trolley: (UK) To be crazy or deranged.

Off the bat: (US) Immediately; right from the beginning.

Off the chain: (Australian) Unrestrained; unrestricted.

Off the hook: 1) To escape punishment; to be forgiven without receiving punishment. 2) (US) Amazing; extremely fun. 3) (Australian) A married man having a night out with male friends.

Off the wall: Strange; eccentric.

Off your head: (Irish) To be drunk or intoxicated.

Off: 1) (US) To kill. 2) Unsatisfactory or inadequate.

Off-side: (UK) Improper behavior; an unfair action.

Off-sider: (Australian) An assistant.

Off-the-wall: (UK) Unconventional; eccentric.

oftc: (Internet/text) Out for the count.

OG: (UK) Original gangster; a gang member with a respected history.

Oggle: (UK) To stare at someone lecherously.

ohic: (Internet/text) Oh, I see.

ohn: (Internet/text) Oh, hell no.

ohnoez: (Internet/text) Oh, no.

ohy: (Internet/text) Oh, hell yeah.

oic: (Internet/text) Oh, I see.

Oil: (UK) An alcoholic drink.

Oiled: (UK) To be drunk or intoxicated.

Oily: (UK) An unsophisticated or foolish person.

oink: (Internet/text) Oh, I never knew.

oiyd: (Internet/text) Only in your dreams.

OJ: (UK) Orange juice.

ojsu: (Internet/text) Oh, just shut up.

OK: (Internet/text) Okay.

Okey-doke (also "okey-dokie"): Okay; sure thing.

Old banger: (UK) An old, run-down car.

Old Bill: (UK) The police.

Old boot: (UK) A mature or old woman, often with severe or unattractive features.

Old chap: (UK) A term of endearment for an older male.

Old coot: (UK) An ill-tempered old person.

Old dart: (Australian) England.

Old fellow: (UK) A term of endearment for an older male.

Old hat: (UK) 1) Old-fashioned; outdated. 2) Something with which one is very familiar or experienced.

Old heave ho: (UK) A rejection; a dismissal; a firing from employment.

Old lady: One's wife or girlfriend.

Old lag: (UK) A lifelong criminal; an acquaintance one made in prison.

Old man: 1) One's father or husband. 2) A term of endearment for a male friend.

Old sweat: (UK) A person with experience in their field.

Old trout: (UK) A woman who is beyond middle-age.

Oldie: (UK) 1) An old person. 2) A parent. 3) A popular song that is now outdated.

Ollie: (UK) A marble.

omdg: (Internet/text) Oh my dear god.

omg: (Internet/text) Oh my god.

omgd: (Internet/text) Oh my gosh dude.

omgn: (Internet/text) Oh my goodness.

omgosh (also "omgsh"): (Internet/text) Oh my gosh.

omgty: (Internet/text) Oh my god, thank you.

omt: (Internet/text) One more time.

omw: (Internet/text) On my way.

omwh: (Internet/text) On my way home.

omwts: (Internet/text) On my way to school.

On a pension: (UK) A corrupt police officer.

On a raft: (UK) On top of toast.

On a roll: (UK) To be enjoying a string of good luck or success.

On canvas: (UK) In prison; in solitary confinement.

On edge: Nervous; tense with anxiety; highly strung.

On hold: 1) For a plan or order to be suspended or delayed. 2) To wait for an operator to connect or field your telephone call.

On holiday: (UK) In prison, especially for a short sentence.

On one: (UK) 1) To be in the know. 2) To be committing a crime, especially theft.

On one's ace: (UK) To be alone.

On one's Jack Jones: (UK) To be alone.

On one's own hook: (UK) To act on one's own initiative.

On one's tod: (UK) To be alone.

On someone's hammer: (Australian/New Zealand) To chase or be in pursuit of someone.

On spec: (UK) At a risk.

On the Abraham: (UK) Pretending to be sick to take time off work.

On the blink: (UK) For a machine to be out of order or malfunctioning.

On the blob: (UK) Menstruation.

On the brew: (Scottish) To be unemployed.

On the bum: (UK) For a machine to be malfunctioning.

On the cards: (UK) For something to be likely or possible to happen.

On the cellar: (UK) To scrounge, especially for money.

On the club: (UK) To be receiving paid sick leave.

On the cross: (UK) Dishonesty; deceitfulness.

On the dot: Exactly; precisely.

On the double: (US) Quickly; swiftly; as fast as possible.

On the elbow: (UK) To be engaged in attempting to borrow money.

On the fly: To do something without preparation; to act or make decisions as the need arises.

On the fritz: (US) For a machine to be malfunctioning.

On the game: (UK) To be working as a prostitute.

On the hook: (UK) To be responsible or accountable for something; to be left in a vulnerable situation.

On the hurry-up: (UK) Quickly; as fast as possible.

On the line: For something of value to be at risk owing to the current situation.

On the money: (US) Exactly; precisely.

On the mud: (UK) A beer glass that is almost empty.

On the never-never: (UK) To purchase something on credit.

On the nose: (Australian) Smelly; pungent.

On the piss: (UK) To be getting drunk.

On the pull: (UK) To be out looking for a romantic or sexual partner.

On the QT: (UK) To do something secretly or discreetly.

On the rag: To be menstruating.

On the razzle: (UK) To be out having a fun time.

On the rocks: 1) To be in a bad or precarious situation. 2) To have an alcoholic drink with ice cubes in it.

On the Rory: (UK) To be poor or poverty-stricken.

On the tap: (UK) To beg for money or seek a loan.

On the thumb: (UK) To hitchhike.

On the up-and-up: To be legitimate; to be legal.

On the wagon: (UK) To be abstaining from alcohol or narcotics.

On the wallaby: (Australian) To look for work, especially by wandering around.

On the way out: (UK) To be dying; to be in the last stage of one's life.

On tick: (UK) To be on duty; to be present.

On tilt: (US) Unbalanced; unsteady.

On top of: In addition to.

On top: (UK) To be caught in the act.

On velvet: (UK) A state of comfort, advantage, or wealth.

On your bike: (UK) An expression telling the listener to go away or leave the speaker alone.

Once every pancake day: (UK) Seldom; very rarely.

Once over: (UK) To inspect something; to check something for obvious flaws.

Oncer: (Australian) A politician who can only serve one term in Parliament.

One for his nob: (UK) A tip or additional payment.

One for the road: A final drink before leaving.

One for the tarmac: (UK) A final drink before leaving.

One over the eight: (UK) To be drunk or intoxicated.

One-eyed trouser snake: The penis.

One-horse: (US) Inferior; second-rate.

One-night stand: An overnight sexual encounter that doesn't lead to a relationship.

One-up: To out-do someone else's efforts.

One-way pockets: (UK) A miser; someone who is stingy with their money.

Onion: (UK) A person's head.

onoez (also "onoz"): (Internet/text) Oh no.

onud: (Internet/text) Oh no, you didn't.

onyd: (Internet/text) Oh no, you didn't.

oob: (Internet/text) Out of business.

oobl: (Internet/text) Out of breath laughing.

OOC: (Internet/text) Out of character.

Oodles: (UK) A large amount; more than enough.

oohm: (Internet/text) Out of his/her mind.

oom: (Gaming) Out of mana.

oomm: (Internet/text) Out of my mind.

ooo: (Internet/text) Out of the office.

Oops: An expression that indicates a mistake or minor accident.

ootb: (Internet/text) Out of the blue.

oow: (Internet/text) On our way.

ooym: (Internet/text) Out of your mind.

OP: (Internet/text) Original poster.

Op: (UK) A surgical operation.

Open a mouth: (UK) To start an argument.

Open slather: (Australian/New Zealand) A free-for-all situation.

Open up: (US) To speak honestly about private or personal matters.

orly: (Internet/text) Oh, really?

Ornaments: (UK) A man's genitals.

OS: 1) (Internet/text) Operating system. 2) (Australian) Overseas.

Oscar: (Australian) Money; cash.

oslt: (Internet/text) Or something like that.

osy: (Internet/text) Oh, screw you.

ot: (Internet/text) Off topic.

otb: (Internet/text) Off the boat.

otc: (Internet/text) Off the chain.

otfcu: (Internet/text) On the floor cracking up.

otfl: (Internet/text) On the floor laughing.

otflmao: (Internet/text) On the floor laughing my ass off.

otflol: (Internet/text) On the floor laughing out loud.

Other half: (US) The rich; the wealthy.

Other side of the coin: The opposite point of view; the flip side of a situation.

oti: (Internet/text) On the internet.

otl: (Internet/text) Out to lunch.

otoh: (Internet/text) On the other hand.

otp: (Internet/text) On the phone.

ots: (Internet/text) Over the shoulder.

OTT: (UK) Over the top; excessive.

otw: (Internet/text) On the way.

Ouch-house: (UK) A pub or bar that caters to a rough crowd.

Out cold: To be unconscious.

Out in the cold: (UK) For a person to be left out or not included in something.

Out in the left field: (UK) To be totally wrong or mistaken.

Out like a light: To fall asleep quickly.

Out of hand: A situation or person that is out of control.

Out of it: To be dazed or semi-conscious.

Out of line: To be impertinent or disrespectful.

Out of one's box: (UK) 1) To be crazy. 2) To be drunk or intoxicated.

Out of one's head: (UK) 1) To be crazy. 2) To be drunk or intoxicated.

Out of one's league: To be outclassed by another person; to lack the necessary skills for a situation.

Out of one's pram: (UK) 1) To be crazy. 2) To be angry.

Out of one's skull: (UK) 1) To be crazy. 2) To be drunk or intoxicated.

Out of one's tree: (UK) 1) To be crazy. 2) To be drunk or intoxicated.

Out of order: (UK) 1) To act improperly. 2) To be drunk or intoxicated.

Out of the blue: For something to happen unexpectedly.

Out of the game: (UK) To be unconscious or incoherent, especially owing to alcohol.

Out of the loop: (US) To be uninformed; to not know what has been going on.

Out of thin air: For something to happen or for someone to do something unexpectedly, as if from nowhere.

Out of whack: To be out of sorts; to not be working properly.

Out of your tree: (Irish) To be drunk or intoxicated.

Out to lunch: (UK) Crazy; eccentric; deranged.

Out: 1) To not conceal one's sexual orientation or gender identity. 2) (US) Something that is no longer popular.

Outfront: (US) Frank; straightforward; honest.

Outing: Publicly revealing another person's sexual orientation or gender identity, especially without their consent.

Outside: The world outside of prison.

Outsider art: Art created by people who are regarded as being outside of mainstream society.

ova: (Internet/text) Over.

Over one's head: Beyond one's ability to comprehend.

Over the edge: To be beyond the ability to think rationally.

Over the hill: (UK) A person who is well past their prime.

Over the mark: (Canadian) To be tipsy.

Over the top: Exaggerated; extreme.

Overall: (UK) A working man.

Overcoat: (UK) A condom.

Overkill: Excessive; extreme; unnecessary.

oways: (Internet/text) Oh wow, are you serious?

Own goal: (UK) A self-harming mistake or action.

Own: (US/gaming) To defeat someone thoroughly.

Owned: (US/gaming) To be defeated thoroughly, often in a humiliating way.

owt: (Internet/text) Out.

oww: (Internet/text) Oops, wrong window.

oyid: (Internet/text) Oh yes, I did.

oyo: (Internet/text) On your own.

oyr: (Internet/text) Oh, yeah right.

Oyster: (UK) 1) A glob of phlegm. 2) A taciturn or withdrawn person.

Oz: (Australian) Australia.

— P —

p/oed: (Internet/text) Pissed off.

p/w: (Internet/text) Password.

p@w: (Internet/text) Parents are watching.

p^s: (Internet/text) Parent over shoulder.

p2p: (Internet/text) Peer to peer.

p2w: (Internet/text) Pay to win.

Pacific slope: (New Zealand) Countries along the Pacific rim.

Pack a rod: (UK) To carry a gun.

Pack a sad: (New Zealand) To throw a tantrum; to lose one's temper.

Pack heat: (US) To carry a gun.

Pack: (Irish) Friendly.

Packet from Paris: (Australian/New Zealand) A baby.

Packet: (UK) A large sum of money.

Pad: (US) A person's home or apartment.

Paddlers: (UK) The feet.

Paddywaggon: (UK) A police van.

pah: (Internet/text) Parents at home.

Pain in the arse: (UK) Someone or something that is irritating or tedious.

Pain in the neck: (UK) Someone or something that is irritating or tedious.

Pain: (UK) A person, task, or situation that is troublesome or annoying; a nuisance.

Paint oneself into a corner: (US) To be in a difficult situation because of one's own actions.

Paint the back seat: (US) To vomit.

Palm off: (UK) To have someone take accountability for something that is not their responsibility.

Palm oil: (UK) A bribe.

Pan out: To happen or conclude in a certain way.

Pan: (UK) A person's face or head.

Pancake: (UK) A flat-chested woman.

Panic attack: To be overwhelmed by anxiety.

panl: (Internet/text) Party all night long.

Pants down: (UK) An embarrassing situation.

Pants man: (Australian) A promiscuous man or womanizer.

Pants: (UK) Something that is of poor quality.

Paper: (US) Money; cash.

Paper-bag job: (UK) An unattractive person.

Paperhanger: (US) A counterfeiter.

Paradise: (UK) A theater or stadium's highest seating area.

Parallel parking: (US) Sexual intercourse.

Parcel from Paris: (Australian/New Zealand) A baby.

Park one's arse: (UK) To sit down.

Park: (US) To sit down.

Parkie: (UK) A park keeper.

Parking: (US) Making out in a car.

Party down: (US) To have a good time; to have a rowdy party.

Party favors: (US) Drugs that are provided or offered at social events.

Party on: (US) To carry on having a good time.

Party-pooper: A killjoy; someone who takes the fun out of a situation.

pas: (Internet/text) Parent at side.

Pash: (Australian/New Zealand) A kissing session; to make out.

Pashing: (Australian/New Zealand) Kissing heavily; making out.

pasii: (Internet/text) Put a sock in it.

Pass in one's ally: (Australian) 1) To surrender; to give in. 2) To die.

Pass muster: (US) To meet expectations; to qualify as satisfactory.

Pass out: To fall asleep from exhaustion; to lose consciousness.

Pass the bone: (US) To impart knowledge or experience.

Pass the buck: To avoid responsibility or blame by shifting it elsewhere.

Passion killer: (UK) Something that lowers a person's sex appeal.

Passion wagon: (UK) A car used for dating or having sex in.

Pasting: (UK) A thorough defeat.

Pat down: To frisk a person.

Patch: (UK) 1) A small area or territory. 2) A bald spot.

Patootie: (US) A person's buttocks.

Patsy: (US/Canadian) Someone who is taken advantage of or deceived.

Pavement pizza: (US) To vomit on the sidewalk or in the street.

paw: (Internet/text) Parents are watching.

Paw: (UK) 1) A person's hand. 2) To handle something roughly.

Pay dirt: (US) A large amount of profit or money (usually used in the expression "hit/strike pay dirt").

Pay one's dues: To work hard or suffer early on in order to earn a better position later.

Pay the freight: (UK) To pay a bill; to take responsibility for an expense.

Pay through the nose: To pay an exorbitant amount for something.

Payoff: The outcome; the end result, especially in terms of what one receives.

Pazzer: (UK) A parent.

PB&J: (Internet/text) Peanut butter and jelly.

pbj: (Internet/text) Peanut butter and jelly.

pbly: (Internet/text) Probably.

pbm: (Internet/text) Parent behind me.

pbp: (Internet/text) Please be patient.

PC: (UK) Politically correct.

pce: (Internet/text) Peace.

pcm: (Internet/text) Please call me.

pco: (Internet/text) Please come over.

PDA: (UK) Public display of affection, such as kissing.

pdg: (Internet/text) Pretty damn good.

pdq: (Internet/text) Pretty damn quick.

Pea: (Australian) The best choice; ideal; favorite.

Pea-brain: An idiot; a fool.

Peach: (US) 1) A nice person. 2) A young, attractive woman.

Peachy: (US) Great; wonderful.

Peanut: (US/Canadian) 1) A short person. 2) Someone who is considered insignificant.

Peanuts: A very small amount of money.

Pearlies: (UK) A person's teeth.

Pearly whites: (UK) A person's teeth.

Pears: (Australian) A woman's breasts.

Pearshaped: (UK) To have gone wrong; to have turned out badly.

Peashooter: (US) A low-powered gun.

Pebble: (Australian) A difficult person.

Pebble-beached: (UK) 1) To be poor; poverty-stricken. 2) To be dazed or forgetful.

Pebbles: (UK) The testicles.

Peck: 1) To nibble at food. 2) Money. 3) A quick, polite kiss, typically on the cheek.

Pecker: The penis.

Peckerhead: An idiot; an unlikeable person.

Peckish: To be slightly hungry.

Pecs: Pectoral muscles.

Pedal: (Australian) To broadcast a radio message.

Pedal-pusher: (US) A cyclist.

Peddle out: (US) To sell one's belongings.

Pee: To urinate.

Peel off: (UK) To undress.

Peeler: (UK) A striptease dancer.

Peepers: (UK) A person's eyes.

peeps: (Internet/text) People.

Peg it: (UK) To die.

Peg out: (UK) To die.

Pelters: (Scottish) A barrage of insults.

Pen pusher: (UK) An office worker.

pen0r: (Internet/text) Penis.

pen15: (Internet/text) Penis.

Pencil geek: (US) An overly studious person; a nerd.

Pencil pusher: (US) An office worker.

Penguin suit: (UK) Formal evening wear for men, such as a tuxedo or suit.

Penguin: (US) A period; menstruation (typically used by trans men to help avoid gender dysphoria).

Pennyboy: (Irish) A person who does menial tasks.

Penny-dreadful: (UK) A sensationalist tabloid or magazine.

Peppy: (US) Lively; full of energy.

Perk up: (Australian) To vomit.

Perp: (US) Perpetrator; a criminal.

Personals: (Australian) Underwear, especially for women.

Perv: Pervert.

Perve: To look at someone lecherously.

Pervy: Perverted.

Pet peeve: Something that you personally find irritating.

Peterman: (UK) A burglar who specializes in breaking safes.

Pew: (UK) A chair.

pex: (Internet/text) Please explain.

pezzas: (Internet/text) Parents.

pfm: (Internet/text) Please forgive me.

pfp: (Internet/text) 1) Profile picture. 2) Picture for proof.

pg: (Internet/text) Page.

ph#: (Internet/text) Phone number.

Phat: (US) Cool; impressive; attractive.

Phenom: (UK) Phenomenal.

Phiz: (UK) A person's face.

phlr: (Internet/text) Peace, hugs, love, respect.

phm: (Internet/text) Please help me.

PI: (UK) Private investigator.

piab: (Internet/text) Panties in a bunch.

pic: (Internet/text) Picture.

Piccadilly Circus: (UK) Crowded with people; bustling; chaotic.

Pick up on: To grasp the meaning or existence of something; to understand; to realize.

Pick up one's drum: (UK) To leave in a temper.

Pickled: (UK) To be drunk or intoxicated.

Picky: Fussy; choosy; particular.

pics: (Internet/text) Pictures.

Picture in the attic: (UK) A young person who tries to act beyond their age.

Piddle about: (UK) To waste time.

Piddle: (UK) To urinate.

Piddled: (UK) To be drunk or intoxicated.

Piddling it down: (UK) Raining.

Piddling: (UK) Insignificant; minor; trivial.

Pie can: (UK) An idiot; a fool.

Pie in the sky: An idea or plan that is unrealistic.

Piece of cake: Simple or easy.

Piece of piss: (Australian/UK) Something that is very easy.

Piece of pudding: (UK) Very easy.

Piece of shit: A horrible or despicable person.

Piece: (UK) An attractive woman. 2) (US) A gun. 3) An artwork.

Pie-eater: (Australian) A poor or unfortunate person.

Pie-eyed: (UK) To be drunk or intoxicated.

Piff: (UK) Nonsense; hogwash.

Piffle: (UK) Nonsense; hogwash.

Piffy: (UK) Doubtful; dubious.

Pig it: (UK) To act in a repulsive manner.

Pig off: (UK) An expression to tell someone to go away.

Pig out: To eat excessively.

Pig: (US/derogatory) 1) A police officer. 2) Someone who eats excessively.

Pig's breakfast: (UK) A total failure; a mess.

Pig-headed: A stubborn or obstinate person.

Piglet: (UK) A cheeky or impertinent child.

Pig-out: To eat excessively.

Pigshit: Rubbish; of no value.

Pigswill: (UK) Nonsense; hogwash.

Pill: (UK) A dull or boring person; a killjoy.

Pillock: (UK) An idiot; an annoying person.

Pillow: (UK) To have sexual intercourse.

Pill-popper: A person with an addiction to pills.

pima: (Internet/text) Pain in my ass.

Pimp: (Australian/New Zealand) An informant; a spy.

Pimpsy: (UK) Something that is easy to accomplish.

Pin down: (US) To make a choice; to identify something from among a group of possibilities.

Pin the rap on: To charge someone with circumstantial evidence.

Pinch: (UK) 1) To steal, especially petty theft. 2) To arrest.

Pineapple: (UK) A hand grenade.

Pinhead: 1) An idiot; a fool. 2) A petty person. 3) A person with a small head.

Pink slip: (US) To lose a job; to receive notification about being fired.

Pinkie: The little finger.

Pinned-up: (UK) Tense; anxious; on edge.

Pins: (UK) A person's legs.

Pin-up: A glamourous female model.

Pip: (UK) A bad mood or temper.

Pipe down: (US) An order for the listener to be quiet.

Pipe one's eye: (UK) To cry; to weep.

Pipes: (UK) The respiratory system; the throat.

Pipsqueek: A small, insignificant person.

pir: (Internet/text) Parents in room.

Piss about: (UK) To mess around; to waste time.

Piss artist: (UK) 1) Someone who wastes time. 2) A drunkard.

Piss down: (UK) To rain hard.

Piss home: (UK) To win easily, especially in a race.

Piss in the swimming pool: (UK) To spoil or ruin something.

Piss in the wind: (UK) A futile or ineffectual action.

Piss in: (UK) To win easily, especially in a race.

Piss it: (UK) To succeed easily.

Piss off: (UK) A rude order for the listener to go away.

Piss oneself: 1) To laugh hysterically. 2) To be very scared.

Piss pot: (UK) 1) A chamber pot. 2) A child's potty.

Piss someone off: To anger or irritate someone.

Piss: 1) To urinate. 1) Weak or watered-down beer. 3) Nonsense; hogwash.

Pissed off: 1) To be angry or irritated. 2) (UK) To be drunk.

Pisser: (UK) A toilet.

Pisshead: (UK) A drunkard.

Pissing down: (UK) To be raining hard.

Piss-poor: (UK) Very low quality.

Piss-take: (UK) A parody; a mockery.

Piss-up: (UK) A heavy drinking session.

Pissy: (US) Ill-tempered in a petty way.

Pit stop: A short break while traveling to have refreshments or go to the toilet.

Pit: (UK) A run-down or sleazy place.

pita: (Internet/text) Pain in the ass.

Pitch: To promote or describe an idea.

pitr: (Internet/text) Parent in the room.

Pits: (UK) Something that is the worst.

pix: (Internet/text) Pictures.

Pixilated: (UK) To be drunk or intoxicated.

Pizzaface: Someone with acne or a lot of pimples on their face.

PJs: Pajamas.

pker: (Gaming) Player killer.

pking: (Gaming) Player killing.

Plank: (UK) 1) A slow-witted person; an idiot. 2) To have sexual intercourse.

Plank-head: (UK) An idiot; a fool.

Plant beets: (US) To vomit.

Plant: Someone who is undercover, such as a police officer.

Planted: (UK) Buried.

Planting: (UK) A funeral (referring to a coffin being lowered into the ground).

plars: (Internet/text) Party like a rock star.

Plaster: (US) To strike aggressively.

Plastered: (UK) To be very drunk or intoxicated.

Plastic: A credit card.

Plat: (Australian) An idiot; a fool.

Play along: To pretend to support what someone else thinks or does.

Play around: To be promiscuous.

Play ball: (US) To cooperate; to reach an agreement.

Play hardball: (US) To act in an uncompromising way; to put the other party in a tough situation.

Play hooky: (US) To play truant.

Play hospitals: (UK) To engage in a sexual activity.

Play it cool: To act in a calm or composed way.

Play silly buggers: (UK) To mess around; to waste time.

Play the hop: (UK) To play truant.

Play the whale: (Australian) To vomit.

Player: (US) A womanizer; a playboy.

pleaz: (Internet/text) Please.

Pleb: (UK) A commoner; someone of lower social class.

pleez: (Internet/text) Please.

plma: (Internet/text) Please leave me alone.

plmk: (Internet/text) Please let me know.

Plod: (UK) A police officer.

Plonk: (UK) Cheap wine.

Plonker: (UK) An idiot; a fool.

Plonko: (Australian) An alcoholic.

Plop: (UK) To defecate.

Plot-up: (UK) To park a vehicle.

Plough: (UK) To have sexual intercourse.

Ploughed: (UK) To be drunk or intoxicated.

pls: (Internet/text) Please.

PLU: (UK) People like us.

Plug: 1) A strike or punch. 2) To shoot. 3) To have sexual intercourse. 4) To promote.

Plugged in: (UK) To stay be aware of the latest trends.

Plugged: To be shot.

Plugged-up: (UK) Menstruating.

Plum: (UK) An idiot; a fool.

Plumbing: (UK) The urinary system.

Plums: (UK) The testicles.

Plunge: (UK) To have sexual intercourse.

Plunger: (UK) The penis.

plx: (Internet/text) Please and thanks.

plz: (Internet/text) Please.

pml: (Internet/text) Pissing myself laughing.

pmo: (Internet/text) Pissing me off.

pmp: (Internet/text) Pissing my pants.

pmpl: (Internet/text) Pissing my pants laughing.

pmsl: (Internet/text) Pissing myself laughing.

pmt: (Internet/text) Pretty much this.

po-po: (Internet/text) The police.

po: (Internet/text) Piss off.

PO'd: (Internet/text) Pissed off.

pob: (Internet/text) Parent over back.

POC: Person of color.

poc: (Internet/text) Piece of crap.

Pock: (UK) A police officer.

Podge: (UK) An overweight person.

POed: (Internet/text) Pissed off.

poggers: (Internet/text/gaming) Awesome; cool (expresses the speaker's enthusiasm or excitement).

POI: (Internet/text) Point of interest.

poidnh: (Internet/text) Pics or it did not happen.

Poison: An alcoholic drink.

Poke fun: To make fun of something or someone.

Poke: (UK) To have sexual intercourse.

Pokey: (UK) A prison or jail cell.

Poler: (Australian) An idle person; someone who takes advantage of other people.

Polish off: (UK) To finish; to complete.

Poll: (UK) A talkative person.

Polluted: (US) To be drunk or intoxicated.

Polly: (Australian) A police officer.

Pom: (Australian/New Zealand/South African) An English person.

Pommy: (Australian/New Zealand) An English person.

poms: (Internet/text) Parent over my shoulder.

Ponce about: (UK) To waste time; to act irresponsibly.

Ponced-up: (UK) Dressed smartly.

Poncey: (UK/derogatory) Effeminate.

Pony: (UK) A small glass of beer.

Pooch: A dog.

Poon: 1) (Australian) A fool; an incompetent person. 2) (US) The vagina.

Pooped: Exhausted; tired.

Pop a vein: (US) To become enraged; to be furious.

Pop a window: (UK) To burglarize, especially by breaking a window.

Pop it: (UK) To die.

Pop one's clogs: (UK) To die.

Pop up: To occur suddenly; out of the blue.

Pop-pop: (UK) A moped.

Poppycock: (UK) Nonsense; hogwash.

Popsy: (UK) An attractive woman.

Pork: (UK) To have sexual intercourse.

Porker: An overweight person.

Porkies: (UK) Lies.

Porky: (UK) A lie.

pos: (Internet/text) Piece of shit; a horrible person.

Posh Sydney: (UK) An upper-class young male.

Posh: (UK) Upper class.

Posse: (US) A gang; a group of close friends.

Postie: (UK) A postman.

Pot: (UK) 1) A toilet. 2) Marijuana.

Potato trap: (UK) A person's mouth.

Potato-head: (UK) A foolish or slow-witted person.

Pothead: A stoner; someone who regularly smokes a lot of marijuana.

Potted: (UK) 1) To be high off marijuana. 2) To be drunk or intoxicated.

Potty: (UK) Eccentric; odd; strange.

Pour it on: (UK) To exaggerate, especially for sympathy.

POV: (Internet/text) Point of view.

POW: (Internet/text) Prisoner of war.

Powder one's nose: (UK) To sniff cocaine.

Powder: (UK) Cocaine.

Pox: (Irish) Someone who is irritating or frustrating.

Pozzy: (Australian) A position.

ppl: (Internet/text) People.

PR: (US) Public relations.

pr0n: (Internet/text) Porn.

Prang: (UK) 1) A collision. 2) To strike against.

Prannet: (UK) An idiot; a fool.

Prannock: (UK) An idiot; a fool.

Prat about: (UK) To play around; to waste time; to act irresponsibly.

Prat: (UK) A fool; an unlikeable person.

Pratfall: (US/Canadian) To fall on one's rear.

Prawn: (UK) An idiot; a fool.

Pray at the porcelain altar: (US) To vomit in a toilet.

Prayer: A hope or wish.

Preggers: (UK) Pregnant.

Preggo: (Australian) Pregnant.

Preppie: (US) 1) A student of an expensive private school. 2) A neat, upper-class style.

Pressure cooker: (US) A high-pressure situation.

Pretty boy: An attractive or effeminate young man.

Prezzy: (Australian/South African) A present; a gift.

Prick: 1) A penis. 2) An unlikeable person; a jerk.

Private parts: Genitals.

Privates: Genitals.

Pro: Professional.

prob: (Internet/text) Problem.

prolly: (Internet/text) Probably.

promo: (Internet/text) Promotion.

Pron (also "pr0n"): (Internet/text) Pornography.

Pronto: Immediately; at once.

Props: (US/Canadian) Proper respect.

protecc: (Internet/text) Protect.

Protein spill: (US) To vomit.

prp: (Internet/text) Please reply.

prv: (Internet/text) Private.

PSA: (Internet/text) Public service announcement.

Psych oneself up: To mentally prepare oneself.

Psych someone out: To make someone nervous.

Psyched: (US) To be very excited.

Psycho: Psychopath.

ptl: (Internet/text) Praise the Lord.

pto: (Internet/text) Personal time off.

Puddle: (UK) To confuse; to make a mess of something.

Puddled: (UK) Crazy; confused.

Puffer: (UK) A smoker.

Pugnose: (UK) A flat nose.

Puke: To vomit.

Pull a rock: (US) To make a mistake.

Pull finger: (New Zealand) To stop being idle; to be more active.

Pull in: (UK) To arrest.

Pull one's finger out: (UK) To stop being idle; to be more active.

Pull one's leg: (US) To playfully deceive or joke someone.

Pull something off: (US) To succeed at something, especially if it was difficult or unlikely.

Pull the plug: 1) To put an end to something. 2) To take someone off life support.

Pull: (UK) 1) To seduce or attract someone. 2) To drink.

Pulling power: (UK) Sexual attraction.

Pump iron: To body build; to lift weights.

Pump up: (US) To flatter someone.

Punctured: (UK) To be drunk or intoxicated.

Punk: A disrespectful person.

Punt: (UK) 1) To promote or sell something. 2) To gamble. 3) (US) To shift a problem to someone else.

Purse: (UK) A vagina.

purty: (Internet/text) Pretty.

Push about: To bully; boss someone around.

Push: (US) To sell drugs.

Pusher: (US) A drug dealer.

Pushing up daisies: To be dead.

Pushover: A weak-willed person; someone who does whatever they are told to do.

Puss: (Irish) A morose or sullen expression.

Pussy: (US) A coward.

Pussycat: (UK) A harmless or gentle person.

Pussy-whipped: (US) Someone who does whatever their girlfriend or wife tells them to do.

Put a sock in it: An exasperated order for the listener to be quiet.

Put away: (US) Eat a lot.

Put down: (US) Insult; criticize.

Put it about: (UK) To be promiscuous.

Put on: (UK) Pretending to act a certain way; an affected manner.

Put one on someone: (UK) To hit or punch a person.

Put one's hands up: To surrender.

Put one's nose out of joint: (UK) To suffer a blow to one's pride.

Put someone away: (UK) 1) To kill someone. 2) To imprison someone.

Put someone down: To insult or criticize someone.

Put someone up: (US) Let someone stay at your home.

Put something on the line: (US) Gamble on something; take a risk on something.

Put the acid on someone: (Australian/New Zealand) To beg or proposition someone, especially for money or a favor.

Put the bite on someone: (UK) To put pressure on someone, especially to have them repay money.

Put the boot in: (UK) To aggravate or antagonize someone, especially when they are already suffering.

Put the frighteners on: (UK) To intimidate someone.

Put the nips in: (Australian/New Zealand) To pressure someone, especially in regard to receiving money from them.

Put the nut on: (UK) To headbutt.

Put the tin hat on: (UK) To finish or complete; to bring to an end.

Put the wind up: (UK) To frighten; to scare.

Put up: (US) To contribute money; to provide someone with financing.

Putdown: An insult.

Put-on: (UK) A scam; a deception.

Putz: (US) A clumsy or foolish person; someone who makes a lot of mistakes.

PvE: (Gaming) Player versus environment.

PvP: (Gaming) Player versus player.

pwd: (Internet/text) Password.

pwn: (Internet/text/gaming) To thoroughly defeat someone; to make a person look bad.

pwnage: (Internet/text/gaming) To thoroughly defeat someone; to make a person look bad.

Pwnd (also "pwned" or "pwn3d"): (Internet/text/gaming) To be thoroughly defeated; to be made to look bad.

pz: (Internet/text) Peace.
pzled: (Internet/text) Puzzled.

— Q —

q33r: (Internet/text) Queer.

q4u: (Internet/text) Question for you.

qfe: (Internet/text) Quoted for emphasis.

qft: (Internet/text) Quoted for truth.

ql: (Internet/text) Cool.

qltm: (Internet/text) Quietly laughing to myself.

qna: (Internet/text) Question and answer.

qotd: (Internet/text) Quote of the day.

qoty: (Internet/text) Quote of the year.

qpr: (Internet/text) Quite pathetic really.

qpwd: (Internet/text) Quit posting while drunk.

qq: (Internet/text) Used as a representation of crying eyes.

qt: (Internet/text) Cutie.

qt3.14: (Internet/text) Cutie pie.

qte: (Internet/text) Cutie.

qtpi: (Internet/text) Cutie pie.

Quack: An incompetent doctor.

Quail: (UK) A girl; a young woman.

Quality: (Irish/US) Great; awesome.

Queen of spades: (UK) A woman who has been widowed several times.

Queen: 1) An effeminate male homosexual. 2) A female icon.

Queer Street: (UK) A strange or difficult situation.

Quick and dirty: (US) To do something quickly at the sacrifice of quality; to get a task done quickly, prioritizing speed over perfection.

Quick: (US) Clever; intelligent.

Quick-fix: (US) A fast, if temporary, solution to a problem.

Quickie: A quick sexual encounter.

Quim: (UK) A woman's genitals.

Quits: To cease an activity; to stop doing something (typically used in the phrase "to call it/something quits").

— R —

R&R: Rest and relaxation.

r: (Internet/text) Are.

Rabbit food: (UK) Vegetables; salads.

Race off: (Australian) To leave in a hurry.

Rack off: (Australian) To leave; to go away.

Rack one's brains: To try hard to recall something; to search one's memory.

Rack up: (US) To accumulate something in steady succession.

Racked-off: (Australian) Annoyed; irritated; peeved.

Racked-up: (US) Tense; agitated; worried.

Racket: A scheme, especially an illegal one.

Rad: (US) Cool; fun; fashionable.

Raddled: (UK) To be drunk or intoxicated.

Radical: (US) Awesome; impressive; fun.

Radish: (UK) An idiot; a dimwit.

Rafferty: (Australian/New Zealand) For there to be no rules in place.

Rag out: (US) To dress up; to wear one's finest clothes.

Rag week: (UK) Menstruation.

Rag: (UK) 1) A newspaper. 2) A sanitary towel. 3) To tease; to criticize. 4) To nag; to pester.

Rag-bag: (UK) A shabbily dressed person.

Rage: (US) To enjoy oneself without restraint. 2) (Australian) A rowdy party.

Ragged out: (US) 1) Smartly dressed. 2) Unpleasant.

Raggedy-arsed: (UK) Poor; shabby.

Ragging: (US) Teasing; harassing.

Rags: (US) Clothes.

Rag-top: (UK) A convertible car.

Railings: (UK) A person's teeth.

Railroad: (US) To coerce someone into doing something; to force something to happen, especially when there is opposition.

Raincoat: (UK) A condom.

Rainmaker: (US) Someone who has a reputation for generating profitable business.

Raise eyebrows: A look of surprise, shock, or disapproval.

Raise sand: (US) A fight; a ruckus.

Raise the devil: (UK) To stir up a lot of trouble.

Rake down: (US) To win at a game, especially cards.

Rake it in: (US) To earn a large amount of money.

Rake over the coals: To criticize.

Rake: 1) To search carefully and meticulously. 2) A comb.

Raker: (UK) A comb.

Ralph: (US) To vomit.

Ram: (Australian) A participant in a petty crime.

Rambo: A tough and aggressive man.

Ram-jam full: (UK) Crammed to capacity.

Rammer: (UK) The penis.

Rampage: (US) To search desperately.

Ranchy: (US) Indecent; dirty.

Rancid: (US) Dreadful; awful; sickening.

Random: (US) Out of the blue; unexpected.

Randy: (UK) Horny; lecherous.

Rank: (US) Foul-smelling; gross; disgusting.

raoflmao: (Internet/text) Rolling around on floor laughing my ass off.

Rap session: (US) A discussion; a conversation.

Rap sheet: (US) A criminal record.

Rapt: (UK) Fascinated; delighted.

Rare: (UK) An expression of agreement.

Raring to go: Very eager to do something.

Rat-arsed: (Scottish) To be drunk or intoxicated.

Rat on: To inform on somebody.

Rat out: To inform on somebody.

Rat race: The cycle of working a full-time job and feeling trapped by it.

Rat: (US) 1) An informant. 2) To inform one someone.

Rat-arsed: (UK) To be drunk or intoxicated.

Ratbag: (UK) A horrible or unlikeable person.

Ratbaggery: (Australian) Nonsense; eccentricity.

Rate: (US) To think highly of someone or something.

Rat-faced: (UK) To be drunk or intoxicated.

Rat-hole: (US) A hiding place, especially for valuables or money.

Rathole: 1) (UK) A squalid or disreputable place. 2) (Australian/New Zealand) A mental hospital.

Rat-run: (UK) Bustling commuter traffic.

Rats: (Australian) Crazy; deranged.

Ratted: (UK) To be drunk or intoxicated.

Rattle someone's cage: To aggravate or provoke someone.

Rattlebrain: (UK) A scatterbrained person.

Rattled: (UK) To be drunk or intoxicated.

Rattler: (UK) 1) A train. 2) A womanizer.

Rattletrap: (UK) A person's mouth.

Ratty: 1) (US) Scruffy; shabby; worn-out. 2) (UK) Irritated; ill-tempered.

Raunchy: Sexual, especially in a graphic way; erotic.

Rave: To be furious.

Ravers: (UK) To be furious.

Rave-up: (UK) A loud, boisterous party.

Raving: (UK) To be furious.

Raw deal: An unfair, bad, or disadvantageous outcome.

Raw meat: A potential sexual partner.

Raw prawn: (Australian) A lie; a scam; a deceitful person.

Raw: (US) Without a condom.

Rays: Sunshine.

Razz: (US/Canadian) To tease; to make fun of someone.

Razzle: (UK) An enjoyable time.

Razzle-dazzle: An exciting and showy display; a flashy style.

Razzo: (UK) A person's nose.

rb@u: (Internet/text) Right back at you.

rbau: (Internet/text) Right back at you.

rbay: (Internet/text) Right back at you.

rbtl: (Internet/text) Read between the lines.

rbty: (Internet/text) Right back to you.

rcvd: (Internet/text) Received.

rdy: (Internet/text) Ready.

re: (Internet/text) Reply.

Reach for the sky: 1) To raise one's arms above one's head. 2) To pursue one's dreams.

Reach: (US) Bribe.

Read between the lines: To understand the meaning of something that is being conveyed implicitly.

Read my lips: An order for the listener to pay close attention to what the speaker is saying; an expression that adds emphasis to a declaration.

Read the riot act: To reprimand someone severely.

Read: (US) To understand.

Ready up: (Australian) To prepare something in a manipulative way.

Ready-up: (Australian) A swindle; an act of fraud or deceit.

Reality check: A realistic reminder or examination of how things truly are.

Reality programming: (US) Television shows that showcase real-world people and situations.

Ream: (US) 1) To cheat; to scam. 2) To thoroughly defeat an opponent.

Rear up: (UK) To become angry; to lose one's temper.

Rec: (UK) A recreation ground.

Recce: (US) Reconnaissance; to scout.

Recco: (Australian) Recognition.

Recon: Reconnaissance.

Record changer: (US) Someone who does menial labor.

Recycle your lunch: (US) To vomit.

Red eye: (UK) A long overnight flight, typically without sleep.

Red ink: (UK) Cheap, low-quality red wine.

Red tape: Bureaucracy.

Red taper: (UK) A bureaucrat.

Red-hot: 1) A new and popular item. 2) (Australian) Unfair; unreasonable. 3) Extreme.

Redneck: (US) A working-class, often rustic, person with conservative political views.

Reeb: (UK) Beer.

Reef: (UK) Pickpocketing; to obtain something dishonestly.

Reefer: (US) A hand-rolled marijuana cigarette.

Ref: Referee.

Regal: (UK) Lager.

Regimental: (UK) A practice of strict discipline.

Rego: (Australian) A vehicle's registration number.

Regular guy: (US) An average, likeable person.

rehi: (Internet/text) Hello again.

Reject: A useless person; a loser.

Relo (also "rello"): (Australian) A family relative.

Rent boy: A male prostitute.

Rent-a-cop: (US) A security guard.

rents: (Internet/text) Parents.

Rep: 1) Representative. 2) Reputation.

Repo: (US) Repossession.

Reptile: (UK) A callous, unlikeable person.

Retch: (US) To vomit.

Retro: 1) Old-fashioned. 2) An old-fashioned style.

Reviver: (UK) The first alcoholic drink of the day.

Revolving door: (US) A situation where people come and go regularly.

Revved up: To be very excited about something.

rez: (Gaming) Resurrect.

rff: (Internet/text) Really fucking funny.

rflmao: (Internet/text) Rolling on the floor laughing my ass off.

rgr: (Internet/text) Roger; affirmative.

Rib: (US) To tease someone, especially playfully.

Ribby: (UK) Seedy; run-down.

Richard: 1) A detective; a private eye. 2) The penis.

Ricket: (UK) A mistake.

Ride someone's ass: (US) To be demanding of someone; to constantly give someone orders.

Ride: To have sexual intercourse.

Ridge: (Australian) Genuine; legitimate; satisfactory.

Ridgy-didge: (Australian) Genuine; legitimate; satisfactory.

Riff: A short piece of music, usually played on a guitar.

Rig: (US) A large vehicle, such as a bus or truck.

Right on: (US) An expression of agreement, approval, or happiness.

Rigid: (UK) To be drunk or intoxicated.

Ring in: (Australian/New Zealand) To deceitfully substitute something.

Ring someone's bell: To strike someone's head.

Ring: (UK) A sphincter.

Ringburner: (UK) A hot curry.

Ringer (short for "dead ringer"): 1) To look almost exactly like something or someone else. 2) (Australian) An expert.

Rinky-dink: (US) Amateurish; low quality.

rino: (Internet/text) Republican in name only.

Rio Grande: (UK) A thousand.

Rio: (UK) A thousand.

Riot: Someone who is funny and lively.

Rip off: To swindle; to cheat; to take advantage of someone.

Rip on: (US) To criticize; to make fun of someone.

Rip: (Australian) To aggravate or annoy someone.

RIP: (Internet/text) Rest in peace.

Ripe: 1) Excellent; ideal. 2) Foul smelling.

Rip-off artist: (US) A con artist; a fraudster.

Rip-off: 1) Counterfeit or stolen articles. 2) To overcharge for a product or service.

Ripped: Well-defined muscles.

Ripper: (Australian) 1) Fantastic. 2) An attractive woman.

Ripping: (UK) Brilliant; awesome.

Rise: (UK) An erection.

rite: (Internet/text) Right.

Ritzy: Luxurious; upmarket; glamorous.

rl: (Internet/text) Real life.

rly: (Internet/text) Really.

rlz: (Internet/text) Rules.

rmr: (Internet/text) Remember.

rn: (Internet/text) Right now.

Roach: (US) The butt of a marijuana cigarette.

Road pizza: A small animal that has been killed and flattened by traffic.

Roar up: (Australian) To reprimand; to chastise.

Roaring: (UK) To be drunk or intoxicated.

Roast: (US) To make fun of someone.

Rob the cradle: To have a relationship with a much younger person.

Robe: (Australian) A wardrobe.

Rock: A diamond; a jewel.

Rocket fuel: (UK) A strong alcoholic drink.

Rocket: (Scottish) 1) A crazy person. 2) An idiot.

Rockfist: (UK) A miser; someone who is stingy with their money.

Rock-head: (UK) A dim-witted person.

Rocking-horse manure: (UK) Something that is extremely rare or non-existent.

Rocking-horse shit: (UK) Something that is extremely rare or non-existent.

Rocks: Ice cubes.

Rocky: A difficult or precarious situation.

Rod: (UK) The penis.

rofalol: (Internet/text) Rolling on the floor and laughing out loud.

rofc: (Internet/text) Rolling on floor crying.

rofl: (Internet/text) Rolling on the floor laughing.

roflmao: (Internet/text) Rolling on the floor laughing my ass off.

roflol: (Internet/text) Rolling on floor laughing out loud.

Roger: 1) (Internet/text) Affirmative. 2) (UK) To have sexual intercourse.

ROI: (Finance) Return on investment.

roids: (Internet/text) Steroids.

roj: (Internet/text) Affirmative.

Roll: (UK) 1) To have sexual intercourse. 2) To rob someone, especially when they are asleep or drunk.

Roll: (US) To leave; to go.

Roller: (UK) 1) A robber who targets people who are asleep or drunk. 2) A Rolls-Royce car.

Rollick: (UK) To reprimand; to chastise.

Rollicking: (UK) 1) A severe reprimand or chastisement. 2) Exuberant and fun.

Rolling: (UK) 1) To be wealthy. 2) To be drunk or intoxicated.

Rollock: (UK) A reprimand or chastisement.

Roll-up: (UK) 1) A hand-rolled cigarette. 2) (Australian) A meeting or assembly.

Roman candle: (UK) A parachute jump where the parachute doesn't open.

Roman collar: (UK) A large head on a pint of Guinness.

Ronk: (UK) Foul smelling.

Roo: (UK) A kangaroo.

Roof: (UK) A hat.

Rook: (UK) 1) A swindler, especially someone who cheats at card games. 2) To swindle or cheat. 3) To overcharge for something.

Rookery: (UK) A fight or disturbance.

Rookie: A newcomer or novice.

Root for: To support; to hope for someone or something's success.

Root: 1) (Australian/New Zealand) To have sexual intercourse. 2) (Australian) A female sexual partner.

Rooted: (Australian) 1) To be exhausted. 2) To be defeated or broken.

Root-faced: (Australian) To look sullen or morose.

Rootin' tootin': (US) Boisterous; exuberant; rowdy and fun.

Ropeable: (Australian/New Zealand) Angry; furious.

Ropey: (UK) 1) Low quality. 2) Dubious; suspicious.

Rort: (Australian/New Zealand) A swindle or scam. 2) A rowdy party.

Rorter: (Australian/New Zealand) A con artist; a swindler.

Rorty: (UK) Rowdy; boisterous.

Rory: (UK) Poor; poverty-stricken.

Roscoe: (US) A pistol; a revolver.

Rosie: (UK) Tea.

Rosin: (UK) An alcoholic drink.

Rosiner: (Australian/Irish) A strong alcoholic drink.

Rot: (UK) Nonsense; hogwash.

rotf: (Internet/text) Rolling on the floor.

rotfl: (Internet/text) Rolling on the floor laughing.

rotflmao: (Internet/text) Rolling on the floor laughing my ass off.

rotflol: (Internet/text) Rolling on the floor laughing out loud.

Rotpot: (UK) A rascal; a scoundrel.

Rotten: 1) (British/Australian) To be drunk or intoxicated. 2) Terrible; awful.

Rotter: (UK) An unlikeable person.

rotw: (Internet/text) Rest of the world.

Rough and tumble: (UK) To have sexual intercourse.

Rough as bags: (Australian/New Zealand) Coarse; vulgar; uncouth.

Rough as guts: (Australian/New Zealand) Coarse; vulgar; uncouth.

Rough as sacks: (Australian/New Zealand) Coarse; vulgar; uncouth.

Rough house: (UK) Rowdy or rough behavior.

Rough scuff: (UK) A disreputable or coarse person.

Rough spin: (Australian) Bad luck; an unlucky outcome.

Rough up: To beat up someone.

Roughie: (Australian) A swindle; an unfair outcome.

Rough-it: To live with only the barest of essentials.

Roughneck: (US) 1) A rough or aggressive person; a thug. 2) Someone who works on an oil-well-drilling crew.

Rough-up: (UK) A fight; a brawl.

Round on: (UK) To betray or inform on someone.

Round the bend: (UK) Crazy; eccentric; deranged.

Round the twist: (UK) Crazy; eccentric; deranged.

Rounder: (US) A temporary railway worker.

Row in: (UK) To conspire with someone.

Row out: (UK) To exclude someone.

Row: (UK) A fight; an argument; a commotion.

Rowdy-dow: (UK) A commotion; an uproar.

Rowdy-dowdy: (UK) A commotion; an uproar.

rox: (Internet/text) Rocks.

Roy: (Australian) A trendy male.

Royal boozer: (UK) A person who drinks heavily.

Royal: (UK) A member of a royalty.

Rozzer: (UK) Police officer.

rp: (Internet/text/gaming) Role-play.

rpg: (Internet/text/gaming) Role-playing game.

rpita: (Internet/text) Royal pain in the ass.

rplbk: (Internet/text) Reply back.

rpo: (Internet/text) Royally pissed off.

rq: (Internet/text) Real quick.

rrb: (Internet/text) Restroom break.

rsn: (Internet/text) Real soon now.

rsp: (Internet/text/gaming) Respawn.

RT: (Social media) Retweet.

rta: (Internet/text) Read the article.

rtbq: (Internet/text) Read the blinking question.

rtf: (Internet/text) Return the favor.

rtfa: (Internet/text) Read the fucking article.

rtfp: (Internet/text) Read the fucking post.

rtfq: (Internet/text) Read The fucking question.

rtg: (Internet/text) Ready to go.

rtl: (Internet/text/gaming) Report the loss.

rtm: (Internet/text) Read the manual.

rtr: (Internet/text) Read the rules.

rtry: (Internet/text) Retry.

rts: (Internet/text/gaming) Real-time strategy.

ru: (Internet/text) Are you?

Rub down: (UK) A search by the police.

Rub out: (UK) To murder; to kill.

Rubbedy: (Australian) A pub.

Rubber boot: (UK) A condom.

Rubber cheque: (UK) A cheque that bounces when someone tries to cash it in.

Rubber Johnny: (UK) A condom.

Rubber: (UK) 1) A condom. 2) A car tire.

Rubberneck: To look back at something, especially while passing by.

Rubbish: 1) (UK) Nonsense; hogwash. 2) (Australian/New Zealand/UK) To disparage or criticize.

Rubbishing: (Australian/New Zealand/UK) An act of disparaging or criticizing.

Rubbity: (Australian) A pub.

Ruby-dazzler: (Australian/New Zealand) Exceptional; of very high quality.

Ruck on: (UK) To reject or disown someone.

Ruck: (UK) 1) To inform on someone, especially regarding illegal activity. 2) To reprimand or chastise. 3) A brawl; a physical fight.

Rucking: (UK) Brawling; fighting.

Ruddy: (UK) An expression of irritation or frustration.

Ruddy-hell: (UK) An expression of irritation or frustration.

Rude bits: (UK) A person's private parts.

Ruffles: (UK) Handcuffs.

Rug rat: (UK) A child.

Rug: (UK) A wig.

Rugcutter: (US) An avid dancer.

Rugger ball: (UK) Nothing at all.

Rugger bugger: (UK) A tough sportsman.

rugta: (Internet/text) Are you going to answer?

Ruined: (UK) To be drunk or intoxicated.

ruk: (Internet/text) Are you ok?

rukm: (Internet/text) Are you kidding me?

rul8: (Internet/text) Are you late?

Rum: (UK) Odd; strange; weird.

Rum-bum: (UK) A drunkard.

rumf: (Internet/text) Are you male or female?

Rummish: (UK) Odd; strange; weird.

Rummy: 1) (UK) Odd; strange; weird. 2) (US) A naive or gullible person.

Rump: (UK) To have sexual intercourse.

Rumpo: (UK) Sexual intercourse.

Rumpot: (UK) A person who drinks heavily.

Run into the ground: (US) To make a series of decisions that result in failure, bankruptcy, or disaster.

Run of the mill: Ordinary; average.

Run off at the mouth: (US) To be verbose; to talk a lot.

Run some off: (UK) To urinate.

Run: To leave, especially quickly.

Runaround: An evasive or indirect response.

Runner: An escape; a getaway. 2) To leave a restaurant without paying for one's meal.

Run-off: (UK) Urination.

Run-out: (UK) An escape; a getaway.

Runs: Diarrhea.

Runt: A small, unlikeable person.

ruok: (Internet/text) Are you ok?

Rupert: (UK) A man in the upper class.

rur: (Internet/text) Are you ready?

Rush: A feeling of adrenaline. 2) To ambush or assault somebody.

Russkie (also "Russky"): A Russian person.

Rust-bucket: An old, rusty car.

rut: (Internet/text) Are you there?

ryt (also "ryte"): (Internet/text) Right.

s: (Internet/text) Smile.

S&M: Sadomasochism.

s.i.t.: (Internet/text) Stay in touch.

s.o.a.b.: (Internet/text) Son of a bitch.

s.o.b.: (Internet/text) Son of a bitch.

s/b: (Internet/text) Should be.

s'pose: (Internet/text) Suppose.

s'up (also "sup"): (Internet/text) What's up?

s2a: (Internet/text) Sent to all.

s2bu: (Internet/text) Sucks to be you.

s2g: (Internet/text) Swear to god.

s2u: (Internet/text) Same to you.

s2us: (Internet/text) Speak to you soon.

s4se: (Internet/text) Sight for sore eyes.

s8ter: (Internet/text) Skater.

Sab: (UK) Sabotage.

Sack artist: (UK) A womanizer.

Sack it: (UK) An order for the listener to stop doing something.

Sack out: (US) To go to bed; to go to sleep.

Sack time: (UK) Bedtime.

Sack: 1) A bed. 2) To fire someone.

Sad sack: (US) Someone who is always depressed or miserable.

Sad sap: A pathetic person.

Sad: Pathetic.

Saddo: (UK) A lonely or dull person.

Sadie and Masie: (UK) Sadomasochism.

Safe: To practice safe sex.

safm: (Internet/text) Stay away from me.

sagn: (Internet/text) Spelling and grammar Nazi.

sah: (Internet/text) Sexy as hell.

Salad basket: (UK) A police van.
Salad dodger: (UK) An overweight person.
Salad: (UK) Money.
Salami: (US) 1) The penis. 2) An idiot; a fool.
Salt water: (UK) Tears; crying.
Salt: 1) Resentment; bitter feelings. 2) Dandruff. 3) (UK) A girl; a young woman.
Salted: (UK) To be drunk or intoxicated.
Salty: To bear a grudge; to be resentful or bitter.
Salve: (UK) Flattery; sycophancy.
Salvo: (Australian) A member of the Salvation Army.
Sammie: (Australian/New Zealand/UK) A sandwich.
Sammo: (Australian/New Zealand) A sandwich.
Sammy: (UK) A sandwich.
Sample: (UK) Urine.
Sand: (US) Bravery; courage. 2) Resolve; determination.
Sandwich: For a person or object to be squeezed between two other people or objects.
Sap: An idiot; a naive, hapless person.
Saphead: (UK) An idiot; a naive person.
Sappy: Overly sentimental.
Sass: (US) Outspoken confidence; insolence; a feisty attitude.
Sauce: (UK) Alcohol.
Sauced: (UK) To be drunk or intoxicated.
Sausage: The penis.
Sausie: (New Zealand) A sausage.
Savage: (Irish) Great; awesome.
Sax: Saxophone.
Saxa: (Australian) Saxophone.
Say goodbye to: (UK) To accept something as gone or lost.
Say goodnight to: (UK) To accept something as gone or lost.
Say what?: (US) An expression of surprise that asks the listener to repeat what they said.
Says who?: According to whose authority?
sbd: (Internet/text) Silent but deadly.

sbt: (Internet/text) Sorry about that.

Scab: (UK) Someone who breaks from an ongoing strike to return to work.

Scabbery: (Australian) To break from an ongoing strike and return to work.

Scaffolding: (UK) Braces on one's teeth.

Scald: (Irish) To chastise; to scold.

Scalder: (UK) A venereal disease.

Scaldy: (Irish) A bald person.

Scale: 1) (Australian/New Zealand) To swindle; to steal. 2) To use public transport without paying for the ride. 3) To climb up or over something.

Scaler: 1) (Australian/New Zealand) A con artist or cheat. 2) A person who uses public transport without paying for the ride.

Scally: (UK) A young, rough working-class man.

Scallywag: (UK) A rascal; a mischievous young person.

Scalp: To resell tickets for a profit.

Scalper: Someone who resells tickets for a profit.

Scalping: Reselling tickets for a profit.

Scammered: (UK) To be drunk or intoxicated.

Scamp: (UK) A rascal; a mischievous person.

Scaredy-cat: A person who is easily frightened.

Scarehead: (UK) A shocking newspaper headline.

Scarf: To eat very quickly.

Scarper: (UK) To run away; to leave quickly.

Scatterbrain: An airhead; someone who can't concentrate.

Scene: 1) A trendy activity or place. 2) A location or situation.

Schitzy: (UK) A person who seems mentally on edge (short for schizophrenic).

Schizo (also "schizzo"): A person who seems mentally on edge or unwell (short for schizophrenic).

Schlemiel: (US) Someone who is unlucky or clumsy.

Schlep: (UK) A hassle; something that is tiresome.

Schlock: (US) Low quality; a cheap, badly made product.

Schlong: (US) The penis.

Schlub: (US) Someone who is lazy or slovenly.

Schluck: (US) Someone who is clumsy.

Schlump: (UK) Someone who is slow-witted or unkempt.

Schmaltzy: Overly sentimental.

Schmo: (US) A foolish or inept person.

Schmooze: (US) To chat at a social event, especially to foster business relationships.

Schmuck: (US) A foolish or unlikeable person.

Schnozz: (US) The nose.

Schnozzle: (US) The nose.

Schoolie: (Australian) A schoolteacher.

Schtum: Silent; quiet.

Scoff: (UK) To eat, especially quickly.

Scone: (Australian/New Zealand) A person's head.

Scoop: The latest news.

Scoot: To run away; to go away; an expression to tell the listener to go away.

Scope out: (US) Investigate; reconnoiter.

Score: 1) To succeed. 2) To get something desirable. 3) To have sexual intercourse.

Scram: To run away; to leave quickly; an expression to tell the listener to go away.

Scrambled: (UK) Disordered; confused.

Scrap iron: (UK) Loose change; pocket change; a few coins.

Scrap: (UK) Loose change; pocket change; a few coins.

Scrape: (UK) 1) To shave; a shave. 2) Butter.

Scraper: (UK) A barber.

Scratch house: (UK) A cheap or low-quality hotel.

Scratch: (US) Money; cash.

Scratcher: (Irish) A scratch card.

Scratchy: (UK) An ill-tempered or overly sensitive person.

Screeve: (UK) A forged or counterfeit document.

Screever: (UK) Someone who makes forgeries.

Screw around: To behave irresponsibly. 2) To be promiscuous.

Screw loose: 1) To be crazy or eccentric. 2) To be reckless or wild.

Screw someone around: To inconvenience someone by breaking an agreement.

Screw the pooch: (US) To make a terrible mistake, especially one that cannot be rectified; to fail badly.

Screw up: To make a mistake; to blunder.

Screw: 1) To have sexual intercourse. 2) To cheat or take advantage of someone.

Screwball: A strange, eccentric, or reckless person.

Screwed: 1) (UK) To be drunk or intoxicated. 2) To be in a hopeless situation.

Screw-up: 1) Someone who always makes mistakes. 2) A delinquent; a miscreant.

Screwy: 1) (UK) To be slightly drunk; to be tipsy. 2) A crazy, eccentric, or reckless person.

Scribbler: (UK) A writer; an author.

Scrilla: (US) Money.

Scrote: (UK) An unlikeable person (derived from "scrotum").

Scrouge: (UK) To crowd; to press or squeeze.

scrt: (Internet/text) Secret.

Scrub: 1) (US) To cancel a plan or activity. 2) An inferior person.

Scrubber: 1) (Irish) A working-class woman. 2) (Australian/New Zealand) A non-professional competitor.

Scruffbag: (UK) A scruffy, unkept person.

Scruffs: (UK) Dirty or shabby clothes.

Scrumptious: (UK) Delicious; tasty.

Scrungy: (UK) Shabby; seedy.

Scuffer: (UK) A police officer.

Scuffle through: (US) To struggle to make a living.

Scuffle: (US) To earn money with difficulty.

Scumbag: A corrupt or reprehensible person; someone without morals.

Scum-sucker: (US) A reprehensible person.

Scunge: (Australian/New Zealand) 1) To borrow. 2) A shabby or pathetic person, especially one who borrows things frequently.

Scungy: (Australian) Dirty; shabby.

Scunner: (UK) A reprehensible or dishonest person.

Scunnered: (Scottish) Exhausted; worn out; tired.

Scupper: (UK) 1) To thwart; to disable. 2) To deliberately sink a ship.

Scusi: (UK) Excuse me.

Scut: (UK) An offensive person.

Scuttlebutt: (US) Gossip; rumor.

Scuz bag: (UK) A sleazy person.

Scuzz: (UK) An offensive person.

Scuzzed out: (UK) Repulsed; disgusted.

Scuzzy: (UK) Dirty; grimy.

Sea bag: (UK) A heavy artillery shell.

Sea dog: A sailor.

Sea dust: (US) Salt.

Seagull: (New Zealand) A dock laborer who doesn't belong to a union.

sec: (Internet/text) Second.

Secko: (Australian) A sex offender; a pervert.

sed: (Internet/text) Said.

Seeing-to: (UK) An assault; a physical beating.

Selfie: A photo taken by and of oneself.

Sell a dummy: (UK) To deceive; to swindle.

Sell a pup: (UK) To deceive; to swindle.

Sell out: To trade one's integrity for profits.

Sell: (UK) To deceive; to cheat.

Seller: (UK) A shop; a store.

Sellout: A person or company that has traded their integrity for profits.

Semi: (US) A partial erection.

Send up: (UK) To send someone to prison.

Sent down (also "sent up"): (UK) To be given a prison sentence.

SEO: (Internet/text) Search engine optimization.

Seppo: (Australian) An American.

Service: (UK) To have sexual intercourse.

Servo: (Australian) A gas station.

Sesh: (UK) A drinking session.

Set of wheels: (US) A motorcar.

set one back: (US) To be expensive; to cost a certain amount.

Settle for: To accept something that is less than satisfying.

Settle: To resolve a bet or grudge.

Set-to: (UK) An altercation; an argument.

Setup: A situation that was engineered to have a specific outcome.

Severe: (UK) Impressive; great.

Sew up: (UK) 1) To swindle; to cheat. 2) To exhaust; to wear out.

Sex bomb: (US) A sexually attractive person.

Sex up: To make someone or something more arousing or sexually appealing.

sexc: (Internet/text) Sexy.

Sexcapade: (US) A sexual escapade.

sexi: (Internet/text) Sexy.

sez: (Internet/text) Says.

sfao: (Internet/text) Sorry for any offense.

sfsg: (Internet/text) So far so good.

sfu: (Internet/text) Shut the fuck up.

sfw: (Internet/text) Safe for work.

sfy: (Internet/text) Speak for yourself.

sfyl: (Internet/text) Sorry for your loss.

sg: (Internet/text) So good.

Shack-up: To live with a romantic partner, especially outside of marriage.

Shade: (US) Contempt; disrespect (often used in the phrase "throw shade").

Shades: Sunglasses.

Shady: Of dubious legality.

Shaft: 1) To treat someone unfairly or badly. 2) The penis.

Shafted: (UK) To be treated unfairly or badly.

Shag: (UK) To have sexual intercourse.

Shagged: (UK) Exhausted; worn out.

Shagging wagon: (UK/Australian) A car used for dating or having sex in.

Shagnasty: (UK) An unlikeable man.

Shake down: (US) To extort someone, especially for money or information.

Shake it: (US) To hurry up.

Shamed-up: (UK) To be disgraced or humiliated.

Shanghai: 1) (UK) To trick or force someone into doing something. 2) (Australian/New Zealand) To launch with a catapult.

Shank: 1) A homemade knife. 2) To stab.

Shape up or ship out: (US) To perform at an acceptable standard or quit.

Shape up: (US) To improve; to stop behaving irresponsibly.

Sharp: (UK) 1) Smart; clever. 2) Fashionable; well-groomed, especially in describing men.

Shattered: (Irish) Exhausted; worn out; very tired.

Shaver: (UK) A man.

Shawl: (Irish) A prostitute.

shd: (Internet/text) Should.

Shebang: (UK) A whole set of circumstances; a situation taken as a whole.

Sheep-dip: (UK) A cheap alcoholic drink.

Sheila: (Australian) A woman.

Shekels: (UK) Money.

Shelf: (Australian) 1) To inform on someone. 2) An informant.

Shell: (US) A bullet.

Shellac (also "shellack"): (US) To defeat thoroughly.

Shemozzle: (UK) 1) A muddled situation. 2) A brawl or altercation.

Sherry: (UK) To run away.

Shicker: (Australian/New Zealand) 1) An alcoholic drink. 2) To be drunk or intoxicated.

Shickered: (Australian/New Zealand) To be drunk or intoxicated.

Shift: To move something quickly, especially goods.

Shifting: (Irish) Kissing.

Shill: An accomplice of a swindler or hawker who helps draw in customers.

Shim-sham: (US) Nervousness; anxiety.

Shindig: A party.

Shindy: (UK) A riot; a disturbance.

Shiner: A black eye.

Shin-plaster: (US/Australian) A low-value bank note.

Ship out: (US) To depart, especially for military service.

Shirty: To be angry; to be ill-tempered.

Shit a brick: To be scared.

Shit on: To criticize severely; to reprimand harshly.

Shit or get off the pot: To stop hesitating and make a decision or take some action.

Shitfaced: To be drunk or intoxicated.

Shit-list: (US) A list of people one has grudges against.

Shit-stirrer: Someone who deliberately causes trouble for others.

Shiv: 1) A knife. 2) To stab.

Shlep: 1) A hassle; something that is tedious or wearisome. 2) To carry or move something.

Shlock: (US) Of inferior quality; cheap goods.

Shlub: (US) A useless person; an oaf.

Shmarmy: (UK) Smarmy; smug; ingratiating behavior.

Shmeg: (UK) A fool; an idiot.

shmexy: (Internet/text) Sexy.

shmily: (Internet/text) See how much I love you.

Shmo: (UK) A naive or foolish person.

Shmooze: (US) To start conversations, especially at social events, for the purpose of networking and building business relationships.

sho: (Internet/text) Sure.

Shoddy dropper: (Australian/New Zealand) A seller of low-quality or knock-off clothing.

Shoo-in: (US) A certainty; a sure thing.

Shoot one's mouth off: (US) To boast; to talk indiscreetly.

Shoot the breeze: (US/Canadian) To chat about trivial matters.

Shoot the bull: (US/Canadian) To chat about trivial matters.

Shoot the shit: (US) To chat about trivial matters.

Shoot through: (Australian) To disappear; to leave.

Shoot up: To inject an illicit drug.

Shooter: 1) (UK) A firearm; a gun. 2) A small alcoholic drink intended to be swallowed in one gulp.

Shooting iron: (US) A firearm; a gun.

Shopper: (UK) An informant.

Shoppy: (UK) A shop assistant.

Short and curlies: Pubic hair.

Short hairs: Pubic hair.

Short of a sheet: (UK) Crazy; eccentric.

Short out: (US) To get angry; to lose one's temper.

Short: To have insufficient money.

Short-arse: (UK) A short person.

Short-change: To swindle; to treat someone unfairly.

Short-house: (UK) A short person.

Short-stuff: A short person.

Shot down: To be rejected, especially when flirting.

Shot stopper: (UK) A condom.

Shot: 1) Exhausted; in bad condition. 2) To be drunk or intoxicated. 3) An injection.

Shotgun: (US) To drink a whole can of beer in one go, especially through a hole in the side or bottom.

Shoulder: To bear a burden or responsibility.

Shouse: (Australian) An outhouse.

Shout at your shoes: (US) To vomit.

Shout out: (US) To promote or give recognition to someone or something on a public platform.

Shout: (Australian) To vomit.

Shove it: (US) An expression to convey that one will not do or accept something.

Shove off: (UK) A rude order for the listener to go away.

Show one's studs: (UK) To be ruthless or callous.

Showbiz: Show business; the entertainment industry.

Showboat: (US) A boastful person; someone who likes to show off their capabilities.

Show-off: A boastful person; someone who likes to show off their capabilities.

Shrapnel: (UK) Small change; pocket change.

Shred: (UK) To defeat thoroughly.

Shreddies: (UK) Tattered underwear.

Shrewd-head: (Australian/New Zealand) A cunning or sly person.

Shrewdie: (Australian/New Zealand) A cunning or sly person.

Shrink: A psychiatrist.

Shrubbery: (UK) Pubic hair.

shtf: (Internet/text) Shit hits the fan.

Shtick: An attention-getting gimmick; a person's go-to talent.

Shtoom: (UK) Silent; non-communicative.

Shtum: (UK) Silent; non-communicative.

Shtup: (UK) 1) Push. 2) To have sexual intercourse.

Shuck: (UK) To cheat or swindle someone.

shud: (Internet/text) Should.

shuddup: (Internet/text) Shut up.

Shufflebutt: (UK) A fretful, fidgety person.

Shush: An order for the listener to be quiet.

Shut it: (US) An order for the listener to stop talking.

Shut up: An order for the listener to stop talking.

Shut your face: (US) An order for the listener to stop talking.

Shut-eye: (US) Sleep.

sic: (Internet/text) Said in context.

Sick: (US) Impressive; cool; fashionable.

Sickie: (UK) A day off work owing to being sick.

Sicko: 1) A mentally ill, often dangerous, person. 2) A pervert.

sicl: (Internet/text) Sitting in chair laughing.

Sidley: (UK) Furtive; stealthy.

Sieve-head: (UK) A very forgetful person.

sif: (Internet/text) As if.

sig: (Internet/text) Signature.

Sight: (Australian) To observe; to tolerate.

Sign on: (US) To be a willing participant; to agree with something.

Sign up: (US) To agree to participate in something.

Silent cop: (Australian) A traffic-management marker embedded in the middle of a road or crossroads.

Silly house: (UK) A mental hospital.

Silly money: (UK) A ludicrous amount of money.

Silly moo: (UK) A foolish woman.

Silo: (UK) An asylum seeker.

Silvertail: (Australian/New Zealand) A wealthy and influential person.

simcl: (Internet/text) Sitting in my chair laughing.

Simp: (US) Someone who is desperate for the affections of a particular person.

Simpatico: 1) Compatible; agreeable. 2) Likeable.

Sin bin: (US) A holding area for players who have committed fouls that require temporarily removing them from the field of play.

Sing to the sink: (US) To vomit in a basin or sink.

Sing: To confess; to reveal secret or privileged information.

Singer: (UK) An informant.
Singleton: (UK) A single person.
siol: (Internet/text) Shout it out loud.
Sir Lancelot: (UK) A womanizer.
Sir Paul: (UK) A condom.
Sis: Sister.
Sissy: A cowardly or effeminate man.
sista: (Internet/text) Sister.
Sit tight: To wait patiently.
sitd: (Internet/text) Still in the dark.
Sit-down job: (UK) Defecation.
sitmf: (Internet/text) Say it to my face.
Sitting pretty: (US) To be in a good or advantageous position, especially financially.
siu: (Internet/text) Suck it up.
Sixer: (UK) A prison sentence of six months.
Six-pack: 1) Well-defined stomach muscles. 2) A pack of six cans of beer.
sk: (Internet/text/gaming) Spawn kill.
sk8: (Internet/text) Skate.
sk8er: (Internet/text) Skater.
sk8ing: (Internet/text) Skating.
Skank: (US) A promiscuous woman.
Skanky: 1) Seedy; dirty; unattractive. 2) Promiscuous behavior.
Skate: (US) To put in the least amount of effort necessary.
skb: (Internet/text) Should know better.
Skedaddle: To run away; to leave quickly.
Sketch: (UK) A tiny amount; a drop.
skewl: (Internet/text) School.
Skid artist: (UK) A talented getaway driver.
Skids: (UK) In a bad state; failing (often used in the phrase "on the skids").
skillz: (Internet/text) Skills.
Skin game: (UK) A swindle.
Skin out: (US) To abscond; to flee.
Skinny: (US) Information.
Skinny-dip: To swim nude.

Skint: (UK) Having little to no money.

Skip bail: To flee from sentencing while out on bail.

Skirt: (UK) A woman, especially a young, attractive one.

Skite: (Australian) Boasting; bragging.

Skive: (UK) To shirk one's duties or responsibilities.

Skiver: (UK) Someone who shirks their duties or responsibilities; an idle person.

Skivvies: (UK) Underwear.

skl: (Internet/text) School.

Skosh: (US) A little bit; a small amount.

Skulled: (UK) To be drunk or intoxicated.

Skunky: (UK) Foul smelling.

skwl: (Internet/text) School.

Sky the wipe: (Australian) To give up; to surrender.

Skyer: (UK) A pickpocket.

Skyman: (UK) A pickpocket.

sl4n: (Internet/text) So long for now.

Slab: (Australian) A carton of beers.

Slack jaw: (US) Impudent talk.

Slag down: (UK) To chastise; to reprimand.

Slag off: (UK) To criticize; to speak ill of someone.

Slag: (Irish) To make fun of someone or something.

Slag: (UK) 1) A promiscuous woman. 2) An unlikeable man. 3) To criticize; to denigrate. 4) (Australian) To spit.

Slagger: (UK) A critic; a reviewer.

Slagging: (Irish) To make fun of something or someone.

Slam: To criticize harshly.

Slammed: (UK) To be drunk or intoxicated.

Slammer: Prison; jail.

Slap-and-tickle: (UK) Heavy petting; amorous activity.

Slap-head: (UK) A bald person.

Slapper: (UK) A promiscuous woman; a prostitute.

Slash: (UK) To urinate.

Slasher (movie): (US) A horror movie where a serial killer primarily uses a knife.

Slate: To criticize harshly.

Slather: (US) 1) To defeat an opponent thoroughly. 2) To chastise.

Slaughter: To defeat an opponent thoroughly.

Slaughtered: (UK) To be drunk or intoxicated.

Slave market: (UK) An employment exchange.

Slay: 1) To impress. 2) To succeed or do something brilliantly.

Sleaze: An immoral, disreputable person.

Sleazebag: An immoral, disreputable person.

Sleazeball: An immoral, disreputable person.

Sleazebucket: An immoral, disreputable person.

Sleazy: Disreputable; seedy; immoral.

Sledgehammer: A lack of subtlety, grace, or tact.

Sleep with someone: To have sexual intercourse with someone.

Sleeper: (US) Someone (often an undercover agent) whose identity and activities are being kept secret.

Sleeping policeman: (UK) A speed bump to slow down traffic.

Slewed: (UK) To be drunk or intoxicated.

Slick: (US) Trendy; cool; fashionable; stylish.

Slickster: (US) A con artist; a swindler.

Slimebag: A despicable, often immoral, person.

Slimeball: A despicable, often immoral, person.

Slimebucket: A despicable, often immoral, person.

Sling your hook: (UK) An expression that tells the listener to go away.

Slingers: (UK) Bread soaked in tea.

Slip a length: (UK) To have sexual intercourse.

Slip into: (UK) To attack; to assault.

Slip it to someone: (UK) To have sexual intercourse with someone.

Slip one over on: (UK) To deceive; to trick; to swindle.

slo: (Internet/text) Slow.

Slob: A slovenly, often overweight, person.

Slog one's guts out: (UK) To work very hard.

Slo-mo: Slow motion.

Slope off: (UK) To leave, especially quietly or discreetly.

Slops: (US/Australian) Beer.

slos: (Internet/text) Someone looking over shoulder.

Sloshed: (UK) To be drunk or intoxicated.

Slosher: (UK) A losing bet.

Slowmo: (UK) An idle, slow-moving person.

Slowpoke: An idle, slow-moving person; someone who drives very slowly.

slt: (Internet/text) Something like that.

Slug it out: (US) To fight; to brawl, especially to resolve a dispute or grudge.

Slug: (Australian) To charge excessively for something.

Slugfest: (UK) A long boxing match, where the opponents trade a lot of punches.

Sluice one's gob: (UK) To drink, especially alcohol.

Sluice the throat: (UK) To drink, especially alcohol.

Slummock: (UK) An unkempt, lazy person.

Slushy: (Australian) An inexperienced kitchen assistant.

Sly: (Australian/New Zealand) Illicit; forbidden.

SM: (Internet/text) Social media.

sm1: (Internet/text) Someone.

Small fry: (US) An insignificant person; someone without much power or influence.

Small potatoes: (UK) A small amount of something, especially money.

Small-time: (UK) Unimportant; minor; insignificant. The lower ranks of an industry or profession.

Smarmite: (UK) A smarmy, obsequious person.

Smarmy: (UK) Obsequious; fawning.

Smart-arse: (UK) Someone who behaves as if they know everything; a person who is arrogant in regard to their intelligence.

Smart-ass: (US) Someone who behaves as if they know everything; a person who is arrogant in regard to their intelligence.

Smartmouth: (US) To speak cheekily or disrespectfully.

Smarts: (UK) Intelligence; know-how; wits.

Smarty pants: (US) An intelligent person.

Smash: (US) A boisterous party.

Smashed: (UK) To be drunk or intoxicated.

Smasher: (UK) Something that is exceptional or remarkable.

Smashing: (UK) Great; awesome; excellent.

Smear: 1) (US) To defeat an opponent thoroughly. 2) To denigrate; to disparage.

Smeg: (UK) An idiot; a fool; an unlikeable person.

Smeggy: (UK) Awful; unpleasant; unsavory.

Smeg-head: (UK) An idiot; an unlikeable person.

Smeller: (UK) 1) The nose. 2) A strike to the nose.

smexy: (Internet/text) Sexy.

smh: (Internet/text) Shaking my head.

smho: (Internet/text) Screaming my head off.

Smidge: (UK) A very small amount.

Smidgen: (UK) A very small amount.

Smoke-ho: (Australian/New Zealand) A short work break.

Smoke-o: (Australian/New Zealand) A short work break.

Smoker: (UK) An old, worn-out car.

Smoko: (Australian) A short work break.

Smoko: (Australian) A smoke break.

Smooch: Kiss.

Smoothie: (UK) A charming, suave person.

Smother: (UK) An overcoat.

smthin: (Internet/text) Something.

smtm: (Internet/text) Sometime.

smto: (Internet/text) Sticking my tongue out.

smtoay: (Internet/text) Sticking my tongue out at you.

Smugged: (UK) To be arrested.

Smush: (UK) A person's mouth.

sn: (Internet/text) Screen name.

Snack: (Australian) Something that is easy or simple to achieve.

Snafu: A confused or disorderly situation.

Snags: (New Zealand) Sausages.

Snail: (UK) A very slow driver.

Snail-mail: (UK) The ordinary postal system.

Snake eyes: (US) The result of rolling two ones with a pair of dice.

Snake in the grass: (UK) An informant; a betrayer.

Snake juice: (Australian) A strong alcoholic drink.

Snakes: (Australian) 1) To urinate. 2) A toilet.

Snaky: (Australian/New Zealand) To be angry or ill-tempered.

Snap: (US) 1) An easy or simple task. 2) To do something quickly.

Snappers: (UK) Dentures; false teeth.

Snappy: (UK) Neat and stylish.

Snaps: (UK) Handcuffs.

Snarf: (US) To eat or drink very quickly or messily.

Snarler: 1) (Australian) A discharge. 2) (New Zealand) A sausage.

Snatch it: (Australian) To resign and take one's outstanding wages.

Snatch one's time: (Australian) To resign and take one's outstanding wages.

Snatch: (UK) The vagina.

Snazz: (UK) Showiness; glamor; pizzazz.

Snazzed-up: (UK) Made to look showy and elegant.

Snazzy: (UK) Attractive and fashionable; stylish.

Sneak: (UK) An informant.

Sneeze chunks: (US) To vomit.

snek: (Internet/text) Snake.

snf: (Internet/text) So not fair.

Sniffer: (UK) The nose.

Snifty: (US) Haughty; condescending.

Snip: (UK) A small, often annoying, person.

Snipe: (US) To criticize; to insult.

Snipes: (UK) Scissors.

Snippy: (UK) Curt; critical in an ill-tempered way.

Snips: (UK) Scissors.

Snit: 1) (UK) A small, unlikeable person. 2) (US) A sulk; a state of irritation.

Snitch: To inform on someone.

snm: (Internet/text) Say no more.

Snob: A pretentious person.

Snockered: (UK) To be drunk or intoxicated.

Snodger: (Australian/New Zealand) Excellent; fantastic; great.

Snog: (UK) To kiss romantically.

Snookered: (UK) To be outmaneuvered; to be thwarted.

Snoot: (UK) 1) The nose. 2) A haughty person.

Snooty: (UK) Haughty; supercilious.
Snooze: 1) Someone or something that is boring. 2) To sleep.
Snorkers: (UK) Sausages.
Snorter: (UK) 1) The nose. 2) A person or situation that is absurd.
Snot groveller: (UK) An obsequious person.
Snot rag: (UK) A handkerchief.
Snotnose: (UK) An unlikeable, often obsequious, person.
Snotty: Haughty; conceited; pretentious, especially in a way that is critical of others.
Snout: (UK) The nose.
Snout-face: (UK) An unlikeable person.
Snow job: A deception; a manipulation, especially for the purpose of persuading someone.
Snow out: (UK) To lose consciousness; to be become lost.
Snowball: (UK) To deceive; to swindle.
Snowball's chance in hell: A situation or outcome that is impossible.
Snowdropper: (UK) A thief who steals clothing from washing lines.
Snowman: (US) A con artist.
Snozz: (UK) The nose.
Snozzle: (UK) The nose.
Snub: To deliberately ignore someone.
Snubs: (UK) Indifference; disdain.
Snuff it: (UK) To die.
Snuff out: To kill; to murder. 2) To extinguish, especially a small flame.
Snuff: (UK) To kill; to murder.
Snuggle: (UK) A bed.
So what?: An expression that conveys the speaker's indifference.
soab: (Internet/text) Son of a bitch.
Soak: 1) (US/Canadian) To overcharge for something. 2) To stay in water for a long time; to take a long bath.
Soaked: (UK) To be drunk or intoxicated.
Soaker: (UK) A heavy drinker.
So-and-so: (UK) A person whose name has slipped the speaker's mind, or who is unimportant to the story being told.
Soap: A soap opera.

Soap-dodger: (UK) A dirty, unkempt person.

sob: (Internet/text) Son of a bitch.

soc: (Internet/text) Same old crap.

Sock puppet: (US) Someone who doesn't think for themselves.

Socked in: (US/Canadian) An airport that is closed owing to bad weather conditions.

Socking: (UK) Very; extremely.

Socko: (UK) Highly successful or effective.

Sod off: (UK) A rude expression that orders the listener to go away.

Sod: (UK) An unlikeable person.

Sod-all: (UK) Nothing at all.

Sodden: (UK) To be drunk or intoxicated.

Sodding: (UK) Very; extremely.

sof: (Internet/text) Smile on face.

Sofa loafer: (UK) An idle person.

sofas: (Internet/text) Stepping out for a smoke.

Soft in the head: To be slow-witted; to be foolish.

Soft: To be overly lenient or sentimental.

Softshoe: (UK) To move or act cautiously or quietly.

Softy: An overly lenient or sentimental person.

Soggies: (UK) Breakfast cereal.

Soggy: (UK) A feeble, incapable person.

sok (also "s'ok"): (Internet/text) It's okay.

sokay: (Internet/text) It's okay.

Sold on: To be convinced of something, especially an idea or plan of action.

Solid: Excellent; reliable.

Sollicker: (Australian) Very large; massive.

some1: (Internet/text) Someone.

Somebody: An important or influential person.

Something else: A person of thing that is exceptional or which defies one's expectations.

soml: (Internet/text) Story of my life.

Son of a gun: A rascal; a scoundrel.

Song and dance: (UK) A fuss; a commotion; a performance.

Sook: (Australian) A crybaby; someone who is overly emotional.

Sooky: (Australian) Sulky; overly sentimental.

sop: (Internet/text) Same old place.

Soppy: Overly sentimental.

Sore: (US) Angry; peeved; offended.

sorreh: (Internet/text) Sorry.

Sort out: To resolve; to settle a dispute or situation.

sorta: (Internet/text) Sort of.

Sorted: (UK) 1) Brilliant. 2) Resolved; taken care of.

Sossie: (New Zealand) Sausage.

Sound on: (US) 1) To criticize; to provoke. 2) To offer an opinion.

Soup strainer: (UK) A moustache, especially a bushy one.

Soup up: To enhance or augment the performance of something.

Souse: (UK) A drunkard.

Soused: (UK) To be drunk or intoxicated.

Sow one's wild oats: To have adventures in one's youth; to have several romantic partners before settling down in a long-term relationship.

Sow: (UK) An unlikeable woman.

sowwy: (Internet/text) A baby-talk variant of "sorry."

Soz: (Internet/text) Sorry.

Sozzled: (UK) To be drunk or intoxicated.

Space out: To daydream; to lose focus.

Spacey: Dreamlike; calm and ethereal.

Spacy: Someone who lacks focus or daydreams a lot.

Spam: 1) Unsolicited mail. 2) To keep posting the message in a forum or thread.

Spank the monkey: To masturbate.

Spanking: 1) A beating. 2) A thorough defeat.

Spanner: (UK) An attractive woman.

Spare tyre: (UK) The loose fat around one's midriff.

Spare: (UK) 1) A single woman. 2) To be out of control; to be furious.

Spark out: (UK) To lose consciousness; to pass out.

Sparkler: (UK) A lie; a deception.

Sparrow brain: (UK) An idiot; a fool.

Spear: (Australian) To fire someone.

Special: (Australian) A convict who receives special treatment owing to their profile.

Specs: Spectacles.

Speeler: (Australian) A fast horse.

Spelunker: (US) A person who explores caves.

Spew: To vomit.

Spiel: (UK) A long-winded or glib speech, especially by a salesperson.

Spieler: (Australian/New Zealand) A swindler; a card sharp.

Spiffed: (UK) To be drunk or intoxicated.

Spiffing: (UK) Fantastic; great; excellent.

Spiffy: (UK) Stylish; smartly dressed.

Spill one's guts: To confess; to reveal all of one's secrets.

Spill the beans: To confess; to reveal a secret.

Spill the groceries: (US) To vomit.

Spill: To reveal a secret.

Spin: To misrepresent or manipulate a story or the perception of something.

Spinach: (UK) Banknotes.

Spine-basher: (Australian) An idle or lazy person.

Spit and sawdust: (UK) A public bar; a simple, modest-looking bar.

Spit cheese: (US) To vomit.

Spit chips: (Australian) To be furious.

Spit tacks: (Australian) To be furious.

Spitball: (US) To share ideas for discussion.

Spit-spot: (UK) Excellent; superb; perfect.

Spitting feathers: (UK) To be very thirsty.

spk: (Internet/text) Speak.

Splash the boots: (UK) To urinate.

Spliced: (UK) To be married.

Spliff: A marijuana cigarette.

Splurge: To spend a lot of money, especially on an indulgence.

Sponge: (UK) A heavy drinker.

Sponk: (UK) Infatuated; smitten.

Spook: (US) A spy; an undercover agent.

Spooked: To be frightened or made uneasy by something, especially if the threat isn't obvious.

Spoon: To cuddle someone from behind, especially while lying down.
Spout off: To talk nonsense.
Spring for: (US) To quickly volunteer to do something.
Sprinkle: (UK) To urinate.
Sprog: (UK) A baby; a child.
Sprogged up: (UK) To be pregnant.
Sprout: (UK) A young child.
Spruce: (UK) To look neat and trim; to look dapper.
Sprucer: (UK)A swindler; someone who exaggerates the truth.
Sprung: (UK) To be tipsy or drunk.
Spud barber: (UK) A person who peels potatoes.
Spud: (UK) 1) A potato. 2) An unattractive person. 3) A hole that has formed in the heel of a sock.
Spud-bashing: (UK) Peeling potatoes as a punishment.
Spunk rat: (Australian) An attractive young person, especially one who is sexually active.
Spunky: Feisty; spirited.
Spurt: (UK) A small amount of something.
sqtm: (Internet/text) Snickering quietly to myself.
Square off: (Australian) To apologize; to pacify; to placate.
Square: Conventional; conservative; old-fashioned.
Squarehead: (UK) A boring or old-fashioned person.
Squashed: (US) To be drunk or intoxicated.
Squat: (US) Nothing at all.
Squeak: (UK) To inform on others.
Squeaker: (UK) An informant.
Squeal: (UK) To inform on others.
Squealer: (UK) An informant.
Squeamish: To be easily nauseated.
Squeeze the lemon: (UK) To urinate.
Squeeze: (US) A girlfriend.
Squib: (Australian/New Zealand) A coward.
Squiff: (Australian) 1) A drunkard. 2) A drinking session.
Squiffed: (UK) To be tipsy or drunk.
Squiffy: (UK) To be tipsy or drunk.

Squiggle: (UK) A signature.

Squillion: (UK) A massive amount; an unthinkably large number.

Squirly: (US) To be fidgety or restless.

Squirrel-food: (UK) To be crazy or eccentric.

Squirt: A small person, especially a child or someone much younger than the speaker.

Squit: (UK) 1) Nonsense. 2) An insignificant person.

Squits: (UK) Diarrhea.

Squitters: (UK) Diarrhea.

Squiz: (Australian/New Zealand/South Africa) To take a curious or inquiring look at something.

Squizzed: (US) To be tipsy or drunk.

srly: (Internet/text) Seriously.

srry: (Internet/text) Sorry.

srs: (Internet/text) Serious.

srsly: (Internet/text) Seriously.

ss: (Internet/text) Screenshot.

ssia: (Internet/text) Subject says it all.

ssry: (Internet/text) So sorry.

Stacked: For a woman to have large breasts.

Stag dance: (US) A dance that is only by men.

Stag party: (US) A social gathering or party of only men, especially to celebrate a bachelor's impending wedding.

Stag: (UK) An informant.

Stagger juice: (Australian) An alcoholic drink, especially a strong one.

Stalk fever: (Australian) Lust; desire.

Stall the ball: (Irish) An expression that asks the listener to wait for a moment or pause what they're saying.

Stallion: A man who is very sexually active; a man with a reputation for being a good sexual partner.

Stamp: (UK) A person's appearance, especially in regard to their overall build.

Stampers: (UK) 1) Shoes. 2) A person's feet.

Stand one's corner: (UK) To contribute one's fair share for something, especially money.

Stand still for: (UK) To tolerate something.
Stand the broads: (UK) To be deceived or swindled.
Stand the three-card trick: (UK) To be easily swindled.
Standers: (UK) Legs.
Stand-over man: (Australian) A person who extorts others, especially through the use of threats.
Stand-up: 1) To arrange to meet someone, especially for a date, and then fail to go without informing that person you won't be there. 2) A comedian.
Starkers: (UK) Totally naked.
Starko: (UK) Totally naked.
Starve the crows: (Australian) An expression of astonishment or surprise.
Starver: (Australian) A saveloy.
Stash: 1) To hide something. 2) A hidden or private store of something.
Stats: Statistics.
stb: (Internet/text) Soon to be.
stbm: (Internet/text) Sucks to be me.
stbx: (Internet/text) Soon to be ex.
stby: (Internet/text) Sucks to be you.
STD: (Internet/text) Sexually transmitted disease.
Steal: A bargain; something that was much cheaper to obtain than it usually is.
Steam in: (UK) To rush in to participate, especially regarding an altercation or brawl.
Steam up: (UK) 1) To excite. 2) To anger or irritate.
Steamboats: (UK) To be drunk or intoxicated.
Steamed up: 1) To be drunk or intoxicated. 2) To be furious.
Steamed: 1) To be drunk or intoxicated. 2) To be furious.
Steamin': (Scottish) To be drunk or intoxicated.
Steaming: 1) To be drunk or intoxicated. 2) To be furious. 3) Very; extremely.
Steamroller: Someone who insists on their ideas or courses of action being implemented, without considering other opinions.
Steamy: Lewd; sexual; erotic.
Steep: Excessive; disproportionate.

Steerer: (US) A swindler's accomplice who helps draw unsuspecting people into the scam.

Step off: (US) An expression that tells the listener to move away from the speaker, or for the listener to stop being confrontational.

Stew: (UK) An alcoholic drink.

Stewed: (UK) To be drunk or intoxicated.

stfu: (Internet/text) Shut the fuck up.

stg: (Internet/text) Swear to god.

sth: (Internet/text) Something.

sthing: (Internet/text) Something.

sthu: (Internet/text) Shut the hell up.

Stick around: To stay in a location for a bit longer.

Stick in the mud: An unadventurous person; someone who resists change and is often considered boring as a result.

Stick one on: (UK) To punch or hit.

Stick: To stab.

Sticks: (UK) Wickets (in cricket); cricket stumps.

Stick-up: To mug or rob, especially with the use of a weapon.

Sticky: A tricky or awkward situation.

Sticky-beak: (Australian) A nosy or meddlesome person.

Sticky-fingered: To be a habitual thief.

Stiff: 1) A human corpse, especially of a person who is recently deceased. 2) To cheat or treat someone unfairly. 3) Strong; powerful. 4) A very conventional, boring person. 5) (Australian) Unlucky.

Stiffener: (UK) An alcoholic drink to strengthen one's nerves.

Stiffy: An erection.

Stilts: (UK) Long legs.

Sting: A law-enforcement operation to catch criminals, especially using undercover officers to infiltrate the criminal group.

Stink: A fuss; a commotion about something.

Stinker: 1) An unlikeable person. 2) A poor performance. 3) Something that is unpleasant.

Stinking rich: Extremely wealthy.

Stinkpot: (UK) A foul-smelling person or thing.

Stinks: 1) For something to be suspicious. 2) For something to be unfair.

Stir-crazy: For someone to be mentally disturbed, especially as a result of being confined somewhere for a long time.

Stirrer: (UK) A troublemaker; an agitator.

stm: (Internet/text) Smiling to myself.

Stocking fillers: (UK) A woman's legs.

Stodge: (UK) Food.

Stogie: (US) A cigar.

Stoked: To be happy or pleased about something.

Stomp on: (UK) To assault; to physically attack.

Stomp: To assault; to physically attack.

Stone end: (Australian) An unbearable situation; an insufferable place.

Stone finish: (Australian) An unbearable situation; an insufferable place.

Stone ginger: (UK) A certainty; a sure thing.

Stone-broke: (US/Canadian) To be without money; to be poverty-stricken.

Stoned: To be intoxicated, especially by marijuana.

Stonefaced: To not reveal any emotion on one's face.

Stones: (UK) 1) Testicles. 2) Bravery; courage.

Stonkered: (UK) 1) To be drunk or intoxicated. 2) To be worn out or exhausted.

Stooge: A subordinate who is used to do menial or unpleasant work.

Stool pigeon: (US) Someone who acts as a decoy.

Stoolie: (US) An informant, especially for the police.

stoopid: (Internet/text) Stupid.

Stop one: (UK) To be shot by a bullet.

Stop one's clock: To kill someone.

Stop the clock: 1) To counting time, especially in a sport or game. 2) To stop the passage of time.

Stop ticking: (UK) To die.

Stoppo: (UK) A rest or break, especially from work.

Storming: (UK) Excellent; brilliant.

Story: 1) An excuse; a lie. 2) An exaggerated account.

Stotter: (Scottish) To stumble.

Stoush: (Australian/New Zealand) 1) To hit; to punch. 2) A brawl; a fight.

stpd: (Internet/text) Stupid.

str8: (Internet/text) Straight.

str8up: (Internet/text) Straight up.

Strafe: (UK) To punish someone severely.

Straight arrow: (US) An honest and upstanding person.

Straight: 1) Heterosexual. 2) An unmixed or undiluted liquid, especially an alcoholic drink. 3) To live a sober lifestyle; to not use illicit drugs. 4) Trustworthy. 5) Satisfactory; good. 6) Fair; even; equal.

Straighten out: To rectify.

Straight-shooter: (US) A frank, straightforward person.

Straight-up: (US) Truly; exactly.

Strain off: (UK) To urinate.

Strain the potatoes: (Australian/New Zealand) To urinate.

Strangler: (UK) A necktie.

Strap: (Irish) A promiscuous woman.

Strap-on: A strap-on sex toy.

Strapped for cash: (US) To be lacking money.

Strapped: (US) To be lacking something.

Straw basher: (UK/South African) A straw hat.

Straya: (Australian) Australia.

Streak: To run naked in public.

Streaker: (UK) A person who runs naked in public.

Street smarts: (US) Practical knowledge that helps one survive and flourish in an urban environment.

Street-smart: (US) To be knowledgeable about how to survive and flourish in an urban environment.

Streetwise: (US) To be knowledgeable about how to survive and flourish in an urban environment.

Stretch: A prison sentence of one year. 2) A tall and thin person.

Stretcher: (Australian/New Zealand) 1) A camp bed. 2) An exaggeration; a falsehood.

Strike it rich: (US) To make a huge profit.

Striker: (UK) A match.

Stringbean: (UK) A tall and thin person.

Stripe up: (UK) To swindle; to cheat.

Stripe: (UK) A police car.

Striped: (UK) To be swindled or cheated.

Strong it: (UK) 1) To act aggressively. 2) To exaggerate.

Strong: (Australian) The truth.

Stroppy: (UK) Irritable; ill-tempered.

Strung out: 1) To be stressed and anxious. 2) To be distressed, especially while under the influence of an illicit drug.

sts: (Internet/text) So to speak.

stsp: (Internet/text) Same time, same place.

stt: (Internet/text) Same time tomorrow.

Stubbies: (New Zealand) Short shorts.

Stubby: (Australian) A small bottle of beer.

Stuck on: To infatuated or obsessed with someone or something.

Stuck-up: (UK) Snobbish and aloof; conceited.

Stud: (UK) 1) A sexually attractive man. 2) A masculine lesbian.

Stuff it: A rude order for the listener to be quiet.

Stuffed: 1) To be broken. 2) To have eaten too much.

Stump it: (UK) To flee; to run away.

Stumps: (UK) The legs.

Stung: (Australian) To be drunk or intoxicated.

Stunned: (Australian/New Zealand) To be drunk.

stw: (Internet/text) Share the wealth.

stys: (Internet/text) Speak to you soon.

Subbie (also "subby"): (UK) A subcontractor.

Suck face: (US) To make out with someone; to kiss romantically.

Suck in: (UK) To swindle; to defraud.

Suck up: (UK) To flatter; to be obsequious.

Sucker: A naive or gullible person, especially one who is easy to take advantage of.

Sucker-punch: (US) To punch someone unexpectedly.

Suckhole: (Australian) An obsequious person; a sycophant.

Sucky: (US) Something that is unpleasant.

Sugar daddy: A rich older man who provides a younger person with money and gifts in exchange for their affections.

Sugar mommy: A rich older woman who provides a younger person with money and gifts in exchange for their affections.

Sugar up: (UK) To bribe.

Sugar: (US) 1) A kiss. 2) A term of endearment, especially for a woman.

Suit: A high-ranking executive.

Suitable case: (UK) A person who is crazy or eccentric.

Suited and booted: (UK) To be smartly dressed.

sul: (Internet/text) See you later.

sum1: (Internet/text) Someone.

Sundowner: (UK) A drink in the evening.

Sunnies: (Australian/UK) Sunglasses; sunshades.

supa: (Internet/text) Super.

Sure look: (Irish) An expression that broadly conveys "It is what it is," hinting at the speaker's indifference or lack of firm opinion on the matter.

Sure thing: A certainty; something that is guaranteed to happen.

Surf: To browse the internet.

Surfboard: (UK) A flat-chested woman.

Surfie: (Australian/New Zealand) Someone whose main activity is surfing, especially a young man.

sus: (Internet/text/gaming) 1) Suspicious. 2) See you soon.

Suss out: (UK) To discern something.

Sussed: (UK) To have been found out or discovered.

Susso: (Australian) Sustenance (referring to welfare payments).

sut: (Internet/text) See you tomorrow.

sux: (Internet/text) Sucks.

sw: (Internet/text) So what?

Swag: (US) 1) Stolen goods. 2) Goods one receives for free.

swak: (Internet/text) Sealed with a kiss.

Swankpot: (UK) A braggart; a pretentious person.

Swanky: 1) Stylish. 2) Pretentious; boastful.

Swap spit: (US) To make out with someone; to kiss romantically.

Swash: (UK) Nonsense; rubbish talk.

Sweat it out: (US) To work hard; to exert oneself.

Sweat on: (UK) To wait for something or someone anxiously.

Sweat: A problem; a hassle (typically used in the negative: "no sweat").

Sweating: To be anxious; to be stressed.

Sweeney: (UK) A barber.

Sweet: (US) 1) Pleasing; satisfactory; all right. 2) Cool; impressive.

Sweetener: A bribe.

Sweet-talk: To persuade someone using flattery.

Swell: (UK) Great; excellent; pleasing.

Swell-head: (UK) Someone who is conceited.

Swig: (UK) To drink heartily.

Swill: (UK) 1) Beer. 2) To drink heartily.

Swillage: (UK) Beer.

Swilled: (UK) To be drunk or intoxicated.

Swing both ways: To be bisexual.

Swing the lead: (UK) To neglect one's duties; to waste time.

Swipe: To steal.

Switch: Someone who alternates between being a dominant and submissive sexual partner.

Switched-on: (UK) 1) Trendy; fashionable. 2) Alert; attentive.

Swizz: (UK) A swindle; a scam.

Swizzle: (UK) To be drunk or intoxicated.

swt: (Internet/text) Sweet.

sya: (Internet/text) See you; goodbye.

syiab: (Internet/text) See you in a bit.

syiaf: (Internet/text) See you in a few.

syl (also "syl8r"): (Internet/text) See you later.

sys: (Internet/text) See you soon.

sysop: (Internet/text) System operator.

syt: (Internet/text) See you there.

— T —

T and E: (UK) Tired and emotional (referring to be drunk or intoxicated).

t/a: (Internet/text) Try again.

t2m: (Internet/text) Talk to me.

t2u: (Internet/text) Talking to you.

t2ul (also "t2ul8r"): (Internet/text) Talk to you later.

t4a: (Internet/text) Thanks for asking.

Ta: (Internet/text) Thanks again.

Tabby: (UK) An attractive young woman or girl.

Tacker: (UK) A child.

Tackle: (UK) Male genitals.

Tacky: (UK) Of poor quality or style.

Tad: (UK) A small amount.

tafn: (Internet/text) That's all for now.

Tag: 1) To graffiti. 2) A graffiti artist's signature mark. 3) To include identifiers in a social media post.

Tagger: (UK) A graffiti artist.

tai: (Internet/text) Think about it.

taig: (Internet/text) That's all I've got.

Tail: (UK) A woman, especially one viewed as a potential sexual partner.

Tailgate: (US) To drive too closely behind another vehicle car.

Take a bath: (UK) To experience a financial loss or failure.

Take a chill pill: (US) An expression for the listener to calm down or relax.

Take a dive: To intentionally lose a competitive game.

Take a pop at: To attack or hit someone.

Take a powder: (US/Canadian) To flee; to run away.

Take a raincheck: To postpone.

Take down: (US) 1) To kill. 2) To put an end to something.

Take five: To have a short break or rest, lasting around five minutes.

Take it easy: Relax; calm down; don't worry.

Take it: (US) To tolerate or endure something.

Take off: 1) To leave. 2) To become popular.

Take on: (US) 1) To accept a responsibility. 2) To fight or confront someone.

Take one's lumps: (US) To accept suffering something unpleasant, especially if regarded as necessary.

Take out: (US) To kill; to obliterate.

Take the biscuit: (UK) An expression that conveys the speaker's great surprise at something (e.g., "That really took the biscuit!").

Take the huff: (UK) To become angry; to lose one's temper.

Take the Mickey: (UK) To make fun of something or tease someone.

Take the piss: (UK) To ridicule or tease.

Take: (US) An opinion.

tal: (Internet/text) Thanks a lot.

Talent: (UK) An attractive person.

Talk to the carpet: (US) To vomit.

Talk to your shoes: (US) To vomit.

Tall poppies: (Australian) Prominent or influential people.

Tam rag: (UK) A sanitary towel; a tampon.

Tan: To beat up someone.

Tank up: (UK) To drink a lot of alcohol.

Tank: (Australian/Indian/New Zealand) 1) A reservoir. 2) To decrease rapidly in value or reputation. 3) (Gaming) A strong character that can withstand a large amount of damage.

Tanked: (UK) To be drunk or intoxicated.

Tanker: (UK) A heavy drinker.

Tapped-out: (US) Exhausted; worn out.

Tarnation: (US) A euphemism for "damnation."

Tart up: (UK) To smarten up one's appearance; to make something look more attractive.

Tart: A promiscuous woman, or one who has that appearance.

Tasty: (UK) Something that is attractive or desirable.

tat2: (Internet/text) Tattoo.

Taters: (UK) Potatoes.

Tats: 1) (US) Tattoos. 2) (Australian) Teeth; dentures.

tau: (Internet/text) Thinking about you.

tay: (Internet/text) Thinking about you.

Tayters: (UK) Potatoes.

tb: (Internet/text) Text back.

tb4u: (Internet/text) Too bad for you.

tba: (Internet/text) To be announced.

TBA: (UK) To be avoided.

tbc: (Internet/text) To be continued.

tbd: (Internet/text) To be decided/determined.

tbf: (Internet/text) To be fair.

tbfu: (Internet/text) Too bad for you.

tbh: (Internet/text) To be honest.

tbnt: (Internet/text) Thanks but no thanks.

tbph: (Internet/text) To be perfectly honest.

tbss: (Internet/text) Too bad, so sad.

tbvh: (Internet/text) To be very honest.

tbya: (Internet/text) Think before you act.

tc: (Internet/text) Take care.

TCG: (Gaming) Trading card game.

tcoy: (Internet/text) Take care of yourself.

tdl: (Internet/text) Too damn lazy.

Teach: (UK) A teacher.

Tear it up: (US) To do something without restraint, especially in regard to partying or having fun.

Tear off a bit: (Australian) To have sexual intercourse.

Tear off a piece: (Australian) To have sexual intercourse.

Tear up: (US) 1) Unrestrained, often aggressive, behavior. 2) To perform impressively.

Tear-arse: (UK) Someone who is always busy.

Tech: Technology.

Teen: A teenager.

Teeny: Very small in size or amount.

Teenybopper: (US) A young teenage girl who is a fan of pop music and follows the related trends.

Teflon-brained: (UK) Forgetful; absent-minded.

teh: (Internet/text) A common typo of "the," sometimes made deliberately.

Tell off: T chastise; to reprimand.
TERF (also "terf"): (Internet/text) Trans exclusionary radical feminist.
tfh: (Internet/text) Thread from hell.
tfic: (Internet/text) Tongue firmly in cheek.
tfl: (Internet/text) Thanks for looking.
tfs: (Internet/text) Thanks for sharing.
tfta: (Internet/text) Thanks for the add.
tfti: (Internet/text) Thanks for the information.
tg: (Internet/text) Thank god.
tgfe: (Internet/text) Together forever.
tgft: (Internet/text) Thank god for that.
tgfu: (Internet/text) Too good for you.
tgif: (Internet/text) Thank god it's Friday.
tgis: (Internet/text) Thank god it's Saturday.
tgtbt: (Internet/text) Too good to be true.
tgws: (Internet/text) That goes without saying.
th@: (Internet/text) That.
thanx: (Internet/text) Thanks; thank you.
That's torn it: (UK) An expression that conveys that something unexpected has thwarted or ruined one's efforts or plans.
Thatch: (UK) Pubic hair.
The Big Apple: (US) New York City.
The big house: (US) Prison; jail.
The big man (upstairs): God.
The Bill: (UK) The police.
The boondocks: (US) A rural or desolate area.
The boot: (UK) Firing or dismissing from employment (e.g., "to be given the boot").
The box: (UK) Television.
The burbs: (US) The suburbs.
The business: (UK) Excellent; top class; first-rate.
The can: (UK) The toilet.
The chair: (US) The electric chair.
The chop: (UK) Firing or dismissing from employment (e.g., "to be given the chop").

The clap: Gonorrhea.
The Company: (US) The CIA.
The drink: (UK) The ocean; the sea.
The god squad: (UK) Evangelical Christians.
The goods: 1) Desired merchandise. 2) Evidence that will help an investigation.
The heat: (US) The police.
The horn: (US) A telephone.
The Jimmies: (Australian) Anxiety; nervousness.
The magic word: Please.
The man upstairs: God.
The man: A very popular, powerful, or influential man.
The mob: (US) The mafia.
The nadgers: (UK) A state of anxiety or nervousness.
The nick: (UK) 1) Prison. 2) A police station.
The night's a pup: (Australian) It's still relatively early.
The nod: Agreement; consent.
The pound: (Australian) A cell or area for solitary confinement.
The pox: (UK) A venereal disease.
The real McCoy: The genuine article or person; the real thing.
The right stuff: The right qualities.
The rough end of the pineapple: (Australian) An unfavorable position.
The royal order: (Australian) To be fired or dismissed from one's job.
The runs: Diarrhea.
The short and curlies: Pubic hair.
The shove: (UK) To be fired or dismissed from one's job.
The skitters: (Scottish) Diarrhea.
The slammer: Prison.
The snip: A vasectomy.
The sticks: The countryside; a rural area.
The strongbox: (UK) A cell for solitary confinement.
The third degree: An interrogation; intense questioning.
The tops: (UK) Someone or something of top quality.
The works: 1) Everything; all-inclusive. 2) A thorough beating.
The Y: (US) The YMCA.

The Yard: (UK) Scotland Yard.

Thicc: (US) A full, voluptuous figure, especially of a woman.

Thick ear: (UK) A slap across the head.

Thick: (Irish) Stupid; foolish.

Thickie: (UK) A slow-witted person.

Thicko: (UK) A slow-witted person.

Thingamajig: Used to reference something that the speaker has temporarily forgotten the name of, or doesn't know.

Thingy: Used to reference something that the speaker has temporarily forgotten the name of, or doesn't know.

Thingy-ma-bob: Used to reference something that the speaker has temporarily forgotten the name of, or doesn't know.

Thinker: (UK) The brain.

thnx: (Internet/text) Thanks.

tho: (Internet/text) Though.

Thongs: (Australian) Flip-flop sandals.

thr4: (Internet/text) Therefore.

Thrash: 1) To defeat thoroughly. 2) To beat severely.

Threads: (US) Clothes.

Three parts gone: (UK) To be drunk or intoxicated.

Three sheets to the wind: (UK) To be drunk or intoxicated.

Throne room: (UK) The restroom.

Throne: (UK) A toilet.

Throw a sickie: (UK) To pretend to be sick, especially to get off work or school.

Throw a wobbly: (UK) To get upset or angry.

Throw one's voice: (Australian) To vomit.

Throw up: To vomit.

Throw: (UK) To lose a game or competition on purpose.

thru: (Internet/text) Through.

Thumbsucker: (UK) 1) A baby. 2) An immature or cowardly person.

Thumping: (UK) 1) Impressively big; excessive. 2) An assault.

Thunder-thighs: A person with fat legs, especially describing a woman.

thx: (Internet/text) Thanks; thank you.

TIA: (Internet/text) Thanks in advance.

Tick off: (UK) To make someone angry.

Ticked off: (UK) To be angry.

Ticker: (UK) The heart.

Ticket: (UK) The correct course of action; something desirable.

Tickety-boo: (UK) All right; satisfactory; to be all in order.

Tickle the ivories: (UK) To play the piano.

Tickled pink: To be very pleased or amused.

Tiddle: (UK) To urinate.

Tiddled: (UK) To be drunk or intoxicated.

Tide's out: (UK) 1) An empty or nearly empty drink. 2) A drink that isn't filled up to the brim.

Tidy: (Scottish) Attractive; beautiful.

Tie the noose: (UK) To get married.

Tied up: (US) To be busy with something.

tif: (Internet/text) This is fun.

Tiger: (US) An energetic or persistent man, especially one who takes the initiative to act.

Tight: (US) 1) Cool; attractive; desirable. 2) A close relationship. 3) Drunk.

Tight-arse: (UK) A frugal or stingy person.

Tightlip: (UK) A person who can be trusted to keep a secret.

Tightwad: (US/Canadian) A frugal or stingy person.

tiic: (Internet/text) The idiots in control.

TIL: (Internet/text) Today I learned.

Time: The length of a prison sentence.

Tin arse: (UK) A very lucky person.

Tin cupping: (UK) Begging for money.

tinf: (Internet/text) This is not fair.

Tinfish: (UK) A torpedo.

Tinhorn: (US) Someone who pretends to have money or power.

Tinkle the ivories: (UK) To play the piano.

Tinkle: To urinate.

tinla: (Internet/text) This is not legal advice.

Tinnie (also "tinny"): (Australian) A can of beer.

Tinsel Town: (US) Hollywood.

Tip off: To provide advance warning of something, especially an illegal activity.

Tip: (UK) A squalid, filthy place.

Tip-off: A warning received in advance, especially regarding an illegal activity.

Tired: (US) Overused; cliched; hackneyed.

tisc: (Internet/text) That is so cool.

tisnf: (Internet/text) That is so not fair.

tisw: (Internet/text) That is so wrong.

Titchy: (UK) Very small; tiny.

Titty: (UK) A breast.

tix: (Internet/text) Tickets.

Tizzy: (UK) A state of agitation or nervous excitement.

tjb: (Internet/text) That's just boring.

tk: (Gaming) Team kill.

tk2ul: (Internet/text) Talk to you later.

tker: (Gaming) Team killer.

tks: (Internet/text) Thanks; thank you.

tku: (Internet/text) Thank you.

tl: (Internet/text) Tough luck.

tl:dr (also "tl;dr"): (Internet/text) Too long, didn't read.

tl8r: (Internet/text) Talk later.

tlc: (Internet/text) Tender loving care.

tld: (Internet/text) Told.

tlgo: (Internet/text) The list goes on.

tlk: (Internet/text) Talk.

tlyk: (Internet/text) To let you know.

tma: (Internet/text) Take my advice.

tmai: (Internet/text) Tell me about it.

TMI: (Internet/text) Too much information.

tmk: (Internet/text) To my knowledge.

tml: (Internet/text) Tell me later.

tmoro: (Internet/text) Tomorrow.

tmoz: (Internet/text) Tomorrow.

tmr (also "tmrw"): (Internet/text) Tomorrow.

tms: (Internet/text) That makes sense.

tmsg: (Internet/text) Tell me something good.

tmth: (Internet/text) Too much to handle.

tmtmo: (Internet/text) Text me tomorrow.

tmtt: (Internet/text) Tell me the truth.

tmw: (Internet/text) Too much work.

tnf: (Internet/text) That's not funny.

tnx: (Internet/text) Thanks; thank you.

To be chuffed: (UK) To be pleased or proud about something.

To cost big bikkies: (Australian) To be very expensive.

To die for: (US) Excellent; first-rate; enviable.

To suffer a recovery: (Australian) To have a hangover.

To the max: (US) To do something to the limit.

Toad: (UK) A liar.

Toasted: (UK) To be drunk or intoxicated.

Toddle off: (UK) To wander off; to leave quietly.

Toerag: (UK) An unlikeable person.

Toey: (Australian) Anxious; nervous; agitated.

Toff: (UK) An upper-class person, especially a man.

Toffee: (UK) Empty talk; nonsense; flattery.

Toffee-nosed: (UK) Pretentious; snobby.

tofy: (Internet/text) Thinking of you.

Together: (US) A person who has their life in order; someone who conducts themselves in a stable way.

Togs: (New Zealand) A swimsuit.

Togs: (UK) Clothes. 2) (Australian/Irish/New Zealand) A swimming costume.

tok: (Internet/text) That's okay.

Tombstones: (UK) A person's teeth.

Tommies: (UK) Tomatoes.

Tommy: (UK) A British private soldier.

Tommyrot: (UK) Nonsense; hogwash.

tomoro: (Internet/text) Tomorrow.

tomoz: (Internet/text) Tomorrow.

Tongue and groover: (UK) An obsequious person.

Tongue wrestling: (US) French kissing; making out with someone.

tonite: (Internet/text) Tonight.

Tonk: 1) (UK) A heavy blow or strike. 2) (Australian/derogatory) An effeminate or homosexual man.

Tonking: (UK) To have sexual intercourse.

Too much: (UK) Fantastic; first-rate; exceptional.

Tookus: (Yiddish) The buttocks.

Tool along: (UK) To move nonchalantly.

Tool around: (UK) To be idle; to laze.

Tool up: (UK) To arm or equip oneself.

Tool: 1) (Irish) An unlikeable person. 2) (US) An idiot; a fool.

Toot: (Australian) A lavatory.

Tootin': (US) An adjective used to add emphasis.

Tootsies: (UK) Toes.

Top banana: (UK) The boss; the leader; the person in charge.

Top dog: The boss; the leader; the person in charge.

Top floor: (UK) A person's head.

Top one: (UK) Excellent; first-rate; the best.

Top storey: (UK) A person's head.

Top whack: (UK) The highest amount possible.

Top: (UK) To kill.

Top: 1) (UK) Excellent; first-rate; the best. 2) A dominant sexual partner.

Toppo: (UK) Excellent; great; the best.

Torch job: (UK) Arson.

Torch: 1) To set fire to something. 2) To destroy evidence.

Torpedo: To sabotage something.

ToS: (Internet/text) Terms of Service.

Tosh: (UK) Nonsense; hogwash; rubbish.

Toss in one's ally: (Australian) 1) To surrender. 2) To die.

Toss your cookies: (US) To vomit.

Toss your tacos: (US) To vomit.

Tosser: (UK) An idiot; an unlikeable person.

Tosspot: (UK) A drunkard.

Total: (US) To destroy something; to ruin beyond repair.

Totally: (US) 1) An expression of agreement. 2) Very; extremely.

totes: (Internet/text) Totally.

Totsie: (UK) A girl; a young woman.

tou: (Internet/text) Thinking of you.

Tough bounce: (UK) Misfortune; an unlucky outcome.

Tough cookie: (UK) A persistent, strong-willed person, especially a woman.

Tough guy: (UK) A persistent, strong-willed man.

Tough it out: To endure a difficult situation.

Tough nut: (UK) A stubborn or unyielding person.

Tough shit: (US) An expression that conveys the speaker's indifference, especially about the listener's situation or plight.

Toughie: (UK) A thug; a tough, intimidating man.

Tourist trap: (US) A popular place that takes advantage of the high number of tourists, especially by overcharging them for goods and services.

Tout: (Irish) An informant.

Towel: (Australian) To beat up someone; to assault.

Town bicycle (or "town bike"): (UK) A promiscuous woman who lives locally.

toya: (Internet/text) Thinking of you always.

Toyboy: (UK) The young male lover of a much older person.

TP: (Internet/text) Toilet paper.

tptb: (Internet/text) The powers that be.

tq: (Internet/text) Thanks; thank you.

Track: (US) A song.

Train wreck: A situation that has resulted in disaster; a terrible outcome, especially one that is complicated and difficult to rectify.

Trainspotter: (UK) Someone who fixates on the minutiae of an interest or hobby.

Tramp: A promiscuous woman.

Trap: (UK) A person's mouth.

Trappy: (UK) Someone who is a gossip or braggart.

Trash: To severely criticize someone or something.

Trashed: To be drunk or intoxicated.

Triff: (UK) Terrific.

Trigger: To make someone agitated, distressed, or angry.

Trilby: (UK) An idiot; a fool.

Trim: (UK) To deceive; to swindle.

Trip: 1) To be under the influence of a hallucinatory drug. 2) Amusing; a weird but enjoyable experience.

Trippy: A weird, hallucinatory-like experience.

Trojan: (US) A condom.

Troll: (Internet/text) Someone who is deliberately offensive or problematic.

Trolling: (Internet/text) Deliberately offensive or problematic behavior.

Tronk: (UK) An unlikeable, blundering person.

Troppo: (Australian) To have one's mental faculties affected by being in a tropical climate.

Trots: (UK) Diarrhea.

Trotters: (UK) The feet.

Trouser snake: The penis.

Trout: (UK) An unattractive woman.

tru: (Internet/text) True.

Trucking: Persevering; persisting.

tsc: (Internet/text) That's so cool.

tsl: (Internet/text) The single life.

tsm: (Internet/text) Thanks so much.

tsnf: (Internet/text) That's so not fair.

tss: (Internet/text) That's so sweet.

tswc: (Internet/text) Tell someone who cares.

ttbc: (Internet/text) Try to be cool.

ttc: (Internet/text) Text the cell.

ttf: (Internet/text) That's too funny.

ttfn (also "tt4n"): (Internet/text) Ta ta for now (i.e., "goodbye for now").

ttg: (Internet/text) Time to go.

tthb: (Internet/text) Try to hurry back.

ttm: (Internet/text) Talk to me.

ttml: (Internet/text) Talk to me later.

ttr: (Internet/text) Time to run.

TTS: (Computer) Text to speech.

ttul (also "ttul8r"): (Internet/text) Talk to you later.

ttus: (Internet/text) Talk to you soon.

ttut: (Internet/text) Talk to you tomorrow.

ttya: (Internet/text) Thanks to you all.

ttyl (also "ttyl8r"): (Internet/text) Talk to you later.

ttyn: (Internet/text) Talk to you never.

ttys: (Internet/text) Talk to you soon.

ttyt: (Internet/text) Talk to you tomorrow.

ttyw: (Internet/text) Talk to you whenever.

tu: (Internet/text) Thank you.

Tub of lard: (UK) An overweight, and often unlikeable, person.

Tubby: (UK) An overweight person.

Tube: (US) 1) Television. 2) (UK) The London underground railway. 3) (Scottish) An idiot; a fool. 4) (Australian) A beer.

Tuck in with: (UK) 1) To have sexual intercourse. 2) To have an affair with someone.

Tuck in: To eat; to start eating.

Tucker: (Australian) Food.

Tuckered out: (UK) Exhausted; worn out; tired.

Tuckered: (UK) Exhausted; worn out; tired.

tuff: (Internet/text) Tough.

tul: (Internet/text) Text you later.

Tumble: To have sexual intercourse.

Turf: (UK) A territory, especially claimed by someone or a group of people (such as a gang).

Turkey: (US) 1) An idiot; a fool. 2) A failure; something that is unsuccessful or of low quality.

Turn a trick: (UK) For a prostitute to service a client.

Turn off: (US) To repulse.

Turn on: (US) To arouse.

Turn someone over: (UK) 1) To swindle; to rob. 2) To attack; to assault.

Turn-off: (UK) Something that is repulsive.

Turn-on: (UK) Something that is arousing.

Turps: (Australian/New Zealand) Alcohol (likening it to turpentine).

Tush (also "tushie"): (US) The buttocks.

tut: (Internet/text) Take your time.

tuvm: (Internet/text) Thank you very much.

Tux: Tuxedo.

TV: (Internet/text) Television.

tvm: (Internet/text) Thanks very much.

Twat: (UK) 1) The vagina. 2) An unlikeable person.

twbc: (Internet/text) That would be cool.

Twerp: An insignificant, unlikeable person.

twf: (Internet/text) That was funny.

twg: (Internet/text) That was great.

Twig: (UK) To understand.

Twigs: (UK) Matches.

Twine on: (UK) To talk long-windedly.

Twit: (UK) An idiot; a fool.

Two cents: (US) An opinion.

Two-bit: (US/Canadian) Worthless; poor quality; cheap.

Two-pot screamer: (Australian) Someone who is greatly or quickly affected by alcohol.

Two-time: To betray; to have an affair.

Two-way street: (US) Mutual cooperation; a situation that calls for give and take.

twyl: (Internet/text) Talk with you later.

twys: (Internet/text) Talk with you soon.

tx: (Internet/text) Thanks.

txt: (Internet/text) Text.

txting: (Internet/text) Texting.

txtyl: (Internet/text) Text you later.

ty: (Internet/text) Thank you.

tyfn: (Internet/text) Thank you for nothing.

tyl: (Internet/text) Text you later.

typo: (Internet/text) A typing mistake.

tys: (Internet/text) Told you so.

tysm: (Internet/text) Thank you so much.

tysvm: (Internet/text) Thank you so very much.

tyt: (Internet/text) Take your time.

tyty: (Internet/text) Thank you, thank you.

tyvm: (Internet/text) Thank you very much.

— U —

u/l: (Internet/text) Upload.

u/n: (Internet/text) Username.

u: (Internet/text) You.

u2: (Internet/text) You too.

u2u: (Internet/text) Up to you.

udc: (Internet/text) You don't care.

udek: (Internet/text) You don't even know.

UI: (Internet/text) User interface.

U-ie: (UK) A U-turn.

ukr: (Internet/text) You know, right?

ukwim: (Internet/text) You know what I mean.

ul: (Internet/text/gaming) Unlucky.

Umpteen: A lot; indefinitely many.

Uncle Bill: (UK) The police.

Uncle Bob: (UK) The police.

Uncle Sam: (UK) The United States government.

Under the table: (UK) 1) To be drunk. 2) Surreptitious; illegal.

Under the weather: To be slightly ill.

Underground: (US) Outside of the mainstream; a subculture.

Unhinged: To be crazy or mentally unstable, often in a dangerous way.

Unit: (US) An attractive person.

Unmentionables: Underwear.

Unreal: (Irish) Great; something so good that it's hard to believe.

Unreal: 1) Amazing; exceptional. 2) Unreasonable.

Unstuck: (UK) Distressed; out of control; highly agitated.

unt: (Internet/text) Until next time.

Unthinkables: (UK) Underwear.

Untied: (UK) Distressed; out of control; highly agitated.

Unwrapped: (UK) Distressed; out of control; highly agitated.

uom: (Internet/text) You owe me.

Up against the wall: (US) In a difficult situation, especially when one's options to act are very limited.

Up and up: (US) Honest; legal.

Up each other: (Australian) For people to mutually flatter one another.

Up for grabs: (US) Something that is available, especially if there is a limited quantity of it.

Up in the air: (US) Unknown; yet to be determined.

Up oneself: (Australian) Conceited; smug.

Up shit creek: In trouble; in a bad situation.

Up the creek: (UK) In trouble; in a bad situation.

Up the duff: (UK) To be pregnant.

Up the spout: (UK) To be pregnant.

Up the wall: To be angry or frustrated.

Up to here: (US) One's tolerance level, especially indicating that it has been reached.

Up to ninety: (Irish) To be very busy with something.

Up to snuff: Up to the necessary standard.

Up to speed: (US) Informed of the latest information.

Up yours: (US) A rude expression that conveys the speaker's contempt for the listener.

Up-and-up: (UK) Improving consistently.

Upchuck: (US) To vomit.

upmo: (Internet/text) You piss me off.

Upriver: (UK) In prison.

Upstairs: 1) A person's head or mind. 2) Heaven.

Upstate: (US) In prison.

Uptight: (UK) Humorless; quick to anger.

upw: (Internet/text) Unidentified party wound.

ur: (Internet/text) 1) Your. 2) You are.

ur2g: (Internet/text) You are too good.

uraqt: (Internet/text) You are a cutie.

url8: (Internet/text) You are late.

urs: (Internet/text) Yours.

urtb: (Internet/text) You are the best.

urtw: (Internet/text) You are the worst.

urw: (Internet/text) You are weird.

usck: (Internet/text) You suck.

Use one's loaf: (UK) To think; to use one's brain.

User: A drug addict.

Using: Habitually using illicit drugs.

usuk: (Internet/text) You suck.

usux: (Internet/text) You suck.

utfs: (Internet/text) Use the fucking search.

utm: (Internet/text) You tell me.

uttm: (Internet/text) You talking to me?

uty: (Internet/text) Up to you.

uwu: (Internet/text) An emoticon that is used to convey cuteness.

$$- V -$$

v: (Internet/text) Very.

Vac: (UK) Vacation.

vajayjay: (Internet/text) Vagina.

Vamoose: (US) To leave in a hurry.

Vamp up: (UK) To improve or repair something; to intensify something.

vbeg: (Internet/text) Very big evil grin.

vbg: (Internet/text) Very big grin.

Veep: Vice-president (from the pronunciation of V.P.).

Veg: Vegetables.

Veggies: Vegetables.

Vego: (Australian) A vegetarian.

Veg-out: To relax; to laze around without thinking.

Ventilate someone's shorts: (US) To chastise or reprimand someone.

Verbal diarrhea: A verbose person; someone who talks relentlessly.

Verboten: (UK) Forbidden (borrowed from German).

Vet: 1) (US) A veteran soldier. 2) (UK) A veterinarian.

vf: (Internet/text) Very funny.

vfm: (Internet/text) Value for money.

vgg: (Gaming) Very good game.

vgl: (Internet/text) Very good looking.

Vibe(s): (US) The atmosphere or mood of a person or place.

vid: (Internet/text) Video.

Vim: (UK) Enthusiasm; energy.

Vino: (UK) Wine, especially that which is cheap or of low quality.

VIP: (Internet/text) Very important person.

vlog: (Internet/text) Video log.

vn: (Internet/text) Very nice.

Voddy: (UK) Vodka.

Voetsek: (South African) A rude command for the listener to go away.

vry: (Internet/text) Very.

vs: (Internet/text) Versus.
vwd: (Internet/text) Very well done.
vzit: (Internet/text) Visit.

— W —

w.e.: (Internet/text) Whatever.

w/: (Internet/text) With.

w/b: (Internet/text) Write back.

w/e: (Internet/text) Whatever.

w/end: (Internet/text) Weekend.

w/eva: (Internet/text) Whatever.

w/o: (Internet/text) Without.

w/out: (Internet/text) Without.

w'sup: (Internet/text) What's up?; what's going on?

w2d: (Internet/text) What to do?

w2g: (Internet/text) Way to go.

w8: (Internet/text) Wait.

w8am: (Internet/text) Wait a minute.

w8ing: (Internet/text) Waiting.

Wack: (US) 1) Lame; uncool. 2) Worthless; stupid.

Wacked: (UK) Exhausted; tired.

Wacko: (UK) To be crazy mentally unstable.

Wacky: (UK) Crazy; eccentric.

wad: (Internet/text) Without a doubt.

wadr: (Internet/text) With all due respect.

Waffle: To talk long-windedly or without a meaningful point.

Wag it: (UK) To play truant.

Wag off: (UK) To play truant.

Wag: (Australian) To play truant.

wai: (Internet/text) What an idiot.

Waldo: (UK) An idiot; a fool.

Walk away: (US) 1) To avoid a confrontation by leaving. 2) To pass on a deal or agreement.

Walk out on: To end a romantic relationship with someone.

Walk: To go free, especially from prison.

Wallop: (UK) 1) An alcoholic drink.

Walloper: 1) (Australian) A police officer. 2) (Scottish) An idiot; a fool.

Wally: (UK) An idiot; a fool.

wam: (Internet/text) Wait a minute.

wamh: (Internet/text) With all my heart.

Wang: The penis.

Wangle: To obtain something by persuasion or manipulation.

Wanker: (UK) An unlikeable person.

Wanky: (UK) Worthless; rubbish.

wanna: (Internet/text) Want to.

Wannabe: Someone who tries hard to fit a certain identity.

Warb: (Australian) A filthy or unimportant person.

Warby: (Australian) 1) Filthy; dirty. 2) Inferior; unimportant.

Warm-ups: (US) A tracksuit.

War-paint: (UK) Cosmetic makeup.

Wart: (UK) An unlikeable person.

Warts and all: To accept something, including all of its negative qualities.

Washed-up: For one's career or ability to no longer be successful or effective; to be passed one's prime.

wassup: (Internet/text) What's up?

Waste: (US) 1) To kill. 2) To beat up; to assault.

Wasted: 1) Exhausted. 2) To be drunk or intoxicated.

Water sports: Urination as a sexual activity.

Watering hole: A pub; a bar.

Waterworks: Tears; crying.

watev: (Internet/text) Whatever.

wateva: (Internet/text) Whatever.

watevs: (Internet/text) Whatever.

wau: (Internet/text) What about you?

waud: (Internet/text) What are you doing?

waug: (Internet/text) Where are you going?

Waxy: (UK) Ill-tempered; irritable.

Way to go: Well done; congratulations.

waycb: (Internet/text) When are you coming back?

wayd: (Internet/text) What are you doing?

Way-out: (UK) Unconventional; eccentric; outlandish.
wayta: (Internet/text) What are you talking about?
wazzup: (Internet/text) What's up.
wb: (Internet/text) Welcome back.
wbb: (Internet/text) Will be back.
wbbs: (Internet/text) Will be back soon.
wbk: (Internet/text) Welcome back.
wbrb: (Internet/text) Will be right back.
wbs: (Internet/text) Write back soon.
wbu: (Internet/text) What about you?
wby: (Internet/text) What about you?
wc: (Internet/text) Who cares?
wcb: (Internet/text) Welcome back.
wd: (Internet/text) Well done.
wdim: (Internet/text) What did I miss?
wdtm: (Internet/text) What does that mean?
wdum: (Internet/text) What do you mean?
wdut: (Internet/text) What do you think?
wduw: (Internet/text) What do you want?
wdya: (Internet/text) Why do you ask?
wdyt: (Internet/text) What do you think?
wdyw: (Internet/text) What do you want?
Weasel: (US) A devious, untrustworthy person.
Web: The internet.
Wedding tackle: (UK) The male genitals.
Wedged: (UK) Wealthy; rich.
Wee: (UK) To urinate.
Weed out: (US) Remove unwanted or unnecessary people or things.
Weenie: (US) 1) A wiener sausage. 2) A timid or cowardly person.
Weensy: Tiny; extremely small.
Weigh in: To add one's own opinion to a discussion.
Weird out: (US) To alienate; to repulse.
Weirdo: A strange or unconventional person.
Well hung: For a man to be well-endowed.
Well stacked: (UK) For a woman to have a large chest.

Well: (UK) Very.

Well-oiled: (UK) To be drunk or intoxicated.

Wench: (UK) An unlikeable girl or woman.

wfm: (Internet/text) Works for me.

wfyb: (Internet/text) Whatever floats your boat.

wgac: (Internet/text) Who gives a crap?

wgo: (Internet/text) What's going on?

Whack: 1) To hit. 2) To murder; to assassinate.

Whacked: (UK) Exhausted; worn out.

Whacko: (UK) A crazy or eccentric person.

whaddya: (Internet/text) What do you …?

Whaletail: (US) A thong.

Whammers: (UK) A woman's (large) breasts.

Whang: The penis.

What gives: (US) An expression of exasperation (e.g., "Why?" or "How come?").

What's happening: (US) What's going on?

What's shaking: (US) What's going on?; how are you?

What's the craic?: (Irish) 1) A general greeting. 2) An inquiry into how a situation is going.

What's up: (US) Hello; what's going on?

whatcha: (Internet/text) What are you …?

whatev (also "whatevs"): (Internet/text) Whatever.

What-for: (UK) A harsh reprimand or punishment.

Whatsit: (UK) An object the name of which the speaker doesn't remember or know.

Wheel and deal: (US) 1) To scheme, especially in an unscrupulous manner. 2) To conduct business in a fast and loose style.

Wheelie: To lift the front wheel(s) of a vehicle off the ground while driving it.

Wheelman (also "wheels-man"): (UK) A getaway driver.

Wheels: A car.

whenevs: (Internet/text) Whenever.

Where's it at: (US) A popular or trendy place.

Whinge: (UK) To complain.

Whippersnapper: 1) A young and inexperienced person, especially one that behaves cheekily or overconfidently.

Whistle bait: (UK) An attractive woman.

White space: (UK) Free time.

White trash: (US) White people who live in poverty.

White-knuckle: (US) Terrifying; anxiety-inducing; stressful.

Whiz: An intelligent person; someone who is very good at something or who knows a lot about it.

Whole hog: (US) Everything; the entire thing.

Whole nine yards: (US) Everything; the entire thing.

Whoopsie (also "Whoopsy"): An expression to convey a mistake (e.g., "Oops").

Whopper: Something that is extremely large.

Whopping: Extremely large.

Whorehouse: A brothel.

whut: (Internet/text) What?

whyb: (Internet/text) Where have you been?

whyd: (Internet/text) What have you done?

Wicked: (UK) Excellent; cool; great.

wid: (Internet/text) With.

Widdle: (UK) To urinate.

wif: (Internet/text) With.

Wig out: (US) To lose self-control, especially in excitement.

wilco: (Internet/text) Will comply.

Wild oats: Indulgences or sexual partners, especially before settling down in later life.

Wilding: (US) Rampaging; acting out of control.

Willie: The penis.

Willies: Nervousness; heebie-jeebies.

Willy: The penis.

Wimp out: To choose not to do something owing to a lack of courage.

Wimp: A coward; a timid person.

Wimpy: Timid; feeble; cowardly.

Wind up: (UK) To annoy; to tease; to aggravate.

Windbag: Someone who talks too much.

Window: The time during which an opportunity is available.

Wind-up merchant: (UK) Someone who often teases or aggravates other people.

Wing it: 1) To improvise. 2) To leave quickly; to run away.

Winkie (also "winky"): (UK) The penis.

WIP: (Internet/text) Work in progress.

Wipe out: (Surfing) 1) To lose one's balance or be knocked over by a wave. 2) To lose one's balance and fall; to crash. 3) To destroy; to eradicate.

Wipe: (Australian) To ignore; to give someone a cold shoulder; to snub.

Wiped out: 1) Exhausted; depleted. 2) Ruined; destroyed.

Wipeout: 1) A crash or fall. 2) A failure.

Wired: Highly strung; agitated and tense.

Wiseass: (US) A smart aleck; an impudent person who believes themselves to be smart.

Wise-up: (US) To become alert or aware of something.

Wishy-washy: Indecisive; a feeble attitude.

wit: (Internet/text) With.

Witch: A mean-spirited woman.

With flying colors: To achieve something impressively well.

With-it: (US) Alert to current trends or information; fashionable.

witu: (Internet/text) With you.

witw: (Internet/text) What in the world?

wiu: (Internet/text) What is up?

wiyp: (Internet/text) What is your problem?

wk: (Internet/text) Week.

wkend: (Internet/text) Weekend.

wlc: (Internet/text) Welcome.

wlcb: (Internet/text) Welcome back.

wlcm: (Internet/text) Welcome.

wld: (Internet/text) Would.

wmao: (Internet/text) Working my ass off.

WMD: (Internet/text) Weapons of mass destruction.

wmgl: (Internet/text) Wish me good luck.

wml: (Internet/text) Wish me luck.

wmts: (Internet/text) We must talk soon.

wna: (Internet/text) Want to.

wnt: (Internet/text) Want.

woa: (Internet/text) Word of advice.

Wob: (UK) A lump; a clump; a piece.

Wobbler: (UK) A state of distress or overanxious behavior.

Wobbly: (UK) A state of distress or overanxious behavior.

woe: (Internet/text) What on earth?

wolo: (Internet/text) We only live once.

wom: (Internet/text) Word of mouth.

wombat: (Internet/text) Waste of money, brains, and time.

Womble: (UK) An inept or unlucky person.

Wonky: (UK) Askew; unstable; crooked.

Woodentop: (UK) An unintelligent person.

Woodie: (US) An erection.

Woolies: (UK) Woolworth's (a store).

woot: (Internet/text) Woohoo; a cheer of excitement or encouragement.

Woozy: To feel dizzy.

Word up: (US) To speak facts; to tell the truth.

Work it in: (US) To incorporate something.

Work out: To exercise.

Work over: 1) To beat up; to assault. 2) To treat unfairly.

Workaholic: Someone who spends all their time working; someone whose entire life revolves around their work.

Working girl: A prostitute.

Worrywart: Someone who worries about everything.

wos: (Internet/text) Waste of space.

wot: (Internet/text) What.

Wotcher: (UK) Hello.

wotevs: (Internet/text) Whatever.

Wotsit: (UK) An object the name of which the speaker doesn't remember or know.

woum: (Internet/text) What's on your mind?

Wowser: (Australian/New Zealand) A person with puritanical views; someone who abstains from alcohol.

wowzers: (Internet/text) Wow; whoa.

woz: (Internet/text) Was.

wp: (Internet/text) Wrong person.

Wrecked: To be drunk or intoxicated.

Wretch: (US) To vomit.

Wrinkly: (UK) An old person.

Write one's name on the lawn: (UK) To urinate outside.

wrt: (Internet/text) With regard to.

wru: (Internet/text) Where are you?

wrud: (Internet/text) What are you doing?

wruf: (Internet/text) Where are you from?

wryd: (Internet/text) What are you doing?

wsi: (Internet/text) Why should I?

wtbd: (Internet/text) What's the big deal?

wtbh: (Internet/text) What the bloody hell?

wtc: (Internet/text) What the crap?

wtf: (Internet/text) What the fuck?

wtfc: (Internet/text) Who the fuck cares?

wtfe: (Internet/text) What the fuck ever.

wtg: (Internet/text) Way to go.

wth: (Internet/text) What the heck?; what the hell?

wtii: (Internet/text) What time is it?

wtmi: (Internet/text) Way too much information.

wtp: (Internet/text) Where's the party?

wtrud: (Internet/text) What are you doing?

wtv: (Internet/text) Whatever.

wtva: (Internet/text) Whatever.

wtvr: (Internet/text) Whatever.

wud: (Internet/text) Would.

wudn: (Internet/text) What you doing now?

wuld: (Internet/text) Would.

Wuss: 1) A coward or timid person. 2) (Welsh) An informal term of address, especially among friends.

Wussy: A coward or timid person.

wut: (Internet/text) What.

wuta: (Internet/text) What you talking about?

wutb: (Internet/text) What are you talking about?

wuteva: (Internet/text) Whatever.

wuv: (Internet/text) Love.

wuwh: (Internet/text) Wish you were here.

wuwt: (Internet/text) What's up with that?

wuwu: (Internet/text) What's up with you?

wuz: (Internet/text) Was.

wuza: (Internet/text) What's up?; what's going on?

wuzup: (Internet/text) What's up?; what's going on?

wwc: (Internet/text) Who would care?

wwhw: (Internet/text) When, where, how, why?

wwikt: (Internet/text) Why would I know that?

WWJD: (Internet/text) What would Jesus do?

wwy: (Internet/text) Where were you?

wwyd: (Internet/text) What would you do?

wwyt: (Internet/text) What were you thinking?

wyas: (Internet/text) Wow, you are stupid.

wyb: (Internet/text) Watch your back.

wyd: (Internet/text) What are you doing?

wyg: (Internet/text) Will you go?

wygac: (Internet/text) When you get a chance.

wygam: (Internet/text) When you get a minute.

wym: (Internet/text) What do you mean?

wyn: (Internet/text) What's your name?

wyp: (Internet/text) What's your problem?

wys: (Internet/text) Wow, you're stupid.

WYSIWYG: (Computer) What you see is what you get.

wyut: (Internet/text) What are you up to?

wywh: (Internet/text) Wish you were here.

— X —

xbf: (Internet/text) Ex-boyfriend.

xcpt: (Internet/text) Except.

xD: (Internet/text) Used to convey a laughing face.

xfer: (Internet/text) Transfer.

xgf: (Internet/text) Ex-girlfriend.

xing: (Internet/text) Crossing.

xit: (Internet/text) Exit.

xl: (Internet/text) Extra large.

Xmas: Christmas.

xmpl: (Internet/text) Example.

xover: (Internet/text) Crossover.

xoxo: (Internet/text) Hugs and kisses.

xp: (Internet/text/gaming) Experience points.

xpt: (Internet/text) Except.

X-rated: 1) Pornographic; sexually explicit. 2) Material that is rated for adults only.

xroads: (Internet/text) Crossroads.

xs: (Internet/text) Excess.

xtreme: (Internet/text) Extreme.

xyz: Examine your zipper.

y!a: (Internet/text) Yahoo! Answers.

y/n: (Internet/text) Yes or no.

y/o: (Internet/text) Years old.

y: (Internet/text) Why.

y'all: (Internet/text) You all; all of you.

y2b: (Internet/text) YouTube.

y2k: (Internet/text) The year 2000.

ya: (Internet/text) Yeah.

Yack: To chatter; to talk verbosely.

Yacka (also "yacker"): (Australian/New Zealand) Work, especially physical labor.

Yackety-yak: (UK) Chatter; idle talk.

Yahoo: A hooligan; a lout.

Yak: 1) To chatter; to talk verbosely. 2) (US) To vomit.

Yammer: 1) To talk loudly and ceaselessly. 2) To complain insistently.

Yank someone's chain: (US) 1) To inconvenience someone, especially on short notice. 2) To tease or provoke someone.

Yank: (UK) An American person.

Yap: To chatter; to talk in a persistent and shrill way. 2) A person's mouth.

yaqw: (Internet/text) You are quite welcome.

Yarn: (New Zealand) 1) A story; a tall tale. 2) A conversation.

Yarra: (Australian) Crazy; mad.

yas: (Internet/text) You are stupid.

yasan: (Internet/text) You are such a nerd.

yasf: (Internet/text) You are so funny.

yasw: (Internet/text) You are so weird.

yatb: (Internet/text) You are the best.

yaw: (Internet/text) You are welcome.

Yawn: (UK) Something that is boring or uninteresting.

yea: (Internet/text) Yeah.

yeh: (Internet/text) Yeah.

Yell at the ground: (US) To vomit.

Yellowbelly: A coward; a timid person.

yer: (Internet/text) You're.

Yes man: (US) Someone who always agrees with their superior; a person who follows orders without question.

yew: (Internet/text) You.

ygg: (Internet/text) You go, girl.

yhl: (Internet/text) You have lost.

yhm: (Internet/text) You have mail.

yhni: (Internet/text) You have no idea.

yid: (Internet/text) Yes, I do.

Yike: (Australian) A quarrel; a brawl.

Yikes: An expression that conveys the speaker's shock or alarm.

yk: (Internet/text) You're kidding.

yki: (Internet/text) You know it.

ykw: (Internet/text) You know what?

ykwim: (Internet/text) You know what I mean?

yme: (Internet/text) Why me?

ymmd: (Internet/text) You made my day.

YMMV: (Internet/text) Your mileage may vary (i.e., your experience may be different depending on your own preferences or circumstances).

ynk: (Internet/text) You never know.

ynm: (Internet/text) Yes, no, maybe.

yo: (Internet/text) Year old.

Yo: (US) An expression that can be used as a greeting or to gain attention.

Yob (also "yobbo"): (UK) A hooligan; a rude, uncouth person.

Yodel in the valley: To perform cunnilingus.

yolo: (Internet/text) You only live once.

Yonks: (UK) A very long time.

Yonnie: (Australian) A stone; a pebble.

You betcha: (US) That's right; an expression that conveys agreement with the listener.

You-know-what: A euphemism for sexual activity.

You-know-who: A reference to someone the speaker doesn't want to name, but whose identity is known to the listener.

Yoyo: (UK) An eccentric or silly person.

ypmo: (Internet/text) You piss me off.

yqw: (Internet/text) You're quite welcome.

yr: (Internet/text) Year.

yrbk: (Internet/text) Yearbook.

yrs: (Internet/text) Years.

ysic: (Internet/text) Why should I care?

ysk: (Internet/text) You should know.

ystrdy: (Internet/text) Yesterday.

yt: (Internet/text) You there?

ytm: (Internet/text) You tell me.

yty: (Internet/text) Why, thank you.

Yuck: An expression that conveys the speaker's distaste for something.

Yucky: Gross; distasteful.

Yummy: Delicious; tasty.

yup: (Internet/text) Yes.

Yuppie: A young, urban (often pretentious) person with a very well-paying job.

yvw: (Internet/text) You're very welcome.

yw: (Internet/text) You're welcome.

ywic: (Internet/text) Why would I care?

yysw: (Internet/text) Yeah, yeah, sure, whatever.

— Z —

Zapper: (UK) A remote control.

Zero out: (US) To run out of money.

Zero: (UK) A loser; an insignificant person.

Zilch: Zero; nothing.

Zillion: A massively big number.

Zillionaire: An extremely wealthy person.

Zinger: (US) 1) Something that is excellent. 2) A punchline; a witty comment or retort.

Zip it: A command for the listener to stop talking.

Zip one's lip: 1) To keep quiet. 2) To keep a secret.

Zit: A pimple, especially on the face.

Zombie: A dull, apathetic person.

zomfg: (Internet/text) Oh my fucking god.

zomg: (Internet/text) Oh my God.

Zone out: (US) To lose focus; to daydream.

Zonk out: (US) To fall asleep quickly; to fall into a deep sleep.

Zonked: 1) To be exhausted. 2) To be drunk or intoxicated.

Zoo: A chaotic situation or place.

zoot: (Internet/text) A cheer of excitement or encouragement (e.g., "Woohoo!").

Zooty: (US) Flashy; showy; smartly dressed.

Zs: (US) Sleep.

zup: (Internet/text) What's up?; what's going on?

Stay in touch!

If you find this dictionary of English slang useful, please consider leaving a short review or comment. Your support is a tremendous help and gives us the opportunity to revise this edition, as well as to write new books for you and others who wish to learn more about the English language.

Follow Easy English on Twitter for more tips and resources: @EasyEnglishPub

Follow Rockwaller Books for all their releases: @RockwallerBooks

www.ingramcontent.com/pod-product-compliance
Lightning Source LLC
Chambersburg PA
CBHW070946250726
48663CB00002B/102